ASPECTS OF GREEK AND
ROMAN LIFE

General Editor: H. H. Scullard

★ ★ ★

FESTIVALS OF THE
ATHENIANS

H. W. Parke

FESTIVALS
OF THE
ATHENIANS

H. W. Parke

3850

CORNELL UNIVERSITY PRESS
Ithaca, New York

First published 1977

International Standard Book Number
0-8014-1054-1
Library of Congress Catalog Card Number
76-12819

Printed in Great Britain

CONTENTS

LIST OF ILLUSTRATIONS

Who are these coming to the sacrifice?
To what green altar, O mysterious priest,
Lead'st thou that heifer lowing at the skies,
And all her silken flanks with garlands drest?
                    Keats, *Ode on a Grecian Urn*

PREFACE

It is more than ten years since Professor H. H. Scullard, soon after becoming editor of this series, suggested to me that I might contribute a book on the Athenian Festivals. This proposal appealed strongly to one who had already worked for long on another aspect of the interaction of Greek religion and society – ancient oracles. But I had to explain that at the time I was too involved in university administration to be able to devote the necessary attention to this new field. So the plan was postponed till after my retirement, when Professor Scullard was kind enough to be willing to renew his original proposal. This is the genesis of the present work.

Modern scholarship owes to Ludwig Deubner the basic formulation of this subject. His book, *Attische Feste*, was published in 1932 and established itself at once as a standard work. But in the intervening years much new evidence has emerged and further research has penetrated some of the problems. Excavation in the Agora has revealed much of the topography of central Athens and has unearthed inscriptions casting new light on its cults. The fragments of the Atthidographers have been collected and furnished with a voluminous commentary by Felix Jacoby. Of particular festivals the *Mysteries* have been examined by George Mylonas and the *Dionysia* by Sir Arthur Pickard-Cambridge and his editors, John Gould and D. M. Lewis. These are only a few examples of the development of knowledge in the last forty-four years. Hence it is appropriate to survey the subject afresh.

Another reason springs from Deubner's treatment of the subject. He classified the festivals under the different deities to whom they were dedicated, and this arrangement corresponded to his general approach which was essentially to treat it as a branch of the science of religion. Professor Scullard originally suggested that the festivals should be taken in their order in the calendar and so discussed as part of Greek life rather than Greek theology. The aim is rather to discover the different parts they played in the experience of an Athenian of the classical period.

In one particular respect there is no attempt to supersede Deubner. He claimed to have cited and reproduced all the significant passages in classical literature bearing on the subject. Though the notes of the present book contain references to what the author regards as the main sources of evidence, those who wish a fully comprehensive catalogue are referred to Deubner. It is hoped that otherwise this restatement of the subject of Athenian festivals will sufficiently describe a significant aspect of Greek life.

H. W. Parke

Trinity College, Dublin 1976

INTRODUCTION

For the purpose of this book by 'festivals' is meant the days set aside by
the Athenian state for the worship of deities. In the ancient Greek city
there were no purely secular festivals. All holidays were really holy
days dedicated to particular gods or goddesses. But also the ancient
Greeks had no rigid distinctions between activities of a religious or of a
worldly character. Not only was feasting an appropriate act of worship,
but even athletics and play-acting were proper institutions for holy
days. The pious psalmist, sure in his knowledge of the nature of Jehovah,
might assert: 'He hath no pleasure in the strength of an horse: neither
delighteth he in any man's legs.' But the Athenian when he took part
in chariot-racing or running at the Panathenaic games believed that
Athena was honoured by these exertions. Similarly when he laughed
at the comedies or wept at the tragedies, he was seated in a theatre
consecrated to Dionysus, and the happenings on the stage, however
pathetic or ludicrous, were governed by the rules of a religious
ceremony.

It would, however, be too large a task for one book to cover in
analytical detail all the events connected with Athenian festivals.
Excellent volumes have been devoted to Greek athletics and Attic
drama. Our present purpose is to describe the chief ceremonial occasions of the city in their order in the calendar, and to try to form a
general picture of the religious year as it presented itself to the Athenian
citizen.

In various ways this is not a simple task. First of all, the Athenian
state did not produce and circulate a brief calendar showing every day
of the year with the fixed dates of the festivals, like that of the Christian
churches with their major holy days and saints' days. The Christians
here were following the pagan Romans who with the *fasti* had available
a diary of the state religion, which was easy to consult, recording the
significance of every day for the purposes of ritual. The festivals of the
Athenians were not available in this handy form. They were originally
a matter of unwritten tradition, but at the beginning of the sixth
century BC Solon (perhaps preceded to some extent by Dracon) reduced
the practices of the state religion to a written code, which formed the

final section of his constitution. It was inscribed and exhibited in public, but our literary or inscriptional evidence for its contents is very slight. No doubt it was not so much a calendar of festivals as a tabulated set of regulations in calendar order.

At the end of the fifth century as part of the undertaking of revising and re-editing this constitution, an Athenian called Nicomachus produced a new code of the state religion. The work took years, and was interrupted by the fall of Athens in 404 and the tyranny of the Thirty, but at last it was completed in 399/8 BC when Nicomachus was unsuccessfully prosecuted by critics of his scheme.[1] The American excavations of the Agora have produced evidence for the form in which the code was published. It was inscribed in both faces of two walls and ran to many columns with much repetition. For one calendar recorded first the annual sacrifices and then a second and third calendar the sacrifices occurring every second year under the year to which they belonged. As this was a codification of the official regulations, it did not merely give the dates and the names of the festivals, but also the particulars of the officials responsible with their perquisites and the specification of the victims to be offered with their cost. The result was a vast document which if printed would have been at least a lengthy pamphlet. It is typical of the antiquarian and essentially conservative approach of the editor that the inscription was written in the archaic form known as *boustrophedon* ('ox-turning'): that is, the lines ran alternately from left to right and from right to left. This method of writing had died out from the early fifth century, except for religious documents, where it was retained like the use of black letter in the printing of prayer books, as Dr Jeffery suggests. This archaism in presentation and the complicated detail of the document, even though it was inscribed in a beautiful script, must have made it discouraging to the reader. Its publication in this form satisfied the principles of Athenian democracy, but one may doubt whether it was often consulted. Perhaps a magistrate or priest of special conscientiousness would occasionally look up the rules governing the ceremony, for which he was responsible, or some religious crank would examine the code with a view to detecting some lapse from strict orthodoxy. That they had such an extensive body of regulations to consult is not surprising when we note that a generation before Nicomachus the author of the pseudo-Xenophontic *Constitution of Athens* had alleged that the Athenians had more public festivals than any other Greek city. (Plate 2)

Unfortunately only a few small fragments of Nicomachus' code have survived. If the document were reasonably complete, we would have a sound and comprehensive basis for any survey of Athenian festivals, but the bits preserved only give a tantalizing amount of detail about a few pieces of ritual with particulars which would otherwise be quite unknown. They thus suggest how much more information remains lost.

Consequently one must fall back on other particular documents dealing with Athenian festivals and the scattered references in ancient literature. None of the books written on the subject in antiquity have survived. This is unfortunate for throughout a period of a century from about 370 to 270 BC a succession of writers known as the Atthidographers, wrote histories of Athens. They devoted much space to what we would class as the legendary origins of religious institutions.[2] This is not surprising, for most of them were by profession Exegetai, experts in sacred law. But their writings were no doubt too technical to interest the general reader and too specialized to make good schoolbooks. So they have vanished, except for many quotations and paraphrases. These come to us almost entirely from the writers of dictionaries and encyclopaedias produced in late-Roman and Byzantine times. These lexicographers were concerned to provide short explanations of the obscure terms of Athenian ritual for those readers who encountered them in classical literature. They were scholarly enough to go back directly or indirectly to the technical writers of the fourth and third centuries BC, but they were content to abridge or paraphrase their sources drastically so long as they could provide a brief definition or explanation of a word. This purely verbal interest meant that they did not attempt to get down to the inner significance of the ceremonies which they listed, nor did they try to combine their separate entries with any general picture of a defunct paganism.

Scholars such as Jacoby by assembling, arranging and annotating the fragments of the Atthidographers have made it possible to form a picture, however scrappy, of the main ancient writings on the origins of the Attic festivals. But from this assemblage it is clear that these ancient historians had certain limited objectives. They sometimes described cult practices if they were peculiar, though these descriptions were rather perfunctorily handled by the late lexicographers. But their main object was to explain the origin of the chief pieces of ritual. In the usual Greek fashion they told the *aition* – the just-so story – which recounted the first occasion of some custom in a context which accounted for the strange features of the practice. Sometimes these legends were isolated episodes from the past history of Athens; at other times they served to link the custom with one of the great figures of Greek mythology and so give it a dignified pedigree. Practically always the *aition* was the product of fantasy and did not actually represent the origin of the ritual, which usually was a piece of primitive cult-practice, best explained in terms of anthropology. Apart from the examples which they give of the Greek power of inventing legends the chief importance of these just-so stories is that they confirm the details of a traditional custom. Special features would not appear in the *aition*, if they were not observed in the custom which it claimed to explain. But the result is that our literary sources tend to concentrate on legends and specialized details rather than to produce an overall picture.

Our other chief source is Attic inscriptions. For the period from the Persian wars to the death of Alexander Athens, except for a couple of years, was ruled by a democracy, and under it was developed the custom of publishing the main activities of the state by inscribing the official documents on marble slabs. The practice of the state religion was one of the most important of these activities, and inscriptions concerning it are plentiful throughout the period. They took several different forms. Some are copies of legislation dealing with cults; others are records of state expenditure on sacrifices and festivals. These must have been some of the chief recurring expenses each year. But also by a regular Greek practice the cost of many religious activities was diverted from the Athenian treasury and fell directly on the shoulders of individuals as a form of annual tax. These functions were known as *leitourgiai* – 'services for the people', and significantly enough the word has gradually changed its usage till it survives in modern English as liturgy, signifying a form of religious ceremony. But to the classical Greek it was a burden, yet at the same time a source of political and social credit. So records of the liturgies were not merely issued officially by the state, but also were cited by individuals in literature or inscriptions when they wished to call attention to their practical patriotism.

For undertaking a liturgy it was simply necessary to be a citizen possessed of a certain amount of means. Though during the festival he could be regarded as carrying out a religious function, this neither involved any form of ordination in advance, nor did it impose any special moral obligations on the holder of the office then or later. It was in modern analogy more like being a churchwarden, but with a prestige and publicity of a much higher order. Besides the holders of liturgies, there were priests of the various deities recognized by the state. Here the Athenian democracy showed its primitive and traditional side, for the priesthoods were normally hereditary in different aristocratic families. Also while liturgies were annual functions, priests and priestesses were appointed for life. However, the state exercised a certain control over the office-holders. Those appointed had to be confirmed by an official board, and their conduct of their office was nominally under state scrutiny. Mostly the holding of an hereditary priesthood, though a highly honourable function, did not impose on the holder any particular religious way of life. He might have to observe some traditional taboos in connection with the performance of his ceremonial, but for the rest his life need not differ from that of other citizens. The one great exception to this generalization appears to have been the Hierophantes or 'Revealer of the Sacred Things' – the chief priest of the Eleusinian Mysteries. He seems to have been regarded as set apart from the other Athenians in virtue of his special control of the initiation.

The important position of aristocratic families in the state religion shows how the particular cults over which they presided went back to highly primitive origins, long antedating the creation of the republican state. The original chief priest of the state was no doubt the king who will have combined in his person the leadership of the community in both its secular and its religious activities. In Athens, as in Rome, when the kingship was abolished as a political institution, it was still retained for ritual functions. The Athenians each year as one of the three high offices of state appointed the Basileus, 'the King', for he still retained the original title. His functions were essentially to preside over the state's worship. Also as judge he directed the court responsible for trying offences against the state religion such as Socrates' trial for impiety. Certain priestly functions fell to him during his year of office. In addition he must have been responsible for the calendar which was a religious institution determining the dates of festivals. But evidently the annual kingship had not retained all the functions of the original kings. The Eteobutadai, who claimed to be descendants of the original royal family of Athens, held reserved to their female members the right to be appointed priestess of Athena Polias, the state's chief deity. The office will originally have been held by one of the king's daughters. The other priesthoods which descended in families probably dated back to a time when the particular cult in each case had been a prerogative of one family or clan, and it had been part of the development of the state religion that certain hereditary cults had acquired sufficient prominence to be taken under the patronage of the state without completely losing their traditional organization. Similarly some local cults of Attica were later received into metropolitan Athens. But also in historic times the worship of a foreign god or goddess was sometimes brought to Athens and accepted by the community and included among its state festivals. This process of adoption of additional cults had no doubt taken place also before the historic period, and some of the deities who were accepted as Athenian had come originally from abroad.

In this way the cults of Athens were a rather miscellaneous assemblage from different origins and at various periods. Such a situation was acceptable under polytheism, when the worship of one deity one day involved no inconsistency in worshipping another deity on the next. In fact, as in classical paganism the importance of worship lay in the thing done rather than in the belief held, it was possible for deities to be combined in ritual, and even one or other to become more dominant without any conscious or deliberate change in religious denomination. But while recognizing this fluidity in ancient cults, for the purpose of the present investigations it is sufficient to establish, if possible, the typical pattern and content of the Attic festivals in the classical period of the fifth and fourth centuries BC without trying to settle their evolution in primitive and archaic times or their subsequent development in the Hellenistic and Roman epochs.

Before looking at the festivals in calendar order it is well to notice briefly what are the typical ceremonies in Greek worship, for generally these had a common character, even when devoted to different deities.[3] The chief action in all Greek cult consisted in offering sacrifice, and the most typical object was some animal, especially cattle, sheep or goats. The particular class of victim, and its appropriate age and gender might differ from deity to deity and occasion to occasion, but this was the normal centre-point of a religious ceremony. Also the sacrifice could generally be treated in one of two quite different ways. Less frequently the victim after being killed could be offered as a whole burnt offering and the carcase completely consumed by fire. Such a ceremony usually implied a view that the deity was angry and required an offering in appeasement. But much more usually after the slaughter of the animal its flesh was cut up into joints and roasted. Some of the larger bones

were stripped of their meat and the entrails were wrapped round them
and burnt, but the main edible parts of the animal were simply cooked
and then consumed by the worshippers. The sacrificing priest often
had the skin and some specified parts of the animal as his prerogative.
The Greeks themselves were somewhat conscious of the anomaly
whereby the deity was given the parts of the victim least appetizing to
the human sacrificer. Of course it was possible to explain that gods
were not like men, and also Hesiod tells a legend how Prometheus
tricked Zeus into accepting his inedible portion, thus providing the
precedent for the practice. Anyway the result was that a sacrifice,
though expensive to the man who offered it, brought with it the
compensation on most occasions of a large meat meal for him and his
family. In ancient Greece where cattle and sheep were never plentiful,
the normal family did not expect to afford meat once a day or even
perhaps once a week. In pagan times, then, the occasion of a sacrifice
was an opportunity for an infrequent feast, whether the family itself
provided the animal or whether alternatively they shared in a state
festivity. The practical importance of this participation explained why
it was often governed by precise and elaborate regulations. All our
evidence suggests that the partaking of the sacrificial meat was not
usually treated as a sacramental communion. It was part of the worship
of a deity, but not much more spiritual in feeling than eating roast
turkey at Christmas. (Plates 67, 68)

However, this association of meat meals and sacrifices worked both
ways. Not only would the worshippers normally have meat when they
partook in a festival, but also it would be obviously absurd and waste-
ful to slaughter an animal on a purely secular occasion. The parts given
to the gods did not seriously detract from the value of the meat as food,
and those concerned in the slaughtering might as well earn such divine
favour as they could. The idea that the gods should show their gratitude
to those who regularly sacrificed to them appears already in Homer.
Consequently we can picture that even the meat in the butchers' shops
had all come from sacrificial victims. It was this situation which in
Corinth in the first century AD presented an awkward problem to
newly converted Christians of a tender conscience who wanted a
meat meal, but did not wish to countenance paganism by accepting
flesh 'offered to idols'. Half a century later when the Christians in
Bithynia had become fairly numerous, Pliny the Younger believed
that some persecution had helped the cattle trade which had been
rather depressed by the difficulty in finding a sale for victims.[4] These

late examples show how the practice of ritual sacrifice interpenetrated the social system of the Greeks.

As the burning of offal and bones was a central feature of cult, it was inevitable that an altar for burnt-offering was the essential feature of most places of worship. It stood in the open air partly no doubt to enable the smoke of sacrifice to ascend to the gods, who were vaguely pictured as in the heavens, but also because the problem of coping with the soot and dirt involved in the operation would have been insoluble if it had been carried on indoors. The altar therefore stood outside the main door of the temple, if there was one, and the building was not so much used directly for worship as to house and shelter the image of the god in a noble setting. No doubt when sacrifice was being offered the doors of the temple would stand open so that the ritual could be related to the deity in whose honour it was performed. But our evidence suggests that many temples remained closed, except on the occasions of festivals. The idea of a church continually open for private worship was quite alien to the practice of antiquity. Homer shows the Greeks as prepared to pray to the gods at any momentary occasion when help was needed. But also the silence of Greek authors suggests that the notion of going into a building for private communion with a deity was equally strange to them. Scipio Africanus the Elder was regarded as very peculiar and probably of superhuman birth because he used to commune regularly in this way with Jupiter Capitolinus.[5]

On the other hand a sacrifice in the open air in a precinct dedicated to a god and in the presence of his image was clearly the most appropriate occasion for formal prayer. Offerings might be in fulfilment of a vow and in acknowledgement of a favour granted, or as an occasion for a request and in anticipation of favours desired. In either event they would be accompanied by prayer and hymns. Though a victim's meat was the most usual offering, different cults gave occasion for all sorts of other gifts to be offered to the gods – fruits, vegetables, cereals, fish – according to the particular deity and the particular festival. The more unusual offerings were often the subject of explanatory legends.

Also, as well as offerings which could generally be classed as food, the Greek gods received gifts of drink, especially wine or milk. This was usually poured out before the deity or on his altar. But as with meat offerings, so with drink: the occasion when the god received such a libation was also one when men too would usually partake in it, or rather in the case of drink it more often appears that the worshipper drank the wine at a festival, but also presented the god with a small quantity as his share. The prayers which accompanied these offerings were not recorded in anything like a breviary or a book of common prayer. They were traditional in so far as they had a fixed form, and, as many priesthoods ran in families, they were probably passed on verbally from father to son. From the New Comedy one gathers also that the recitation of prayers might be a function of the professional sacrificer. He would be employed by private individuals or societies to kill their sacrificial victim on the occasion of a festival, but it appears that he would also take over the liturgy. Menander in his play, *The Flatterer*, gave a delightful vignette of such a professional at work. The Tetradistai (a guild who worshipped Aphrodite on the fourth of each month) have hired a sacrificer, who speaks as follows, declaiming the liturgy in a loud voice and adding *sotto voce* instructions to the slave ministrants.

LIBATION! (aside to the slave) Follow me and pass me the entrails. What are you looking at? LIBATION! (aside), Come on, slave Sosias. LIBATION! (aside) Pour on a good drop. TO THE GODS AND GODDESSES OF OLYMPUS LET US PRAY; TO ALL THE GODS AND ALL THE GODDESSES – (aside), catch hold of the victim's tongue – THAT IN ADDITION THEY MAY GIVE TO US ALL PROTECTION, HEALTH, MANY BLESSINGS AND THE ENJOYMENT OF OUR PRESENT BLESSINGS, LET THAT BE OUR PRAYER.

Such a comparatively simple and generalized formula of supplication seems to have been typical of ancient prayers rather than the much more specific petitions of modern religious services.[6]

Besides presenting the god with food and drink – the essential enjoyments of human life – the Greek might offer any other of the things which he enjoyed – music and incense for example. He had a more highly developed sense of smell as a source of pleasure than modern man and at feasts scents were normally provided as well as things to eat and drink. So it is not surprising that the Greeks at times burnt incense or poured out scent in ritual. It may have been also a convenient antidote to the all-pervading smell of cooking flesh and burning bones which must have been the inevitable accompaniment to Greek worship. Similarly, the Greek at his banquets regularly enjoyed music and so could appropriately play the harp or blow the flute at a sacrifice. Once more as with incense there may have been a secondary function too. For the unaesthetic Roman at any rate believed that music on ritual occasions served to drown the noise of inauspicious words or sounds. But the Greek in this matter is more likely to have been interested in the positive beauties of melody. In the same way the association of athletic games and the performing of plays with certain Greek festivals was partly determined by the fact that the Greeks enjoyed these activities and were prepared to believe their gods looked on them in the same way.

There was one kind of public ceremony which was particularly frequent and important in Greek ritual. This was the procession. The Greek word for it (*pompe*) meant literally 'a sending', and the procession usually was concerned with sending an offering to the deity. It would be conducted along a traditional processional route, sometimes with particular ritual performed at stops on the way. The order of the procession would be determined by conventional rules, and the right to hold positions in it might be strictly controlled. As it was an occasion for expensive robes and elaborate equipment the business of arranging and fitting-out a procession might be of itself a liturgy in the sense of a public service imposed as a tax.

The importance of processions in the public worship of the Athenians is well illustrated by the fact that they erected a special building in connection with these events. Called the Pompeion (Procession Building), it occupied the space between the Sacred Gate and the Dipylon Gate in the Kerameikos. This was the traditional starting point for the great processions such as those of the *Panathenaia* heading inwards to the Acropolis or of the Mysteries heading outwards to Eleusis. It was set up early in the fourth century B C, and consisted of a large open court measuring some 140 ft by 50 ft surrounded by a colonnade with rooms opening off it. We can picture these rooms as providing offices for the secretarial work of organizing the events and store-rooms for the secure housing of the many consecrated vessels and much other apparatus used in processions.[7] Something of the scale and value of these sacred utensils can be judged by the fact that late in the fourth century the politician Lycurgus furnished the state with 'gold and silver processional vessels and ornaments for one hundred bearers of baskets' (Kanephoroi). The extensive oblong courtyard will have provided a suitable space for marshalling the chief participants in the procession and inspecting them to make sure that the equipment was all in order before the *pompe* got under way. Prior to the erection of the building these preliminaries must have been managed in the street. (Plate 88)

A humorous impression of how the ordinary citizen saw these processions is provided by Aristophanes in his *Ecclesiazousai*. The situation is that a decree has been passed for all property to be shared in common. Chremes, the simple honest citizen, is bringing out his household goods with the help of his slaves so as to take them to the Agora for the sharing-out. He arranges them like a religious procession with a series of complicated jokes. A sieve and two pots represent the maiden carrying a sacred basket (Kanephoros) who usually headed the *pompe*, and her attendants one of whom carried her chair and the other probably her sunshade. Then there is a water-carrier represented by a water jug: a singer to the harp by a rooster, and other vessels to represent the carriers of honeycombs and branches. Finally the small crockery was to represent the miscellaneous populace crowding in at the tail of the procession. The scene was calculated to raise a laugh as the various items listed by Chremes can mostly be paralleled in the great *pompe* of the *Panathenaia*.[8] Standing somewhere between a procession and an athletic contest was a curious competition largely confined to Athens. This was the torch-race sometimes run as a relay on foot, sometimes as a straight foot-race, and even in one instance converted into a horse-race.

There should also be mentioned the fact that while most Greek ritual took place in public and was accessible to any citizen, there were certain exceptions to this generalization. First of all certain rites were confined to one or other sex. Women were often excluded from shrines of Heracles. But more prominently there were various festivity rites, especially those associated with Demeter, which were performed by women, when the intrusion of a man would have desecrated the ceremony. Again there were in Attica several mystery cults recognized by the state, as distinct from private mystery religions operated by private individuals. All citizens who were not disqualified by a few obvious ritual impurities were entitled to be initiated in such state mysteries. So that in fact, though it was forbidden to divulge in public description of the ceremonies, many Athenians must have been completely aware of what was in some ways an open secret. But the prohibition worked with such effectiveness that in spite of some alleged disclosures in Christian authors, the arcane rites of the Eleusinian Mysteries still remain undiscovered.

These were the most conspicuous features of Greek cult. The festivals on which the rites took place were distributed through the year on fixed dates of the calendar. In fact the calendar was clearly established so as to provide a proper frame for the celebration of annual festivals. Athenian holy days were normally celebrated on the same date of the same month annually and were not movable feasts. The management of the Athenian calendar has become a highly controversial subject among scholars, but for our present purposes these difficulties can be put on one side, as our only concern is with a typical year. The Athenian year consisted of twelve lunar months, which usually were alternately of thirty and twenty-nine days. As the period from one new moon to another is approximately twenty-nine and a half days, this system roughly kept the months in step with the changes of the moon. As, however, it produced a year of 354 days, it soon got out of step with the solar year of $365\frac{1}{4}$ days. The Greek solution was to insert an extra month at intervals by repeating one of the current twelve. But we need not concern ourselves with the problems of this inter-calation, but take instead the typical twelve months of the Attic year and their associated festivals. The system of the twelve months itself was probably not very ancient. It does not appear in Homer at all and only doubtfully in one place in Hesiod. So scholars have conjectured that it was established not earlier than the first half of the seventh century BC. The relation between the calendar and the festivals is shown by the fact that though the Greek names for their months varied a great deal from city to city, they are almost all derived from the name of some festival falling in the month. But in Athens this has some curious features. None of the months is named after festivals of Athena in spite of the fact that she was the city's goddess. The ex-planation probably is that the names of the months were at least partly borrowed from Ionia where the festivals were often similarly named to those celebrated in Attica. The names show a marked bias in favour of feast days of Apollo or Artemis, and Nilsson may be right in supposing the influence of Apollo behind the system. Again the month in which the great initiation of the Eleusinian Mysteries took place was called Boedromion after a minor rite in the cult of Apollo – the Boedromia. The reason why the Mysteries did not lend a name to the month was no doubt that Boedromion was in current use before Eleusis and its cults were absorbed by Athens. The names of other months also recall festivals which were not prominent in the classical period, but earlier had evidently been of greater relative significance. In this way it is clear that the prominence and popularity of different deities and their cults could wax and wane with the passage of time. It is a process which is not mentioned by our literary sources, which do not describe

the history of Greek religion and only occasionally indicate the introduction of a new cult in classical times. These variations in worship
make it rather doubtful whether a picture drawn from sources of
different epochs can be correct for any one point in time. But it is only
by combining our sources that a general view can be produced; the
overall conservatism of Greek polytheism moreover tended to guarantee the continuance of cults even when they had lost importance with
the people.

The Christian year shows the working of two systems – the distribution of major festivals according to the pattern of events in the life of
Jesus, and the recurrence of other holy days to fit the progress of the
farmer's year. Greek polytheism had no gospel story which could
relate festivals to one another, but Greek religion was very closely
derived in much of its concerns from the need to insure fertility of
crops or animals or man. However, in the fifth and fourth centuries
Athens was undergoing a process of urban development not unlike, on
a small scale, what happened in Great Britain from the nineteenth
century. At the beginning of the Peloponnesian War, as Thucydides
records, the majority of Athenians still lived on country estates, and
must therefore have still felt the agricultural aspects of religious cult
as very real. But after the evacuation of the Attic countryside in face
of the Spartan invasions and the devastation of the olive-trees which
followed, the Athenian populace became more and more based on the
city and the Peiraeus. So though the old agricultural festivals of
Athens were preserved, they must have lost somewhat in significance.
The result may never quite have reached the anomaly familiar now-
adays of a city congregation enthusiastically singing 'We plough the
fields and scatter . . .', but it must have become more appropriate for a
citizen to join in the celebrations which were less concerned with the
seed-time and harvest. This may have encouraged an interest in new
deities not too closely linked to the Attic soil. But such questions as this
are better considered after a survey of the festivals themselves.

CALENDAR OF ATHENIAN FESTIVALS

	Hecatombaion	Metageitnion	Boedromion	Pyanepsion	Maimakterion	Poseideon
1						
2						
3						
4						
5			Genesia	Proerosia		
6			Artemis Agrotera, Boedromia			
7		[Metageitnia]		Pyanepsia, Oschophoria		
8				Theseia		Poseidea
9				Stenia		
10						
11				Thesmophoria (Halimus), The Road Up		
12	Kronia			The Fast ⎫ Thesmophoria		
13				Kalligeneia ⎭		
14			M —			
15			Y — Agyrmos (Gathering)			
16	Synoikia		S — 'Seaward, Initiates'			
17			T — 'Hither the Victims'			
18			E — Epidauria ⎫			
19			R — March to Eleusis ⎭			
20			I — Initiation			
21			E — Plemochoai			
22			S —			
23						
24						
25						
26						Haloa
27						
28	Panathenaia					
29						
30						
Festivals of uncertain date		Herakleia at Kynosarges		Chalkeia, Apaturia (Supper Eve, Sacrificing, Day of Youths, Morning after)	Maimakteria, Pompaia	The Country Dionysia

	Gamelion	Anthesterion	Elaphebolion	Munichion	Thargelion	Skirophorion
1						
2						
3						
4				Festival of Eros		
5						
6			Elaphebolia	Procession to the Delphinion	Thargelia →	
7						
8			Asclepieia			
9			Proagon			
10			City Dionysia →			
11		Pithoigia ⎫				
12	Lenaia →	Choes ⎬ Anthesteria			Skira	
13		Chytrai ⎭				
14			Pandia			Dipolieia
15						
16				Munichia		
17						
18						
19				Olympieia	Bendidia	
20						
21						
22						
23		Diasia				
24						
25					Plynteria	
26						
27						
28						
29					Kallynteria	Diisoteria
30						
Festivals of uncertain date	Gamelia					

Principal Sanctuaries of Athens

Part One

FESTIVALS IN THE CALENDAR

I HECATOMBAION

The first month of the Attic year, called HECATOMBAION, began about midsummer with the new moon before the summer solstice. The name of the month, like most of the others in the Attic year, was derived from a cult-title of Apollo as the god to whom hecatombs – hundreds of victims – were appropriately offered. But the festival of the *Hecatombaia*, had vanished from importance in Attica before classical times, leaving only the name of the month as its survival. It is noticeable that the Athenians had no state festival for New Year's day. To them as to other Greeks the month rather than the year was the significant religious unit, and they did not count their year from a great event in the past, like Christians reckoning the year of Our Lord. Similarly also in commerce the month, not the year, was the unit: interest was calculated monthly and due on the last day of the month. To the individual Athenian the significant annual day was his birthday, and there is no sign that for instance he celebrated the beginning of the first month by making New Year resolutions or saw the New Year in with a party, even a secular one.[1]

The only recorded religious ceremony performed at the start of the year was actually held on the last day of the previous month. It was a sacrifice to Zeus the Saviour and Athena the Saviour. The title was applied to Zeus as a protector of cities, and the Athenian festival was evidently not one for the citizens in general but for the magistrates and council of the old year appealing to the gods for the protection of Athens in the coming year. In this respect it is referred to in an official record as an inaugural ceremony, even though it actually took place before the new year had begun.[2]

Only three festivals occurred in Hecatombaion: one – the *Panathenaia* the most famous and important in Athens, and the others – the *Kronia* and the *Synoikia* – among the least renowned. The *Kronia* on the 12th of the month was dedicated to Kronos who seems to have been originally a god of the grain harvest with the reaping hook as his symbol. But his place in agricultural worship had gradually been taken

by other deities, and he chiefly survived in literature as the father of
Zeus according to mythology. In the days when Kronos was still an
important god his festival must have been intended to mark the final
end of the grain harvest and as such may have had some importance.
Athenians believed that in earlier times it had given its name to the
month, which had once been called Kronion and only later Hecatombaion. Actually the name was used in Samos and its colonies for
the last month of the old year, pointing to the existence of a similar
festival in Ionia somewhat earlier in the season. But by the classical
period in Athens there was only one feature surviving of the day's
ritual. It was a holiday for slaves and they were allowed to dine with
their masters. This was, as one may suppose, originally a celebration
of the end of the farmer's activity, and a kind of harvest supper in
which all who worked on the farm took part. But with the growth of
Athens as a city and the decline of arable farming as a main occupation
the only survival was a traditional privilege for the slaves. There was a
sanctuary of Kronos near the temple of Zeus, and presumably an
annual sacrifice took place there. But it has left no trace in our records.
Aristophanes can treat the festival as out of date and otherwise it is only
mentioned by Demosthenes because it was once ignored. In 353 B C
the politician, Timocrates, arranged for a meeting of the Ecclesia (the
popular assembly) to be held on the 12th of Hecatombaion. Demosthenes in prosecuting him later, of course implies that this was so as
to get through a piece of crooked legislation. But it is interesting to
notice that he says 'when this was the *Kronia* and on that account the
boulē [the state council] had been let go'. Evidently the day was
reckoned an occasion on which normally no state business was trans-
acted. How far this was regularly true of state festivals it is impossible
to tell. Elsewhere references to such dates as an occasion for work to be
suspended are not found. But presumably the day when the slaves had
holiday was so socially disorganized that it was easiest to treat it as one
on which usual activity was suspended. One may also wonder whether
in sophisticated periods to dine with one's slaves was more than a
perfunctory gesture. Some centuries later the dignified Plutarch
remarks that 'whenever the servants are having their *Kronia* banquet –
you would not endure their howling and uproar'. Probably the master
only appeared for the first course or two and then took an early
opportunity to leave the slaves to their for once rather uninhibited
enjoyment.[3] (Plate 1)

The other minor festival of Hecatombaion fell on the 16th. It was the *Synoikia* which, as its name implied, celebrated the Synoecism or combining into one community of the people of Attica. Traditionally this union was created by Theseus and should therefore have predated the Trojan War. But modern scholars would doubt his historical existence, and also reject the legend that the union of Attica took place as a single act so far in the past. Yet it is obviously true that at one time Attica was divided into a number of local communities, each ruled no doubt by its own separate king. When we first have historical evidence of a dependable kind, these had all been combined politically, except for Eleusis, and the kingships had all fallen.

In the time of Thucydides the Athenians held a state festival to Athena under this name, *Synoikia*. So at some point in the history of Athens' development, it had been resolved to celebrate in honour of the city's goddess the political union of Attica, but when we cannot tell. Thucydides mentions the festival in the place where he is carefully establishing early history from contemporary survivals. He accepts this origin of the celebration as dating from Theseus. The lack of later references to the feast-day is sufficient proof that it was not one of popular interest in the classical period.[4]

Some light on the subject comes from a fragment of the fifth-century code of sacrificial regulations found in the Agora. It records among the festivals held every second year as the earliest in the calendar sacrifices held on the 15th and 16th of Hecatombaion. This is evidently the *Synoikia* though the name does not appear in the inscription. Thucydides did not mention anything about a two-yearly celebration, and one would naturally expect the commemoration of an historic event to take place annually. But the part of the code dealing with the annual festivals of Hecatombaion is lost, and it probably contained a reference to the annual *Synoikia* on the 16th, and one should picture the celebration as taking place on this one day every year, and every second year being held in a larger and more extended form over the two days of the 15th and the 16th. The inscription confirms the belief that it was a primitive institution and to this extent justifies Thucydides in his belief that it dated from Theseus. The whole celebration is closely linked with the Phylobasileis (the kings of the four Ionic tribes, which only survived in classical times as an archaic religious system). The expenses of the festival were paid from a fund named after them and presumably under their control, and the code is mainly concerned with specifying the shares which they are to have in the sacrifices. The regulations include puzzling primitive features. On the first day one third (*trittys*) of the tribe of the Geleontes, described as 'those of the white head-bands', have a special right to the sacrifice. On the second day when the sacrifice was offered to Zeus Phratrios (god of the tribal brotherhoods) the tribe of the Geleontes are once more specially mentioned. The victims were not considerable: one young ewe on the 15th and two young bullocks on the 16th. The whole picture indicated is of a highly archaic rite involving out-of-date forms of aristocracy. It is not likely to have been instituted before the Trojan War, but there is nothing improbable in supposing that it might date from the eighth century B C at least.[5] (Plate 2)

Another inscription proves that some at any rate of the *demes*, the local territorial (and political) divisions, had a traditional part in the ceremony. The *deme* Skambonidai offered a mature victim – presumably a bull – to Athena. The record adds a further specification: 'The meat is to be sold raw.' This implies that it was not roasted on the Acropolis and shared out among the worshippers, but, after the parts reserved for the goddess had been burnt, the rest was disposed of by sale. Again we are left with the picture of a limited rite treated as a formality with no suggestion of a throng of feasters rejoicing in the celebration.[6]

In the fourth century B C another goddess was also worshipped on the same date. The people of Athens had become tired of the constant strains of recurring wars, and when in 374 B C an armistice with Sparta was achieved the occasion was celebrated by the institution of a new cult of Eirene, the goddess of Peace. This deity had existed in Greek literature as a personification since the time of Hesiod and had been used dramatically by Aristophanes in the war-weary years of the Peloponnesian conflict. But she had not received official worship previously and probably had not been thought of in personal terms by the ordinary citizen. It was in accordance with the new trend of the fourth century that more specific aspects of deities were personified and associated with them. Eros (Love) was accompanied by Himeros (Desire) and Pothos (Longing). So the worship of a specific deity of Peace was appropriate to the spirit of the time. It may also have had political overtones expressing the views of those who thought that Athenian imperialism was a mistake and any return to it a disaster. The cult was celebrated in the Agora at an altar and was fortunate enough to have the cult image produced by Cephisodotus, the father of Praxiteles. It was his masterpiece which can be identified in various late copies. The goddess was shown holding the child Ploutos

(Wealth), another associated personification, which by rather obvious allegory indicated that the wars of Athens had led to her impoverishment. In 374 the peace with Sparta only lasted a year or so but the cult evidently continued. It can be traced that forty-one years later in 333 BC the generals offered a considerable sacrifice on this date. Four centuries later when Plutarch records that the Athenians still sacrifice the *Synoikia* one may wonder whether this was the form of the festival which had survived.[7] (Plate 3)

A great contrast in importance was presented by the other festival of Athena held in Hecatombaion. This was the *Panathenaia*. In the classical period it truly became the ceremony in which all the inhabitants of Attica and even of the Athenian empire combined to do honour to the great goddess of the city. The 28th of Hekatombaion, three days from the end of the month, was the traditional date. From what were primitive and simple beginnings it became a most elaborate institution.

Originally Athena, like any other god or goddess, had one day in the year particularly dedicated to her, and legend chose to identify the date of the *Panathenaia* as her birthday. But also evidently from early times the day had another significance. Athena as a goddess was entitled to expect to have a new dress periodically, and her annual festival was the appropriate occasion for it to be presented to her. Such a presentation also required a suitable procession which would bring the dress to the goddess. When the archaic statue of Athena was only life-size, the dress itself will have been of ordinary human scale. Perhaps even earlier when the Athenians were unable to produce a life-size statue, the goddess may still have received a full-scale robe. Later, as we shall see, when the size of Athena's statue became colossal, her robe was proportionately enlarged.[8]

The festival day and the presentation of the *peplos*, as it was called, will have existed at least from the seventh century BC and probably much earlier. But a further element that greatly enhanced the popular interest of the festival was added in the sixth century. In 566/5 BC a programme of athletic contests was attached to the religious occasion. It was the period when gatherings of this sort were established as regular institutions in Greece. The Olympic games had been founded in the eighth century, but nothing on a similar scale and pattern had been celebrated till the Pythian games at Delphi became a regular institution from 582 BC. They were followed by the Isthmian games from 581 and the Nemean games from 573. So Athens was very much in a contemporary fashion in founding a recurrent series of contests. They were like the Olympic and Pythian games in being held every four years, and the occasion was known as a *Great Panathenaia* to distinguish it from the annual ceremony. But unlike the four great Panhellenic games which we have mentioned, the prizes at the *Panathenaia* were not merely garlands of leaves. They had a very real value as well as a spiritual and competitive significance. The reward was olive-oil made from the sacred olive-trees of Attica which were legendarily supposed to be all descended directly from the primal olive-tree created by Athena in her contest with Poseidon for the sovereignty of Attica. To contain the precious liquid for presentation to the victors a handsome jar of pottery was designed – the Panathenaic amphora – and remained the standard conventional pattern for two centuries with no great change in its shape and ornament. On the front was represented the armoured Athena brandishing her spear with the inscription 'from the games at Athens'; on the back a picture of the particular contest – chariot-race, foot-race, boxing and so forth.[9] (Plates 4–6)

The actual founder of the games was probably Hippocleides, a famous Athenian nobleman, who was chief magistrate (archon) in 566/5. He was a remarkable character – the subject of Herodotus' famous story of the suitor who lost the hand of Agariste, the daughter of the tyrant Cleisthenes of Sicyon, because he persisted in performing a dance on his head. This youthful indiscretion must have taken place a dozen or more years earlier. At the time of the founding of the games there was much political rivalry in Athens, and though we have no evidence on the subject in our ancient authorities, it is likely that one of the motives behind the institution was its appeal to the populace. Later when Peisistratus made himself tyrant he developed the festival further. From his time at least the procession had already become an elaborate affair. Also he laid down the rules for a competitive recitation of the works of Homer by the rhapsodes – an event which did not occur at Olympia or Delphi, and which may have had a permanent effect on the transmission of the *Iliad* and the *Odyssey*, the poems chosen for performance. In addition to the rhapsodes there were various musical contests. It is not certain when they were included in the programme of the festival. Whilst they possibly may have been established by Peisistratus, the latest date for their introduction would have been under Pericles, who built the Odeion as a concert hall for their performance.[10]

The dates when particular events were included are not known, nor is there any record of how many days were devoted to them. A minimum of some three or four days needs to be allotted even if we allow for the overlapping of some of the competitions. A general picture of the programme, though with some gaps, can be found in an inscription of the first half of the fourth century BC which lists the value of the prizes. It is preserved in two fragments, but covers many of the competitions.[11] (Plate 8) It starts with the awards for the events in the Odeion. The prizes for the rhapsodes which probably were listed first are lost. They were followed by the singers to the harp (Citharoidoi). It is noteworthy that these and the other musicians did not receive jars of olive-oil, but gilded crowns of wild olive together with money prizes. Also there were prizes in descending value for a number of the competitors. The victorious singer to the harp received a crown worth 1000 drachmas and 500 silver drachmas. The second a crown worth 700 drachmas and 50 in cash. The third a crown worth 600 drachmas and 10 in cash. The fourth a crown worth 400 and the fifth one worth 100. The explanation of the form of prize selected is probably that in the fourth century these musical performers were professionals of high standing. These celebrities were the object of much popular admiration and they could no doubt easily win handsome rewards anywhere in Greece, and to attract them to Athens there was needed not merely the renown of a great occasion, but also some decoration which could be worn at future performances and a tidy fee which at least covered expenses for even the third performer. Singers to the flute were reckoned cheaper. They only got as first and second prizes crowns worth 300 and 100 drachmas respectively, and apparently cash of 50 and 10 drachmas. There were also solo performers on the harp and the flute who received crowns, but no cash prizes. The singers to the flute and the solo harpists are described as men, which seems to imply that there were also competitions for boys in these two events; but no prizes are listed. Presumably they were not old enough to be reckoned of professional standing and were simply awarded plain crowns of olive which as of no specific value did not need to be recorded in the catalogue of the value or amount of the prizes.

The athletes are listed next. Their competitions comprised the five standard events in Greek sports meetings: the foot-race (*stadion*), the pentathlon, wrestling, boxing and all-in-wrestling (*pancration*). The competitors were divided into three classes by age: boys, beardless youths, and men. This contrasted with the Olympic games where the competitors we only divided into the two classes of boys and men. Unfortunately the men's awards are missing through the loss of the latter part of a column in the inscription. But in the case of the boys and the beardless youths a recurring pattern can be noted. There are first and second prizes for each event always consisting of jars of olive oil. The boy winner of the foot-race received fifty jars, the second, ten, and this proportion of five to one between first and second was maintained throughout the athletic events. The boy winners of the other four events were reckoned less meritorious and only got thirty jars and the seconds six each. The value of the prizes was stepped up for the beardless youths – sixty jars for the *stadion* victor and twelve for the second, while the other events received forty and eight respectively. What the further stage was for the men victors unfortunately is lacking. The only remaining column of the fourth-century inscription gives some details of the equestrian programme. Again the prizes were jars of olive oil and were awarded to firsts and seconds. The amounts varied a good deal and the proportions were sometimes five to one and at other times four to one. Horses were raced in four-horse chariots, two-horse chariots or ridden singly. There were races for foals as well as for full-grown horses and there were other special classifications. A race of pairs is for war horses, but a late Byzantine commentator who seems to have known the rules explains that these horses need not be trained for war but carried equipment as though going into battle. There was even a contest for javelin-throwing from horseback.

At the end are listed the team events, for which only the winner was recognized for an award. There were three classes – boys, beardless youths and men – who competed in the Pyrrhic dance. This was a traditional evolution performed in armour. Legend said that it had first been danced by Athena to celebrate the defeat of the Titans. [12] (Plate 7) This mythical origin made it particularly appropriate as an event in the *Panathenaia*. A relief from the Acropolis represents eight men performing a dance in hoplite armour which has been identified as this ceremony. It was probably dedicated by a successful team. The reward was 100 drachmas in money and an ox in each of the three classes. Presumably the cash was divided between the team members and the ox sacrificed to Athena, and its meat shared between them and their families and friends in a feast of celebration. The next two listed events were special to Attica. One was a contest in Manly Excellence (*evandria*). From a passage in Xenophon it is clear that this form of competition was reckoned unique to Athens. It was organized by tribes, each of which supplied a team, and it was one of the public duties (*leitourgiai*) to act as team manager. From Xenophon's allusions it is shown that large size and strength were qualities which scored points: but what tests and demonstrations the competitors had to undergo we do not know. In the list of prizes in the early fourth century the tribe winning in Manly Excellence was given the same award as the victors in the Pyrrhic dance – an ox and 100 drachmas. In Aristotle's time the individual members were given shields.[13] (Plate 7)

The next item on the list was the torch-race, but as it was incorporated in the ritual of the Panathenaic sacrifice it is best considered in that context.[14] Finally there is a prize 'for the contest of ships'. This again was organized on a tribal basis. The winning tribe received 300 drachmas for the crew and 200 more which are especially designated 'for the feasting'. So evidently a special celebration was held by the victorious tribe.

The regatta must have taken place in the Peiraeus, probably over the same course from the main harbour to Munichia which we shall see was used again at other festivals.[15] The horse-races were run somewhere on the open ground between the city and Phaleron. The athletic events were held in a stadium roughly on the site of the present one in Athens, which was reconstructed for the modern Olympic games, and the musical events by mid-fifth century were held in Pericles' Odeion. The contests involving tribes and the torch-race and regatta were confined to citizens as competitors. The musical contests and the athletic games were Panhellenic, and though Athenians could of course compete, they were open to musicians and athletes from anywhere in the Greek world. Pindar praises an Argive wrestler to whom 'by earth baked with fire the fruit of the olive came (as a prize) in the highly decorated walls of jars'.[16] Many foreigners must have thronged to Athens every four years, whether to take part in these competitions or as spectators. They will have seen not only the contests, but the great procession which embodied the united power and glory of Athens.

It was a remarkable spectacle even in Greece where this kind of public ceremony was highly developed. It has also been perpetuated in a unique representation on the frieze of the Parthenon. No other instance exists where an architectural decoration of this sort on a Greek temple shows, not some events of Greek legend, but a contemporary ritual. This innovation was appropriate on the Parthenon which was not just a restoration of the temple destroyed by the Persians, but a victory memorial to Athens' triumph over her enemies. The pediments showed the birth of the City Goddess and her establishment of her claim to Attica. The metopes in various myths depicted the victory of Greeks over savage monsters and of Athenians over their invaders. So the frieze displayed the contemporary life of the Athenians as dedicated to the honour of their goddess. Behind it we can see the purpose of Pheidias to express for Pericles those ideals which Thucydides was later to put into Pericles' mouth in the Funeral Speech.[17] (Plates 12–19)

So it is not surprising that the frieze was not simply a series of pictures reproducing the procession but rather a selection of episodes suitable for representation in carved relief worked up into one great imaginative unity. Our literary sources mention many details which cannot be traced in the Parthenon frieze, but on the other hand no extant author attempted to give a detailed description of the procession. So our two types of sources are complementary to each other, but even when combined do not enable one fully to picture the event.

The central feature was the *peplos*. This was the dress for the goddess, and so it was a very special object whose production was surrounded by much traditional ritual. It was woven by a team of maidens, the Ergastinai (Workers) who were chosen from the aristocratic families of Athens. The warp was set on the loom on the last day of the month Pyanepsion – the festival of the *Chalkeia*. This was nearly nine months before the *Panathenaia* and presumably in earlier days this had been found sufficient time to produce the *peplos*. Also the date, a festival of craftsmen, as we shall see, was probably felt to be appropriate for a beginning. Our late source which mentions the date also states that the work of setting up was done by the priestesses together with the Arrephoroi. As we shall later see, these latter were little girls specially dedicated each year to the worship of Athena. Evidently the solemn act of starting the work on the robe was begun by a group of people particularly linked to the goddess's service, and then it was carried on by the Ergastinai. The material used was wool, the traditional stuff of early Greek clothing. The main preoccupation was not the weaving of the material so much as its decoration. This was woven into the dress in the manner of tapestry, judging by the terms used to describe the pictures produced. The traditional subject mentioned repeatedly in our ancient authors was Athena's exploit in overcoming Enceladus in the battle of the Gods and Giants. It had been the myth represented on the pediment of the temple destroyed by the Persians and was a popular subject on Attic vases after the Persian wars had ended victoriously for Athens. The design of the *peplos* was executed in bright colours – yellow and blue are mentioned – and the general effect was evidently most striking. It was a conventional motive in the New Comedy to describe a maiden leading a sheltered life in the country as only coming to town to see the *peplos*.[18] (Plate 10)

Presumably the original garment had been of human scale or not much larger, but by the late fifth century at least the offering was made of such colossal size that it was as big as a ship's sail. To convey it to the Acropolis it was fixed on a model of a ship mounted on wheels, where it was rigged to the yard-arm of a mast in the centre. The ship-cart had a crew of priests and priestesses wearing golden and colourful garlands. One of these priests is honoured in a late inscription for having three times driven the vessel to the temple of Athena. Actually this elaborate cart was hauled from the Kerameikos Gate to the shrine of the Eleusinian Demeter on the slopes of the Acropolis. To have conveyed it up the final climb to the Propylaia was obviously too great a task. But presumably the *peplos* was struck at that point. How it was brought the remainder of the route to the Parthenon we are not told. The ship-cart itself was docked near the Areiopagus where Pausanias, the guide-book writer, records it among the sights for the tourist, as it was kept there from one *Panathenaia* to the next.[19]

One may ask why a model of this sort was used. Athena has no associations with the sea in her cult or her epithets. The explanation which has been suggested is that the idea of a ship-cart was borrowed from the worship of Dionysus where it seems to have been a long-established tradition. Probably the use of this form of vehicle for Athena's robe was devised at the time when the robe itself was first made of colossal size and that may well have been in the mid-fifth century when with the design of the Parthenon the cult-image of Athena was planned on a similar scale. Pheidias' statue of gold plates and ivory was over 30 feet high and needed a huge *peplos* as an appropriate offering. Also at the same period the power and glory of Athens was based so clearly on its fleet that the introduction of a ship in the procession must have seemed peculiarly appropriate.

The ship-cart was kept from festival to festival, but the robe was re-made for each occasion. Its design even if bound by convention in its handling was evidently the subject of severe competition. Aristotle records that 'once the council used to judge the samples for the *peplos* but now they are judged by a court appointed by lot. For the counsellors appeared to show favouritism.'[20] But only once is a change in the design recorded and the innovation had disastrous results. In 307/6 BC Demetrius Poliorcetes occupied Athens and his overthrow of the government of Demetrius of Phaleron was greeted with frantic delight by a group led by Stratocles who voted extravagant honours to Antigonus and his son. Among other distinctions meant to raise them above ordinary human level their portraits were to be woven into the pattern of Athena's *peplos* in the company of the goddess herself. This may not have been done in time for the *Great Panathenaia* of 306 BC, but certainly it was introduced into the *peplos* in 302 BC. However, when the ship-cart with the *peplos* as sail was passing through the Kerameikos in the procession a sudden squall struck it and broke the mast tearing the middle of the robe. A more disastrous omen could scarcely have been imagined, and appropriately next year in the battle of Ipsus Antigonus was killed and his army defeated. Athens rejected its allegiance to Demetrius and a dramatic poet, Philippides, attacked Stratocles for their misfortunes:

> Through him it was that hoar-frost blasted all the vines,
> Through his impurity the robe was rent in twain,
> Because he gave the god's own honours unto men.

As he was a personal friend of King Lysimachus, Demetrius' great opponent, Philippides went to Thrace and in private negotiations with the king arranged for him to supply a new mast and yard-arm for the sacred cart. This was obviously largely a political gesture, but also it came specially appropriately from Lysimachus' kingdom of Thrace – one of the chief Greek sources of forest timbers. The royal gift was in time to be used in the *Great Panathenaia* of 298 BC.[21]

The ship-cart does not appear on the Parthenon frieze, but this is not surprising as it would have been quite out of scale with the human figures which are the main element in the composition. The *peplos* probably is represented, but in a somewhat mysterious manner. At the central point of the frieze over the main east door of the temple was set a panel containing five figures. From the left two young girls are approaching the central figure of a tall dignified woman. The girls each carry on their heads a four-legged stool with a cushion on top. The tall woman who is the priestess of Athena Polias is assisting the nearer girl to remove the stool from her head. On the right, back to back with the priestess a bearded man is holding the edges of what is evidently a large oblong piece of cloth which is held on the opposite side by a boy facing him. They are represented as folding this cloth between them. The latter part of this scene can best be interpreted as the ultimate stage in the reception of the *peplos*. It is being folded so as to be laid away. How far this part of the scene links with the other half is difficult to determine. It all depends on the function of the stools. The most favoured interpretation is that they were set out at the entrance to the temple as a symbolic gesture to invite the presence of the goddess and other deities. The alternative possibility would be that they were intended to hold the *peplos* when it was folded so that it could lie before the temple until the conclusion of the ceremony. The idea of seats for the deities is supported by the fact that on either side of the central panel the nearest parts of the frieze showed the Twelve Gods seated on just such stools. They are shown in two animated groups either talking to each other or looking towards the procession which approaches them along the frieze. The charming picture represents Athena and her fellow deities as interested, but invisible, guests at her great festival. (Plate 12)

This interpretation of the central panels of the frieze is reasonably satisfactory, except for one difficulty. The oblong cloth representing the *peplos* is much too small for the robe as big as a sail which we have described from our literary sources. A. H. Smith has accurately recorded that it is shown on the frieze as 'folded once lengthwise and twice breadthwise. According to the scale of the figures it would measure four feet by seven.' These dimensions suggest a *peplos* of rather more than human dimensions, but not equal to that described by our ancient authors.

Two alternative explanations are open. Either the colossal size of *peplos* had not yet been introduced when the frieze was designed, and this is possible as our earliest literary reference to it is from the early fourth century BC, or else in spite of the fact that the vastly larger robe was already instituted, the designer chose, probably for aesthetic reasons, to represent the *peplos* as it used to be handled. If the colossal *peplos* had to be folded before storing it in the temple, the operation would certainly have been of an awkward scale to show on the frieze, and not easy to render in beautiful forms. So perhaps here as elsewhere in the translation of the Panathenaic procession into relief sculpture we encounter an obvious clash between the reality of the ceremony and the ideal representation in art.

On either side again of the two groups of gods come standing figures of older and younger men. They are unaware of the invisible deities, but like them are either talking among themselves or looking towards the approaching procession. On the southeast side there are six of them of whom the farthest from the centre is perhaps to be thought of as leading the procession and being greeted on arrival by the man next to him. At the opposite end four of the men are talking together, a fifth makes a gesture which is to call their attention to the arrival of the procession while the sixth and seventh face outwards towards it as it approaches. On either side the head of the procession itself consists of maidens but on the northeast side one standing man is included facing towards the approaching ranks. He is perhaps to be reckoned a fourteenth member of these groups of men at the receiving point of the route. But as this section of the frieze is defective, a detailed interpretation is impossible. (Plates 14, 15)

It is usually supposed that these male figures are human, though some scholars have preferred to see in them groups of heroes as a descending rank after the gods. If they are mortal, as is more probable, they must represent some Athenian officials. But the numbers shown do not fit neatly into any identification. They might be the nine archons or again the ten Agonothetai. But in either case there must be some extra persons present. Most likely the group of officials who waited to receive the procession consisted of various members of magisterial and other boards, and the designer has reduced them to a convenient pattern of standing male figures without distinguishing between the different categories.

The Agonothetai deserve a word of explanation. They were the board specially appointed to organize the *Great Panathenaia*. The other four-yearly festivals were run by an annual board of ten Hieropoioi appointed by the *boulē*. But the Agonothetai had responsibility for no other festival and were in office for four years from one *Great Panathenaia* to the next. The *boulē* chose them by lot, one from each of the ten tribes, so that representation was spread evenly among the Athenians. How the short list for allotment was prepared is not explained. As Aristotle records, 'they manage the procession of the *Panathenaia*, the musical and gymnastic contests and the horse-racing; they arrange for the making of the *peplos* and the oil jars in association with the *boulē* and they present the olive oil to the athletes.' Considering the elaboration of the festival the Board must have had a seriously responsible task especially as the days of the *Panathenaia* drew near. Starting on the 4th of Hecatombaion they remained in continuous session for the last twenty-four days and were given dinner at the public expense in the Tholos where the *boulē* dined.[22]

If we return to the procession, the head of it on either side consists of a group of maidens. Most of them were shown carrying bowls, jugs and an incense-burner – evidently the apparatus for the sacrifice. But the leading pair on either side are empty-handed and are therefore usually identified as the Ergastinai who now that their work is completed are given the place of honour at the head of the procession when the *peplos* is presented to Athena. The designer has probably chosen four to represent them. Our literary sources do not say how many there were, but late inscriptions give lists which if complete would be likely to hold 100 names at least in one year. (Plates 13, 16) Similarly in the rest of the procession the artist chose to show what would make a beautiful composition. He lays particular stress on the young men who represented the cavalry and the older groups who drove chariots. That the Panathenaic procession had always contained a large military component is suggested by our literary sources, but while they mention foot-soldiers, the frieze shows horsemen. Again no doubt the artist was deliberately selective and omitted the rank after rank of somewhat monotonous infantry while depicting with beautifully subtle variations the cavalry in all the stages from mounting to gallop. Also the frieze depicts an element which was no doubt present in this procession but had long ceased to play a part in warfare: the four-horse chariots. Each of these is drawn by a charioteer in the long robe traditional for the function. His passenger is a mature man in full hoplite armour. Technically he was called an *apobates* (dismounter) for his task was to leap from the chariot when it was in motion, run beside it and then remount again without stopping it. This was no doubt a good training exercise, and made an interesting spectacle at a festival. As a piece of military archaism on ceremonial occasions the *apobatai* can be compared to the Yeomen of the Guard.[23] (Plate 17)

Those taking part in the procession, however, were not confined to the religious officials and the army. An effort was evidently made to find a place for all ages and classes to be represented. Our literary sources supply a great deal of casual evidence on the subject. Besides the Ergastinai the maidens mentioned most are the Kanephoroi. They were chosen before each festival from the noble families and their function was to carry on their heads baskets containing the meal which would be sprinkled on the victims. They are not shown on the frieze, but one must picture them as elaborately equipped for the occasion.

It is recorded that Lycurgus in the late fourth century provided out of state funds gold ornaments for a hundred Kanephoroi. Associated with them are the Diphrophoroi or chair-bearers. We have seen already on the frieze two young girls carrying chairs, but they were probably quite different. The chair-bearers are described as following the Kanephoroi, and besides chairs they are also sometimes mentioned as carrying sunshades. So their purpose was probably not so much ritual as to provide for the comfort of the aristocratic Kanephoros during the lengthy ceremony in the blazing sun.[24]

The old men also had a place in the procession besides those of military age. Those selected were called the Thallophoroi (green branch bearers) because they carried boughs, probably of Athena's olive-trees. The frieze shows a group of older men in the middle of the procession. They have come to a halt and one is adjusting his garland, but as they are not actually shown carrying anything, it is perhaps unsafe to call them Thallophoroi. In one respect, however, they are well fitted for the part. They are notably handsome and it is an interesting fact that we are told that the old men appointed as Thallophoroi were chosen for their good looks. It is typical of the aesthetic sensitiveness of the fifth-century Athenian that, while he respected old age, it was not in itself enough to qualify for a part in a procession which was meant to be a beautiful spectacle. In this respect it is perhaps significant that there was no place in the procession for old ladies. The Greeks, unlike Rembrandt, do not seem to have recognized beauty in the face of an aged woman.[25] (Plate 18)

So far the participants whom we have mentioned were all citizens, but a place was also found for those resident non-Athenians (the Metoikoi) who were a prominent and wealthy body in fifth-century Athens. Their young men who could not be in the proper military procession were called Skaphephoroi (tray-bearers) as they carried trayfulls of offerings. The trays themselves like much of the apparatus of the festival were supplied by the state and were made of bronze or silver. The offerings on them were cakes and honeycombs, and the bearers themselves wore purple robes. The daughters of metics also were present carrying water jars. These groups cannot be identified on the frieze. The only young men shown carrying anything are bearing jars of some liquid, water or wine.[26] Finally, of the residents in Attica we are told in one reference that 'the freed slaves and other barbarians' (non-Greeks) carried branches of oak-trees. Again they are not identifiable on the frieze, but it may well be of set purpose that the designer omitted the participants who were not citizens.[27] (Plate 19)

One must also mention one class of participants in the festival who came from outside Attica. Under the Athenian empire an effort was evidently made to treat the great festival of the city's goddess as not only for all Athenians, but for all Greeks who were under an obligation to Athens. The inhabitants of Athenian colonies and Athenians overseas were expected to participate in the festival by sending a cow and a suit of armour on each occasion as an offering. This was a usual requirement from Greek colonies, which, though they did not normally owe any political allegiance to their mother city, were expected to share in its major religious festivals. But the Athenians from at least the mid-forties had been applying this to the cities of her empire, and in 425/4 BC she passed a general order requiring these offerings from them all. Considering that officially some four hundred communities were assessed for tribute the resulting procession of victims would have been vast. Actually one may suppose that many of the smaller places escaped the requirement through it not being fully enforced. The designer of the frieze includes some cattle and sheep escorted as sacrificial offerings, but one cannot distinguish whether they are supposed to come from Attica or overseas. They merely serve to indicate that after the presentation of the *peplos* the slaughter of victims was the other main ritual act.[28]

The sacrifice at the *Panathenaia* was associated with a remarkable piece of ritual. The fire on the altar of Athena was lit by a torch brought in a race to the Acropolis. The fire was taken from the altar of Eros in the Academy outside the Dipylon Gate, and it was not a relay-race but a contest of single runners each with a torch. As Pausanias explains, the object was to run as fast as one could, but also to keep the torch alight. Those who arrived first and second, if their torches were out, did not count. But the winner's torch was used to light the altar flame to burn the sacrifices. Peisistratus had dedicated the altar of Eros. So it is natural to suppose that he was responsible for this remarkable practice. The ritual idea behind it may have been to bring fresh fire as speedily as possible from one site to another, and the element of competition may also have suggested, like the drawing of lots, that the gods were allowed room for choice in the matter. But on a more mundane level it fitted with the athletic contests of the Panathenaic games as part of the festival. The precinct of the Academy probably had much earlier connections with torch-races. For in it was situated the altar of Prometheus, the primitive Athenian god of fire and, as we shall see, the site of another torch-race, which is likely to have been older than the *Panathenaia*. It provided the model on which Peisistratus founded his race to light the fire on Athena's festival. The distance must have been over two miles and ending in the steep ascent of the Acropolis. So it is not surprising that one ancient commentator described this as 'the long race'. The list of prizes of the mid-fourth century which we have already discussed records that the winner was given the sum of thirty drachmas and a water jug (*hydria*). It is strange, and unexplained, why he should not have received jars of olive oil like the athletic victors.[29]

In Aristophanes we have a sarcastic caricature of what could happen in this torch-race. In the *Frogs* Aeschylus is represented in the Other World as accusing Euripides of being responsible for producing a generation of Athenians of whom 'no one is able to carry a torch any longer through lack of athletic training'. Dionysus supports this charge with a reminiscence: 'No indeed, by Jove, and at the *Panathenaia* I split myself laughing when a slow fellow was running, doubled up, white and flabby, left behind and in a terrible state. Then the men from the Kerameikos [the workmen's quarter through which the course went] in the gates were butting him on the belly and ribs and flanks and buttocks. When he was beaten on the road he gave a fart, blew out his torch and fled.' The episode is perhaps not all mischievous fantasy and is certainly a corrective to any romantic and sentimental notion of classical Greeks who were all perfect athletes.[30]

To many Athenians the sacrifice rather than the procession must have been the most important event of the festival. The *peplos* and its many accompanying attendants will have made a magnificent spectacle, but one with which the older inhabitants of the city were familiar enough. With its narrow streets and low houses Athens will not have been built so as to enable people to see the procession well in the town itself. When it crossed the open spaces in the Agora and the slopes leading towards the Acropolis a better view would be possible. We never hear of public stands, only of a private platform erected by a politician in the mid-third century. He was Demetrius, a descendant of Demetrius of Phaleron and like him a virtual dictator under the Macedonian supremacy. He aroused indignation by setting up a stand in the Agora, 'higher than the stoa of the Hermai' so that his Corinthian mistress might view the *Panathenaia*.[31]

The sacrifices had a practical interest for many Athenians because they were able to get a meat meal at the city's expense. The complicated procedure involved is well illustrated by a decree of about 335 BC which was part of the great revival and reorganization of ceremonies undertaken by Lycurgus, the able finance minister.[32] Actually this document deals with the annual *Panathenaia*, not the Great (four-yearly) festival. But one can take it that the kind of regulations which it makes applied on an even larger scale on the more important occasion. The preamble is missing but otherwise the most important parts are preserved: '. . . in order that the procession may be equipped as well as possible when it is sent each year to Athena on behalf of the people of Athens and that in other respects all that is needed be managed well to do with the festival held in honour of the goddess by the Hieropoioi on every occasion, the people has voted the resolution of the *boulē* and that the Hieropoioi are to sacrifice the two sacrifices, one to Athena, Goddess of Health (Hygieia), and the other at the old temple as previously. They are to assign five portions to the Prytaneis (the committee of the *boulē*), three to the archons, one to the treasurers of the goddess and one to the Hieropoioi, three to the generals and divisional officers and to those Athenians who took part in the procession and to the Kanephoroi in the usual manner. They are to apportion the remainder of the meat to the Athenians.'

The part of the decree evidently deals only with a special group of the sacrifices. The proposals of the *boulē* which may have dealt with any other matters concerning the festival were passed en bloc by the people and are not recorded. But the rules for disposing of these special sacrifices are preserved and also, as we shall see, for the more general offering. The method is interesting. Various officials have a right to share in certain 'portions'. What a portion (*meris*) was is not defined as it was evidently something already understood. It was not an individual helping, for the Prytaneis, for instance, who were fifty in number have five portions to divide between them. The individual shares must have varied between the different groups of officials. The nine archons do much better than the Prytaneis. They have three portions between them, working out at three to a portion, while the Prytaneis were ten to a portion. Similarly the ten Hieropoioi and the ten treasurers each have to share one portion. 'The usual manner' in which the members of the procession shared is not explained. As for the general body of the Athenians, the rest of the document gives some notion how they were probably treated.

'From the 41 minas [4100 drachmas] derived from the lease of the

fallow land the Hieropoioi are to buy cattle in consultation with the
"cattle buyers".' Evidently the Athenian state had already set aside some
public land as an endowment for the festival, and the proceeds from
the lease amounted to 4100 drachmas. One can vaguely estimate the
value of this sum by reckoning that the day-wage of an Athenian of
the period would vary from one and a half to two drachmas. It is
interesting to notice that Athens had a special commission, little
mentioned in our literary sources, who were responsible for the
buying of cattle for sacrifice.

The document continues:

> When they have led the procession they are to sacrifice to the
> goddess all the cows on the great altar of Athena, except for one on
> the altar of Victory having chosen it in advance from the best
> quality cows. When they have sacrificed to Athena the City Goddess
> and Athena Victory out of all the cows bought from the 41 minas
> they are to distribute the meat to the people of Athens in the Kera-
> meikos as in the other distributions of meat. They will assign the
> portions to each *deme* in proportion to those in the procession as
> many as each *deme* provides.

The main sacrifice was to be supplied from the income derived from
the lease. It was evidently to be spent in full each year and the number
of cows purchased would presumably fluctuate somewhat in accordance
with the current price of cattle. These victims were to be driven in
procession to the Acropolis and sacrificed on the altar in front of the
Parthenon, except for one selected animal which would be offered in
front of the temple now popularly called that of the Wingless Victory.
Then all the meat was to be distributed to the people (apart of course
from the portions burnt in offering to the goddess). This distribution
did not take place on the Acropolis, but down in the town at the
Kerameikos, where the procession had started. The source does not
explain how the large quantity of meat from no doubt at least a
hundred cows was transported this considerable distance. Presumably
this was one of the familiar tasks of the Hieropoioi. One may note
that the distribution to the people was made on the basis of the local
districts (the *demes*). These varied greatly in size, some being very
large and populous, some quite small. Also one may imagine that the
distant *demes* may not always have been enthusiastic in providing
members to travel to Athens so as to take part in the procession. How-

ever, each community was to have its quota of portions in accordance with its participation in the ritual. How the *demes* distributed their portions individually was presumably left to them. (Plate 9)

The document ends the arrangements for the sacrifice by recording:

> For the expenses of the procession and the butchery and the fitting of the big altar and all the other things that need to be provided in advance to do with the festival and the all night service 50 drachmas are provided. The Hieropoioi who manage the yearly *Panathenaia* are to make the all-night service as well as possible in honour of the goddess and are to send the procession at sunrise and anyone who fails to obey they are to punish with the penalties provided by law.

Evidently the 50 drachmas represented a small cash advance intended to cover the sundry minor expenses which the putting-on of the festival involved. The tone of the final summary of instructions to the Hieropoioi perhaps suggests that recent performances of the procession had not been up to time and had been laxly done through a failure to enforce discipline.

The final instructions also mention the all-night service. Such *Pannychides* were a common feature in Greek worship. Actually this one in honour of Athena is scarcely mentioned in our literary sources where it was evidently taken for granted as part of the festival. The one noteworthy passage is in a patriotic chorus in the *Heraclidai* of Euripides. The poet with obvious appropriateness to the date of production early in the Peloponnesian War makes his Athenian maidens in face of a Dorian invasion invoke Athena. 'Since to you the honour of many sacrifices is accomplished and the day is not missed when the moon wanes and there are songs of young men and choirs of dancers. On the windy mountain ridge the shrill voices of maidens echo to the rhythmic beat all night of dancing feet.'[33] The scene of the *Pannychis* was the breezy top of the Acropolis round the Parthenon, and the ritual events were hymns sung by young men and dances of singing maidens all performing in honour of the goddess. We must remember here that Greek and Roman festivals, like those of the Hebrews, could be reckoned strictly to begin at sunset. So it could be regarded that the *Pannychis* was the preliminary ritual to the great procession which would start as soon as the sun rose. If the young men and girls began their activities at nightfall one can imagine they would have been rather exhausted by the time the procession was over and the meat distributed in the Kerameikos. The tail-piece is provided by Aristophanes. In the *Clouds*, when Socrates is expounding the material explanation of thunder, he asks the simple Athenian who has enquired of him: 'When at the *Panathenaia* you have filled yourself with stew, then were you disturbed in your tummy and did a roaring noise suddenly rumble through it?' The scholiast rather unnecessarily comments that 'because of the abundance of meat they all filled themselves, eating beyond what they ought.'[34]

2 METAGEITNION

It is perhaps appropriate that after the great exertions and excitements of the *Panathenaia* a pause comes in the sequence of the Athenian festivals. The month that followed, METAGEITNION, contained no major event. Its name like that of the months that immediately preceded and succeeded it was derived from a cult-title of Apollo – in this instance Metageitnios – and there was evidently a festival of that name in his honour. But it was not treated as one of importance in our literary or inscriptional sources. The derivation of the name, suggesting the idea of 'changing neighbours' is peculiar, and modern scholars would prefer to regard it as some festival involving the neighbourhood. It was celebrated as a holy day in various Ionian centres – certainly in Miletus, and on the evidence of the month name at Delos, Ephesus and Samos, but no more can be said of it.[35]

The only other festival which is known to have occurred in this month was the annual celebration of Heracles in the gymnasium at Kynosarges. Heracles was an appropriate patron deity for athletics, but at Kynosarges there was a curious rule that the club was specially open to residents of non-citizen birth, who would not elsewhere have been accepted. These were particularly the children of mixed marriages between an Athenian and a foreign wife. Even the officials of Heracles' cult were drawn from this class. According to the popular picture of Heracles he was a hero who indulged greatly in eating and drinking. Hence his cult generally included feasting as a prominent element in the ritual, and at Kynosarges, as elsewhere also, to guarantee the god company at his meal twelve members were chosen as Parasitoi – probably the earliest use of the word which was to become 'parasite'. At Kynosarges a law passed by Alcibiades laid it down that 'the priest and the Parasitoi were to have a monthly sacrifice. The Parasitoi were to be drawn from the base-born and the sons of the base-born in accordance with ancestral custom. If any one refused to act as Parasitos, he was to be brought to court on the question.' The sacrifice falling in the month Metageitnion must have been the chief annual feast at Kynosarges, but we have no further particulars about it.[36]

However, one peculiar practice which was typical of festivals of

Heracles may perhaps be conjectured as occurring there. Theophrastus in his *Characters* when describing that remarkable, but not unfamiliar, human type, the Late Learner, says: 'Of course if ever he is invited to a shrine of Heracles, he throws off his coat and lifts the bull so that its neck can be cut.' The Late Learner is depicted as a rather pathetically eager extrovert trying to imitate the young. At a number of state festivals, as we shall see, it was the custom not simply to pole-axe the victim and cut its throat and then dismember the carcase and put the appropriate pieces, bit by bit, on the altar. Instead the animal was lifted bodily aloft and placed on the altar for its throat to be cut. A number of references in classical literature make the reality of this practice reasonably certain, though some classical scholars have boggled at the feasibility of the ceremony. The struggling bull would certainly present a problem. But it may first have been stunned with a blow of a mallet or thrown and roped. We shall see later that at a feast of Hephaestus as many as two hundred Athenians were selected to lift the bulls. The number of victims is not stated, but evidently such a large contingent could be divided into a number of teams to deal with them in turn. Theophrastus pictures a less formal procedure as typical of the feast of Heracles. The young men probably volunteered for the task and the Late Learner cannot be prevented from throwing off his coat and joining in. Just as the providing of an ample banquet of meat fitted the character of Heracles as the god to be honoured, so also a display of strength such as was involved in lifting his victims bodily on to the altar may have seemed to suit his worship. But the occurrence of the custom at other festivals makes this explanation doubtful.

3 BOEDROMION

The next month, BOEDROMION, also derived its name from an Apolline festival, which as usual was held on the 7th of the month. Unlike the *Metageitnia* this had a local Attic legend to explain its origin, though as the cult-title and month are known elsewhere in Greece the story is not to be taken as authentic. According to it the Athenians were at war with the Eleusinians in the reign of Erechtheus, and their enemy led by Eumolpus was winning when Ion came hastily to help the Athenians and brought about victory. In gratitude for this service he was made king after Erechtheus, who had fallen in the battle. Ion in legend was closely associated with Apollo, sometimes even made his son. So it was to be expected that the victory would be celebrated by a feast of Apollo. Also the title, 'Boedromios', was correctly enough derived from a word meaning 'to run to help in response to a shout'. The assistance of Ion was pictured as explaining this title. The legend is a typical story invented to explain a cult, but is unnecessary. Obviously the festival was a general thanksgiving to Apollo as the god who rescued in war. It may have been fixed at this date because September represented the close of the campaigning season and was therefore appropriate for such a festival. There is only one reference in ancient literature which indicates the form of the celebration and this mentions a procession. It is a sarcastic allusion in Demosthenes to the way in which contemporary politicians have induced the Athenian populace to eat out of their hands. 'You are content if they give you a share of the festival funds or mount a procession at the *Boedromia* for you.' This suggests that there was some amount of popular display at the *Boedromia*, but evidently nothing very grand.[37]

Two days earlier in the month, on the 5th, took place a festival which also may have had some connection with the end of the campaigning season. This was the *Genesia* – a state celebration in honour of the dead. Its name implies that it was a family festival, and Jacoby may be right in supposing that originally it belonged to the aristocratic clans who may have separately reverenced their dead in their private burial grounds on this day.[38] Then Solon, in whose legislation it appeared, may have converted it into a national celebration. This would be consistent with the policy of a legislator, such as Solon, to control the aristocratic clans and convert their practices into functions for the community. So the *Genesia* as established by him may have been a kind of Remembrance Day, on which the state recognized its debt to the dead, which in early times would be mainly their sacrifice in battle. We have one famous description of what could be such an occasion: Thucydides' account of the setting for Pericles' funeral speech.

Two days before the ceremony the bones of the fallen are brought and put in a tent which has been erected, and people make whatever offerings they wish to their own dead. Then there is a funeral procession in which coffins of cedarwood are carried on wagons. There is one coffin for each tribe, which contains the bones of the members of that tribe. One empty bier is decorated and carried in the procession; this is for the missing, whose bodies could not be recovered. Everyone who wishes to, both citizens and foreigners, can join in the procession, and the women who are related to the dead are there to make their laments at the tomb. The bones are laid in the public burial place, which is in the most beautiful quarter outside the city walls . . . When the bones have been laid in the earth, a man chosen by the city for his intellectual gifts and for his general reputation makes an appropriate speech in praise of the dead and after his speech all depart.[39]

This ceremony took place at the end of the campaigning season, during a major war, but it is not safe to equate it with the annual *Genesia*, which in peace-time will not have had the same material for a public funeral. However, it does express beautifully the spirit of fifth-century Athens in such ceremonial with its balanced association of dignified public mourning and restrained private participation. Apart from the *Genesia* there is no evidence of a public festival of the Athenian dead. Private families went to the tombs of relatives with offerings on their anniversaries. But the state was not otherwise concerned except in the cult of some heroized dead such as Harmodius and Aristogeiton or the dead at Marathon.

The battle of Marathon itself was associated with the 6th of Boedromion, and the anniversary became an important festival. The day had in earlier times been established already as the feast of Artemis Agrotera (the Huntress). Her temple stood outside the walls of Athena at Agrai on the Ilissos, and legend maintained that this was the place where she had first engaged in hunting after she left her native Delos. Just as Apollo's birthday and festival day was the 7th of the month, his twin sister was evidently thought of as being born a day earlier and usually had her festivals on the 6th. Before the battle the Athenians made a vow to the goddess that they would sacrifice to her a she-goat for every Persian whom they killed. Artemis was not normally a goddess of war in Athens. So it is reasonable to suppose that the vow was made because of some connection in date between the campaign and Artemis' traditional festival. Actually in later times it was asserted that the battle itself had taken place on the 6th of Boedromion, but this is impossible to square with the refusal of the Spartans to march because they were waiting till the full moon of the *Carneia* was past. The more reasonable supposition is that the 6th was the date on which the resolution was passed by the Athenian army to set out from Athens, and the vow was made in anticipation of the battle which did not actually take place till ten days later. The victory which followed put the Athenian state in a curious quandary. According to Herodotus, who probably represents the reasonable estimate of the time, 192 Greeks had fallen and about 6400 Persians. This figure of numbers slain had far exceeded the wildest conjecture before the battle. The Athenians, as Xenophon was later to explain, could not find sufficient she-goats to reach the number vowed. The goat population of Attica would have been wrecked. So as a compromise it was vowed to sacrifice 500 yearly to Artemis and this continued to be done a century later in Xenophon's day when the original total of the Persian dead had long been passed. The effect of the decision was to convert the 6th of Boedromion into a commemorative festival for the victory of Marathon, which led again to the mistaken popular belief that it was the actual anniversary. Also as there is no evidence that the she-goats were burnt as a holocaust, it must have meant a feast of goat flesh for some thousands. The Polemarchos, as the traditional official responsible for military affairs, conducted the festival and in later times at least it was made a military occasion. The young soldiers in training (Epheboi) paraded under arms and marched in procession to the temple of Artemis. Probably they had a share in the ensuing feast.[40] (Plate 20)

After this cluster of festivals early in the month, the next occasion fell on the 15th when the celebration of the Eleusinian Mysteries commenced. These ceremonies to the modern reader suggest something more like what he would expect of a religious rite. The *Pana-thenaia* would seem more like a Lord Mayor's show combined with an

athletic and musical competition. The participants would not need to
do so with religious feeling, nor would they be expected to acquire any
personal merit or spiritual reward from their performance. But the
Mysteries both laid some stress on the fitness of those initiated and in
return initiation promised some religious benefits to those taking part.
Also some of the methods used – fasting and congregational worship
led by a minister – suggest superficially Christian ritual. It is probably
because of this general resemblance that the Eleusinian Mysteries were
bitterly attacked in the polemics of some of the Christian Fathers. This
hostile attitude, while understandable, is unfortunate. For these late
Christian writers are the only authors who set out to expose the heart
of the Mysteries, and their testimony is correspondingly suspect through
their obvious prejudice. Pagan authors on the other hand clearly felt
themselves bound by the silence which was the reason why these
ceremonies were called mysteries. They were not supposed to be
mysterious in the sense of containing some recondite teaching difficult
to understand, but were things about which one must shut one's
mouth in the literal meaning of the word 'mystery'. Those who had
been initiated must not subsequently mention the content of their
initiation even among those who have shared in the rite. It was possible
to be prosecuted in Athens for this kind of profanation, as it is said
Aeschylus was. [41]

Actually in the classical period, at least, the Great Mysteries of
Eleusis were not the first stage in initiation. This was properly begun
at the Lesser Mysteries held at Agrai some seven months previously in
Anthesterion. Those who wished to be initiated at Eleusis should first
have received initiation at Agrai. This previous festival can best be
discussed in its proper place in the calendar. But also there was a
further stage of higher initiation at Eleusis itself. Those who had taken
part in the rites in one September could return next year or later and be
advanced to the final stage then. In this way the Mysteries were
ultimately developed into quite an elaborate pattern of ritual.

The origin of the cult, however, was probably quite simple and
local to Eleusis itself. Demeter was the goddess of the corn crop and
was linked at Eleusis with the original royal palace in the manner of
other Mycenaean goddesses. The legend associated with her told how
when her daughter Persephone was carried off to Hades by the King of
the Underworld she wandered the earth in grief seeking for her and
came disguised as an old woman to the town of Eleusis. She was
received in a kindly way by the royal family and appointed nurse of

the boy prince. Later her divinity was revealed and she commanded the building of a temple in her honour and instituted the Mysteries as an expiatory ceremony. This myth is enshrined in the beautiful *Homeric Hymn to Demeter*, a composition probably to be dated to the latter half of the seventh century BC. At the time it was composed Eleusis was still a community independent of Athens with a little port in the Bay of Salamis and the fertile Rarian plain behind it where legend said that corn had first been sown. Evidently the Mysteries at this early date were fully established, though the exact form of the festival at this archaic period would be beyond proof. However, already they made a claim to confer spiritual benefit as is proudly recorded in the lines 'Blessed the man among mortals on earth who has seen these things. But he who has not partaken of the rites and is without a share in them, he never has a lot in similar good things when dead beneath the grim darkness.' So the initiate was promised a blessed hereafter as a consequence of his participation.[42]

Athens is not mentioned in the *Homeric Hymn*, but some time in the last years of the seventh century not long after it was written Eleusis fell finally under the control of her great neighbour and was incorporated in Attica. This led to the taking over of the festival by the Athenian state, and clearly the form in which it was celebrated in the classical period was the result of a combination of the cults of Eleusis and Athens. But the original priesthoods were not displaced. Though the organization of the festival was controlled by the King Archon, the regular official for the state religion at Athens, the chief priesthood of the Mysteries – the Hierophantes or 'Revealer of the Sacred Things' – was appointed from the family of the Eumolpidai who claimed to be descended from the kings of Eleusis. So the local hereditary right was maintained. The possible trace of Attic intrusion in the priesthoods concerns the second rank – the Daiduchos or 'Torch-holder.' At least by the fifth century and probably earlier this important post had become hereditary in the family of the Kerykes ('Heralds') who alternated the family names of Callias and Hipponicus. They seem to have been an Athenian not an Eleusinian clan, and it is probable that it was as representatives of Athens that they managed to win a post in the hierarchy second only to that of the high priest.[43]

A word or two may be said in parenthesis about these religious officials. For in several respects they differed from the normal Athenian priests. First of all, when performing their ceremonies they wore elaborate robes, which can be compared to sacred vestments. So far as one can tell, the other Athenian clergy simply wore their ordinary secular clothes and at most assumed an appropriate garland, but since the worshippers too would often be garlanded at a festival this was not the exclusive mark of the officiating cleric. The vestments of the Eleusinian priest were so elaborate that they were compared to the dignified costume which Aeschylus was said to have invented for his kings in tragedy. Even in private life they retained some features of this garb. For instance the Daiduchos wore a beard and long hair which he confined in a special headband. The effect was to mark him out and convey the effect of royalty. This is illustrated by an extremely malicious story which was told to account for the great wealth of the family of Callias the Daiduchos, whose nickname was 'Pits of riches'. It tells that on the field of Marathon a Persian seeking mercy mistook Callias for a king because of his long hair and headband, and to win his life showed him a pit full of gold. But Callias appropriated the treasure and slew the man, to conceal the evidence. The story need not be believed, but it would have had no plausibility unless one is to picture the Daiduchos as garbed unlike other Athenians even on the field of battle.[44] (Plate 28)

It is possible that as time went on the reverence for these offices and the recognition of their peculiar character actually increased. Certainly in the Roman period the personal name of the Hierophantes was subject to a taboo and must not be spoken or written in his lifetime. Priests engaged in religious rites were normally expected to observe ritual taboos including abstention from marital intercourse at the time of festivals, but for the Hierophantes this was carried much further. Late authors allege that he was drugged at the time of the Mysteries so as to ensure his bodily chastity.[45]

In another direction too, besides the share in the priesthoods, the Athenian state won a place for itself in the pattern of the Eleusinian Mysteries. There evidently was a local cult of Demeter (called simply 'The Mother') at Agrai on the Ilissos. This site had its own Mysteries which included the worship of Persephone, and were held in the springtime in the month Anthesterion. When Eleusis was incorporated in Attica the relation between these two cult centres was conveniently worked out on the basis of the arrangement that the Mysteries at Agrai were the Lesser Mysteries where initiation must be sought before applying to be admitted to the Greater Mysteries of Eleusis. This suited both centres. Agrai obtained a certain priority in time and a link with the more important Eleusinian rites by accepting a technically lesser status.[46]

In a third direction, too, Eleusis and Athens were combined in the worship of Demeter. After their union a consecrated area was set aside for the goddess of Eleusis above the Agora and immediately below the Acropolis. This bore her name and must have contained some building to act as a shrine, for annually in the festival of the Mysteries the 'Holy Things' were brought from Eleusis to Athens to be lodged temporarily there and then were returned in a great procession to their traditional home. As Nilsson points out, this curious procedure shows that the Athenians may have wished actually to transfer the cult from Eleusis to Athens, in the way in which, as we shall see, the local cult of Dionysus of Eleutherai actually was transferred. But Eleusis was too important a place and the local attachment of her goddess was too strong to be broken in this way. So the Athenians had to be content with a symbolic visit of the 'Holy Things' to Athens as an admission of the importance of the ruling city. By these tactful compromises between different officials the two cult centres and political capitals were all successfully fused into a complicated pattern of festivals which came to be recognized in the Greco-Roman world as one of the greatest of its religious occasions. [47] (Plate 21)

The first day of the Mysteries fell on the 15th of Boedromion. The full moon in this lunar month would make an auspicious beginning. But as a preliminary preparation two days previously on the 13th of the month young men on military training (Epheboi) went out to Eleusis and on the 14th escorted the 'Holy Things' from their shrine there to the Eleusinion in Athens. They had to be shielded from the sight of the uninitiated, and so were brought out in round boxes (*kistai*) which were tied with purple ribbons. (In 322 BC when Athens had to submit for the first time to a Macedonian garrison, it was recognized as an omen of this disaster that the dye on the ribbons had turned out a sickly hue.) The 'Holy Things' themselves must have been quite small as the boxes containing them could be carried by the priestesses. Mylonas has conjectured that they were the appurtenances of a Mycenaean palace shrine which had survived in Eleusis through the Dark Ages.[48]

The priestesses and the *kistai* were conveyed in a wagon which was paid for by the state. About half-way to Athens they had to cross the streams known as Rheitoi. About 421 BC the Athenians built a bridge over them, using the stones left over from the temples at Eleusis demolished by the Persians, but the decree authorizing the work specified that the bridge was to be only 5 feet wide and was not for carts, but so that the priestesses could better carry the 'Holy Things' over the bridge. They must have dismounted from the wagon which went round by the ford to pick them up again on the other side of the streams.[49]

On arrival at the Eleusinion the minor official known as the Cleaner (Phaidryntes) of the Two Goddesses went to the Acropolis and reported to the priestess of Athena that the 'Holy Things' and their escort had arrived. By this charming piece of etiquette the senior importance of the city's goddess over all other divinities was maintained in dignity.[50]

The conveying of the 'Holy Things' to Athens was a high state occasion, but it did not involve the participation as yet of those about to be initiated. That began on the 15th – the day known as *Agyrmos* (the Gathering). It was so named because those seeking initiation were required to assemble in the Agora at the Painted Portico, where in the presence of the Hierophantes and the Daiduchos a formal proclamation was delivered. In later times there was a special official, the Sacred Herald drawn from the clan of the Kerykes charged with this duty. The proclamation invited candidates for initiation to declare themselves and also contained prohibitions against those who could not take part without the guilt of sacrilege. The postulants were to be of pure hands, particularly in respect of blood-guilt, but also it would appear that the Herald specified more spiritual fitness. The would-be initiate must have 'a soul conscious of no evil and have lived well and justly'. There was no distinction of age or sex, and free men and slaves were in theory equally entitled to admission. The only racial exclusion was directed against barbarians (i.e. non-Greeks), but in later times Romans were accepted. As the stress seems to have been placed not so much on foreign birth as on 'intelligible speech', the underlying motive may have been less to exclude the alien than to ensure that those taking part in the Mysteries could understand what was said and, if necessary, respond correctly.[51]

It is not clear how far there was a formal registration of candidates, but it is probable that this was the point where they were required to pay their fees, and, if so, some sort of roster was probably prepared. It would give occasion, if necessary, for excluding barbarians and also for ascertaining whether the candidate had already received initiation in the Lesser Mysteries, if this was actually made a pre-condition. As for the deeper matters of personal fitness, whether ritual purity or spiritual preparedness, one can scarcely suppose that the candidates were catechized. There were too many of them for it to be satisfactorily performed in one day. Evidently by the proclamation of the Sacred Herald the onus was put on the would-be initiate not to present himself or herself if they were unfit, as it was declared that the goddesses would punish the unworthy.

The cost of initiation was quite high. In the late fourth century it ran at a total of 15 drachmas each, which one can estimate as some ten days' wages. This sum was made up of contributions paid to each of the officials responsible. In a fragmentary inscription of a century and a half earlier recording the restored regulations after the Persians had destroyed the sanctuary, we find that 'the Hieropoios is to receive a half obol a day from each initiate: the priest of Demeter at the Great Mysteries is to receive an obol a day from each initiate'. Evidently there were other officials listed above in the broken record. Also quaintly enough at the end of the lengthy regulations a footnote had been inscribed later in a different, less careful, hand recording that 'the priest at the altar and the cleaner of the Two Goddesses and all-holy priest each receive a half obol from each initiate consecrated to the Two Goddesses'. It appears as if the perquisites of both these minor officials had been overlooked when the official rules were drawn up. Perhaps even they had been undisclosed tips which were belatedly added to the table of rules.[52]

We must not suppose that these fees collected by the priestly officials simply went into their private pockets. The same decree lays down that the whole amount received for the Two Goddesses is to be more than 15,000 drachmas and from this sum the priestess is to pay the customary expenses. So presumably the priesthood could only divide among themselves the balance left over after all expenses had been met. If we take the later figure of 15 drachmas per person, it seems to be implied that a minimum of a thousand will take part, and for the fifth century a figure of this sort may not be unreasonable. On the other hand perhaps the registration at the *Agyrmos* may also have made sure that the numbers coming forward for admission would not exceed the space in the Hall of Initiation.

The would-be initiates, as we have seen, were not merely Athenians, but came from all over the Greek world. Already in the fifth century heralds were sent out in advance to all the cities that recognized the festival inviting them to declare a truce of fifty-five days to allow safety of travel to and from Eleusis for the pilgrims. [53] These foreigners, many of whom might never have seen Athens before, and had likewise to take part in an elaborate programme of ritual in which a mistake might cause a serious offence, obviously had to be guided through the routine. For this purpose there were Mystagogoi – guides to the initiate – who accompanied their charges through the ceremonies. The clans of the Eumolpidai and the Kerykes from whom the priestly officials were drawn supplied from their lay members the chief cicerones. Andocides, when actually on his trial for impiety against the Eleusinian Mysteries, as he belonged to the Kerykes, can tell the jury that in three years after he returned from Cyprus he had 'initiated a Delphian and other guest-friends of mine'. Evidently in this way foreigners going to Eleusis linked up with those Athenians with whom they had social connexions. Otherwise can one surmise that the *Agyrmos* provided the opportunity for introducing strangers to suitable Mystagogoi? In one way one must not picture the proceedings too flippantly in terms of modern tourism. There were no throngs of bewildered foreigners shepherded by a single guide. The regulations specify that the Kerykes and the Eumolpidai are to initiate the new Mystai individually, and if they deal with them in a body they are liable to a fine of 100 drachmas. So one is to suppose that each pilgrim had personal attention throughout, and the Mystagogos is likely to have been more in the nature of a father confessor, who may for instance have recommended spiritual exercises for the remainder of the day after the meeting in the Agora.[54]

After the registration came purification. (Plate 23) For though the proclamation had warned the would-be initiates from approaching in a condition of impurity, it was not sufficient to trust to the negative state of being unconscious of defilement. A positive act of ritual cleansing was needed before the awesome experience of initiation itself, and the second day of the festival was devoted to this purpose. It was known as 'Seaward, Initiates!', a name which was the command for the occasion and perhaps also a watchword shouted by those who took part. The purification was performed by two methods, a sea-bathe and a sprinkling with pig's blood. The salt sea was a traditional purifier; also traditionally sacrificial pigs were used for atonement. Besides, the animal was specially appropriate on this occasion as it was the conventional victim offered to Demeter, perhaps as a natural emblem of fecundity.[55] (Plate 25)

The Mystai set out in carriages and carts to drive the eight miles to the port of the Peiraeus or the beach of Phaleron. Though they may not have gone in a formal procession, the cavalcade was to some extent organized for they left the city by one gate and in the third century B C at least there were superintendents arranging the proceedings who were thanked by the state for their services. When they reached the coast, they had to walk out into the water carrying a piglet. This animal had been supplied by the authorities as part of the return for the fees paid, but it was the responsibility of the would-be initiate to convey the victim to the sea and purify it as well as himself by immersion in salt water. Then when the party had returned to Athens each Mystes sacrificed his pig and was sprinkled with the blood. We are not told that the pig had to be made a holocaust. So it is to be supposed that the evening of the 'Seaward, Initiates' was spent in eating a feast of sucking pig. The whole procedure, even if done for a serious purpose, sounds as if it must have had its more flippant and comical side. Mylonas has well suggested that the trains of carriages making for the coast would be more like a holiday outing in modern Athens than a solemn religious rite. Also one cannot picture the entry into the sea holding a struggling piglet in one's arms as being conducted in quiet dignity. Actually it could have its alarming incidents. In 339 B C a Mystes at one of the creeks in the Peiraeus rashly cut the throat of his piglet while in the water. The blood attracted a shark which attacked the Mystes with fatal results. At the time this was taken as an omen for the destruction of the state.[56]

The third day of the festival is much less noticed in our sources. It was probably called 'Hither the victims' and, if so, was the date of the main state sacrifice in Athens for the Two Goddesses. (It was usual as part of the secrecy connected with the festival to treat the names of Demeter and Persephone as too sacred to utter and to substitute for them this paraphrase.) Also presumably the private persons who could afford to show their piety in that manner would make their own personal offerings.[57]

The fourth day, following on these rather festive occasions was evidently intended to bring the Mystai back to the proper solemn attitude, in which they should approach their initiation. They were expected to spend the day indoors; an even more unusual restriction than it would appear in modern times. For in ancient Athens much of the male citizen's life was spent outside. This quiet time will then have been a suitable preparation for the spiritual experience of the two final days.[58]

The vacuum created by the retirement of the Mystai from public life was curiously filled by another religious festival in honour of Asclepius, the god of healing. His cult had been introduced to Athens in 420/19 from Epidaurus, its chief centre in southern Greece. Until that date healing in Athens seems to have been mainly the concern of local hero shrines. Apollo was recognized as the god who sent plagues and sudden death and could therefore avert these, but he was not much consulted on casual illness. So the introduction of Asclepius filled a functional need. The year 420/19 was particularly appropriate as, during the interruption in the Peloponnesian War caused by the Peace of Nicias, Epidaurus was open to friendly relations with Athens. In the summer of 418 Argos and Epidaurus went to war and as Athens was allied to Argos she was drawn into hostile action against Epidaurus. But by then the cult of Asclepius had been safely installed. A fragmentary chronicle inscribed in the early fourth century recorded that the god had 'come at the time of the Great Mysteries to the Eleusinion (in Athens) and sent for his snake from home and brought it thither on a chariot when they were met by Telemachus', (the Athenian who was responsible for establishing the cult in Attica). 'Hygieia [Asclepius' daughter, the goddess of Health] came with him and thus there was founded all this sanctuary in the archonship of Astyphilos' (420/19 BC). Evidently the worship of Asclepius must have been introduced with the approval and active co-operation of the priesthood of the Eleusinian Mysteries. Otherwise the god would not have put up on arrival at the sanctuary of the Eleusinian Demeter in Athens. It must have been one of the problems in bringing in a new major cult that the deity needed to be accommodated temporarily somewhere until his own shrine could be built and fitted up to receive him. Apparently the Eleusinian Demeter extended this hospitality to Asclepius. The sacred snake often shown with him in art was one of the features frequently mentioned in references to Epidaurus; one of the tame specimens from the sanctuary there must have been sent over. Also Hygieia his daughter, as the goddess of Health, was associated with him in worship at Epidaurus.[59] (Plate 29)

The advent of Asclepius was worked up into a myth which told that in his own lifetime on earth Asclepius had come to Athens to seek initiation, but had arrived too late for the preliminary ceremonies, so that they had all to be rushed through again for his benefit on this, the fourth day. His privilege provided a mythical justification for any other would-be initiates who had started belatedly on the ceremonies. Evidently the arrival of Asclepius in 420 BC took place on the 18th of Boedromion, and the date became the occasion for an annual festival in commemoration. A procession arranged by the archon may have re-enacted the original coming. Anyway there were the usual women carrying offerings and a banquet was spread for the god with a couch on which he was supposed to recline. The occasion was known as the *Epidauria* and continued to be celebrated in the middle of the older festival of the Eleusinian Mysteries. As we shall see later Asclepius had a second annual festival, the *Asclepieia*, which also was closely linked in date to another important older festival, the *City Dionysia*. They were neatly spaced at six-monthly intervals. The whole arrangement suggests the conscious planning of a careful priesthood working in harmony with the authorities of Athens.[60]

The fifth day of the Eleusinian festival reached the climax. The 'Holy Things' of Demeter were escorted back to Eleusis by the procession of the Mystai going to receive initiation. The 'Holy Things' had been stored in the Eleusinion, on the northern slope under the Acropolis, and for the return to their home they were accompanied by another sacred object – the image of Iacchos. He was represented as a young man bearing a torch. In origin he seems to have been simply a personification of the triumphant shout (*iacche*) uttered by those in the procession, just as Hymenaios appears to be a personification of the wedding song. But he gradually developed into a young male attendant on the Two Goddesses and became more and more assimilated to Dionysus. This process was probably assisted by the nearness in sound of Bacchus and Iacchos. It could not be truly said that Dionysus penetrated into the cult of Demeter and Persephone at Eleusis, but the great procession from Athens became as much a triumphant march of Iacchos as a return of the Goddesses' 'Holy Things'.[61]

The procession probably formed up near the Dipylon Gate as it is indicated that the shrine of Iacchos was somewhere in the humbler quarter of Athens near there. The young military escort of Epheboi accompanied the march and all the officials of the Eleusinian cult will have had their places. Iacchos was escorted by a special priest of his own called the Iacchagogos (the Leader of Iacchos). (Plates 24, 30) The would-be initiates and their Mystagogoi formed the core of the procession. Those taking part wore garlands of myrtle and also often carried objects connected with the rite, known as *bacchoi*. These were branches of myrtle tied together with strands of wool, which are frequently shown in artistic representation of the Mysteries.[62] In addition they often carried a stick from which a bundle of provisions hung. This equivalent of the medieval pilgrim's scrip was no doubt needed in the next two days when the Eleusinians must have been quite incapable of catering for the vast influx of worshippers. For, besides the priests and the band of the would-be initiates with their companions, many other Athenians who had been initiated in the past joined the pilgrimage. The distance from Athens to Eleusis was 14 miles, and most of the pilgrims traversed it on foot with the help of donkeys or mules to carry their luggage or give them a ride at intervals. The procession was no doubt interspersed with bands of flute and harp players and choirs of singers, and the mixed company will have joined in the choruses of hymns or in shouts of '*iacche*'. The sacred route was traditional and passed a number of religious sites at which we may imagine there may have been a halt for ritual observances and an opportunity to take refreshment. For example, soon after leaving Athens at the Dipylon Gate they passed the Gymnasium of Academus. Then as they climbed the pass over Mount Aegaleus they reached the sanctuary of the Pythian Apollo where now stands the famous Byzantine church of Daphni, and as they descended to the shore of the Bay of Eleusis there was a sanctuary of Aphrodite. Beyond this they passed over the bridge at the streams of Rheitoi. They had reached at this point the original territory of Eleusis and the spot was associated with a legendary king of the country called Krokos. The family who claimed to be his descendants had a curious privilege. They bound the right hand and the left leg of each Mystes with a yellow woollen thread. The rite presumably took place at this point, and though this is not mentioned by our authorities, one may conjecture that the Krokidai expected some traditional tip for the service. The real meaning of the custom is buried in the myth, for the alleged ancestor Krokos simply derives his name from the yellow woollen thread (*kroke*). It suggests some magic purpose in protecting the initiates by these bands. Further out on the Eleusinian plains the Mystai crossed another bridge, this time over the local river named Kephisos. It was the scene of a traditional custom (the *gephyrismos*) which may have been religious in origin, but obviously gave scope for human entertainment. Men with heads covered to conceal their identity sat on the bridge and hurled ribald insults at distinguished persons in the procession. It is impossible to decide how far this had a magic intention to forestall any ill-luck, or again how far it was just a traditional opportunity for popular licence of this sort.[63]

At last after dark the procession reached Eleusis itself, the final stages of the pilgrimage being completed by torch-light. The older pilgrims will have been glad to bivouac or put up where they could and rest, but some of the more enthusiastic young made it an occasion for an all-night celebration. Also a special offering may have been made to Demeter at this point in the festival, as Mylonas suggests. This was the presentation of *kernoi*, which were circular earthenware dishes to which were attached numbers of tiny cups. This vessel was evidently designed simply for ritual as a means of making a number of offerings simultaneously by putting small samples into each of the receptacles. It was used at Eleusis to thank the goddess by offering her the fruits of the earth, and somewhat various lists are recorded of the different kinds of grain, peas and beans which were put in the cups. The *kernos* was carried aloft and the bearer tasted the contents of the vessel, thus joining in some ritual fashion in the goddess's share.[64] (Plate 22)

The *kernoi* have been the subject of controversy in modern times, because a very similar type of vessel has been found on Minoan sites and at the other extreme in time the Greek Orthodox Church uses similar multiple cups on a tray. Some scholars such as Nilsson are prepared to accept that a continuity of tradition runs from Minoan times. On the other hand Mylonas, though he believes in a consecutive tradition at Eleusis from Mycenaean times, since excavation has failed to find early examples of the *kernos* there, proposes to regard it as having been independently re-invented twice; once in the archaic Greek period and again in Christian times. This seems a rather unsafe supposition on the basis of negative evidence, which is so risky to argue from in archaeology.[65]

The fifth day of the festival with its great pilgrimage from Athens was one of the chief religious occasions in the Athenian year, and consequently it figured at times in the course of history. The earliest occasion was just before the battle of Salamis. Herodotus in a vivid narrative obviously derived from first-hand sources, describes how, when Attica was evacuated and the Persian army was ravaging the country Dikaios, an Athenian exile on the Persian side in company with Demaratos, the renegade Spartan king, was crossing the Thriasian plain and saw a cloud of dust proceeding from Eleusis as though raised by thirty thousand men. They were wondering what body of men this could be when they heard a sound which seemed to Dikaios to be the Iacchos call of the Mysteries. Demaratos, who was uninitiated, wanted to know what this strange call meant and Dikaios explained, adding:

'This cannot but mean destruction for the Persian King's forces.

For clearly as Attica is deserted, the cry is supernatural and is proceeding from Eleusis to avenge the Greeks and their allies. If it
strikes toward the Peloponnese, then the danger to the King and his
forces is on land, but if it turns towards the ships at Salamis, then the
King is in danger of losing his navy.'

Demaratos warned Dikaios that he would have his head cut off if this
got to the ears of the Persian King.

'So they watched till out of the dust-storm and the voice a cloud
arose and floated aloft towards Salamis and the Greek camp. Then
they knew by this that Xerxes' navy was fated to be destroyed.'[66]

This pious legend of Eleusinian deities intervening to avenge themselves on the Persian invader was probably susceptible of some natural
explanation so far as the phenomenon was concerned. But it serves to
illustrate and prove the highly emotional and credulous feelings which
the Mysteries and the procession to Eleusis evoked. This story in
Herodotus is the earliest evidence for the Iacchos shout: as for his
description of the procession as one of thirty thousand men, this
number need not be taken strictly as an estimate for the pilgrims at
this time. It is Herodotus' standard estimate for the total Athenian
population, as is shown by his use of this figure elsewhere.

The respect for the procession may have been great, but during the
latter part of the Peloponnesian War when the Spartans had a base in
Attica, the Athenians gave it up because of the risk involved and
conveyed the 'Holy Things' of Eleusis to and fro by sea. This must
have altered the whole character of the occasion and reduced greatly
the popular participation in it. So it was one of Alcibiades' most
picturesque performances when in 407 B C he conducted the procession
as a military operation. Eight years before he had been exiled from
Athens on charges of impiety. The chief charge being that he and a
group of friends had parodied the Eleusinian Mysteries at a drunken
party. One Theodorus had played the part of the Sacred Herald, their
host Pulytion that of the Daiduchos, and Alcibiades himself the leading
role of the Hierophantes while the remainder of the guests as Mystai
had submitted to a mock-initiation. It was a superb reply to these
charges that Alcibiades himself in the end should re-establish the
traditional procession when it had been suspended. He advised the
Eumolpidai and Kerykes of his plans and stationed sentries on the
mountain tops and sent out ahead an advance-guard at dawn. Then

after picking up the priests and Mystai and Mystagogoi he enveloped
them in an armed escort and led them with dignity and without
disturbance to Eleusis and back. The occasion won him great temporary
applause from the fickle Athenian populace.[67]

The only time recorded when the Mysteries were broken off was in
334 BC when Alexander the Great shocked the Greek world by his
sudden descent on the rebellious Thebans and his destruction of their
city. The Athenians at the time were celebrating the festival when some
Thebans arrived coming straight from the action. At their news the
Athenians were so alarmed that they abandoned the ceremonies and
summoned everyone to take refuge inside the city walls. But this panic
measure proved unnecessary as Alexander did not proceed to invade
Attica.[68]

The sixth and final day of the festival took place entirely in Eleusis
itself. Already our ancient authorities become vague as we approach
the secret part of the ceremonies. Sacrifices were made to the Twin
Goddesses and other deities. Also as was appropriate to Demeter the
goddess of corn, a vast offering of meal was made. It was known as the
Pelanos, and on one occasion, as recorded in an inscription, the Athenian
authorities approved the use of '21 *medimnoi* less three *choinices*' of corn
for the purpose. Since a *choinix* was reckoned a day's corn ration for a
man, this extraordinary repast would have sufficed to feed just over a
thousand men for a day. The regulations frequently state that the
Eumolpidai should expound the sacred law determining what offerings
were to be made from the *Pelanos*. But probably, as Mylonas suggests,
the correct picture of this last day was of the spiritual preparation for
the rite of initiation and of the physical discipline of fasting. In this the
Mystai may have been thought to be imitating the mourning Demeter
fasting at the loss of her daughter, Persephone. Also there are references
to the Mystai drinking a special mixture known as the *kykeon*. This was
probably their way of breaking the fast at the end of the day and if so
they were certainly imitating Demeter in this action. The *Homeric
Hymn* describes how Meteneira, the queen of Eleusis, had offered the
mourning Demeter a cup of wine which she refused, thus setting the
precedent for the prohibition of wine in her cult. But she commanded
her instead to mix with water flour and the herb pennyroyal. When
this had been presented to her the goddess drank it 'for the sake of the
rite'. Evidently this gesture of acceptance by Demeter established this
potion as the proper drink for the initiates to use to break their fast
before the ceremony itself.[69]

This began in the evening. The whole of the precinct of the Two
Goddesses was a consecrated area, but for the purpose of the Mysteries
themselves there was a special building – the Telesterion, or Hall of
Initiation. It was not designed like ordinary Greek temples, for unlike
them it was intended for congregational worship under cover. Hence
in the fifth century it was a building approximately 150 feet square.
It had developed to this size through earlier stages, each time being
enlarged to hold a bigger audience. This process of growth suggests
the increasing demand for accommodation for initiates. In its final
form the building may have held ten thousand worhsippers. In the
centre of the building was a walled-off holy of holies, the Anaktoron,
which only the Hierophantes himself might enter.[70] (Plate 27)

The nature of the initiation remains ultimately a secret. The Christian
Fathers, who are the only writers claiming to lay bare the mystery, were
doing so to discredit it, and either suggested that it was indecent – an
obvious charge against everything kept hidden – or else that it was
trivial. The suggestion that the cult of a goddess of vegetation might
also have been linked with the fertility of animal and of man is plausible
enough and quite in keeping with primitive origins. But if critically
examined the evidence of Christian writers for a sexual symbol as the
centre of the Eleusinian cult is not convincing. There is more plausibility in the ironical statement of Hippolytus that 'the Athenians, when
they initiate in the *Eleusinia* exhibit in silence to the *epoptai* the mighty
and marvellous and most epoptic mystery, an ear of cut-wheat'. Just
as the old Eleusinian legend represented Demeter as bestowing on them,
first of mankind, the gift of corn, wheat may have played a central part
in the Mysteries. But it is not likely that it was such an isolated anti-
climax as Hippolytus suggests.[71]

The elements of the final ceremony are traditionally divided into
'things said', 'things done', and 'things revealed'. Nothing suggests that
the 'things said' were in any real sense the exposition of an esoteric
doctrine or the delivery of moral sermons. Mysteries frequently contained ritual formulae uttered by the priests and repeated by the people
and something of the sort is to be supposed. The 'things done' may
have included not merely ritual acts performed by the priests, but also
actual mimetic reproduction of some of the myths of Demeter. But the
climax was the 'things revealed'. These must have been the 'Holy
Things' which had just previously been escorted under a veil of secrecy
to the Eleusinion in Athens and back. They were otherwise kept in the
Anaktoron, an innermost sanctuary at Eleusis which only the Hiero-

phantes – 'The revealer of the Holy Things' – might enter. References in Plutarch and elsewhere suggest that after the initiates had been for a period in darkness the Hierophantes appeared in a brilliant light revealing these objects. The ultimate point of the Mysteries in this way was not an intellectual exposition, nor even a general participation in some ritual act, but the sharing of a visual exhibition which as a result of all that the initiates had undergone was of high emotional content. This is confirmed by the fact that the technical term for those who had received the highest degree of initiation was the epoptai, meaning 'those who gazed at something'. One may presume that either they had been allowed to see what the other initiates had not yet seen or had been allowed to have a closer look at the 'Holy Things'.[72]

This corresponds to the aphorism attributed to Aristotle that the initiates rather had something done to them than received instruction. Plutarch for his part compared the progress of the initiate and the development of the philosopher – that at first it was all noise and confusion in a jostling throng, but at last it was a great light beheld in fear and silence. These are among the few more explicit tributes to the impressive effect of the Eleusinian Mysteries. Otherwise the greatest testimony to their spiritual efficacy is that they continued from the archaic period throughout classical antiquity and even survived after the official adoption of Christianity. The hordes of Alaric the Goth in AD 395 finally devastated the site. Within this period of more than a thousand years the Mysteries had been approached by all manner of persons, Athenian and other, seeking spiritual sustenance. Evidently many must have come away satisfied. For the universal respect with which the Eleusinian rites are treated in pagan tradition cannot simply be the result of superstitious panic. In a civilization where official religion did little to support the soul, Eleusis provided some comfort to those faced with the anxieties of this world and the next.[73]

After the rite of initiation lasting through the night between the seventh and the eighth day of the festival, the eighth day itself must have come as rather an anti-climax. It was called *Plemochoai* after a form of vessel used in its ritual: this was shaped like a spinning top, but with a firm base. The initiates took a pair of such vessels and filled them with water. Then they tipped one over to the east and the other towards the west, uttering a mystic formula. Unfortunately the words are not recorded. So there is little clue as to the meaning of the ceremony. Taken by itself it perhaps suggests a magic rite meant to encourage rain, and such may have been the original purpose in the ceremonies of the goddess of corn. The early rains in autumn were of great importance as a preliminary to the sowing.[74]

Mylonas has also suggested that on this day the initiates dedicated to the Two Goddesses the clothing they had worn at the time of their initiation. The existence of the practice is proved by a joke on the subject in Aristophanes. Also there is evidence that at Eleusis there was a room set aside for storing clothes. Evidently the simple idea behind the practice was that the garments themselves had acquired some holiness, like their wearer, from the ceremony which they had shared. Hence they could not well be used in future for secular occasions, but should be laid up in the sanctuary. The ancient commentary on Aristophanes tells of an alternative practice which was derived from the same belief in the acquired holiness of the clothes. They could be taken home and cut up to make swaddling clothes for infants. The notion evidently was that consecrated cloth could protect the child at the dangerous period immediately after birth.[75]

4 PYANEPSION

The next month, PYANEPSION, began with another festival to Demeter – the *Proerosia* – which was essentially agricultural in purpose. Its name signifies by derivation 'the preliminary to the ploughing', and it was evidently centred on Eleusis. The legend told to explain its origin describes how the whole of Greece was smitten with a plague, and when the Delphic oracle was consulted for a remedy, Apollo commanded that the Athenians were to sacrifice to Demeter on behalf of all. In return for this service tithes of the crops were to be sent from the rest of Greece to Athens. Our best evidence for this practice is an inscription from the period of uncertain peace during the Peloponnesian War, when an attempt was made to revive and reorganize the collection of the first-fruits which had no doubt been interrupted by the hostilities. Attic farmers were to set aside a six-hundredth of their barley crop and a twelve-hundredth of their wheat to be delivered at Eleusis by their local magistrates (demarchs). Also similar proportions of first-fruits were to be collected from the cities of the Athenian empire. In addition an invitation was to be sent to all other Greek cities as far as possible, asking them voluntarily to contribute in the same way. In the case of Attica and the empire this collection could be imposed by authority, and may be compared to the way in which offerings were officially required for the *Panathenaia*. In the case of the other Greek states the invitation based its claim on 'ancestral custom and the oracle from Delphi'. The legend of Apollo's command had probably some basis in fact, even if the pious picture of the whole of Greece or even of the whole world suffering from a plague is much overdrawn. Our literary authorities seem to point to a date in the early sixth century, which would be plausible enough. This also would be possible to reconcile with the archaeological remains at Eleusis, where storage buildings of sixth-century date have been conjecturally identified. The fifth-century inscription contains instructions for the building of three storage containers at Eleusis to hold the yield of the renewed collection, and there are remains which approximately belong to that period. The first-fruits were evidently an offering to Demeter made to invoke her blessing annually before the ploughing and sowing began the season of agriculture.[76]

At Eleusis on the 5th day of Pyanepsion the Hierophantes and the Sacred Herald publicly announced the feast of the *Proerosia*, and were assigned a small sum of money for the expense of the midday meal. The form of the announcement is not recorded, but we may assume that the Herald, prompted by the Hierophantes, proclaimed the purpose of the festival, and invited those contributing to make their offerings. In later periods also there was a sacrifice of oxen as it is recorded that the victims were lifted by the Epheboi – a practice which we shall see again in connection with the festivals of Hephaestus. But no doubt the main offering was the first-fruits of the cereals. Generally one gets the impression that the *Proerosia* was a state-ceremony centred on Eleusis, but only established after Athens had incorporated that city in Attica. The comic writers who are a good index of popular interest never mention the festival, and only one late rhetorician refers to it as though it was an occasion for cereal offerings by farmers privately. Instead we find that it is one of the very few Attic festivals which is represented in tragedy. The scene of the *Suppliants* of Euripides is set in front of the temple of Demeter at Eleusis. This was appropriate as the subject of the play was the burial of the Seven Against Thebes whose graves were shown there in historic times. The prologue is spoken by Aithra, the mother of Theseus, who addresses Demeter in prayer for Athens and her own native land of Troizen. She explains:

‘. . . I happen to be offering preliminary sacrifice on behalf of the ploughing of the land, and have come from my house to this sanctuary, where first the fruitful ear was seen to bristle above this soil.’

Clearly the occasion which Euripides suggests is the *Proerosia* and the festival provided a convenient motive for bringing Aithra to Eleusis where she could meet the suppliant mothers of the dead heroes. But also there may be a further purpose in the choice of the occasion. As Gilbert Murray points out, though the style of the play might suggest an earlier date for the writing the treatment of the subject suggests the time of the Peace of Nicias. Otherwise it was probably produced at the same time when the collection of corn for the *Proerosia* was being elaborately revived, and delicately alludes to this contemporary effort.[77] (Plate 31)

From its absence from comedy and its place in tragedy and in the inscriptional record one can conclude that the *Proerosia*, though an important official occasion, was not what could be called a popular festival.

To the Athenian it must merely have seemed like something managed by the state to which he had to pay a tithe.

At Eleusis two days after the *Proerosia* there was a sacrifice to the Pythian Apollo of a he-goat and a lamb with other offerings, and a table was set out for serving a meal for the god. The 7th of the month was the day specially devoted to the worship of Apollo, and in Athens this particular date was the occasion of the *Pyanepsia* – a festival of Apollo which gave its name to the month, Pyanepsion. The fact that at Eleusis the sacrifice was made to the god under the title 'Pythian' has been taken, probably rightly, by modern scholars as an indication that it was made the occasion for showing gratitude to the Delphic oracle for the foundation of the *Proerosia*. If so, the Eleusinian authorities had simply linked their specific offering with a date already dedicated to a popular Apolline feast.[78]

The name *Pyanepsia* is derived from the two words 'beans' and 'boiling', and referred to a special dish cooked on the occasion. It was very typical for Greek festivals to be associated with particular foods. Even if beans gave their name to this dish they were not the sole ingredient, though they may have been the most prominent one. Any leguminous vegetables could be included, and also cereals. In fact it was a hotch-potch of the sort which the ancient Greeks called *panspermia* (all seeds), boiled together in one pot. That this was its nature is shown by the legend told to explain it. This was part of the story of Theseus for, as we shall see, since traditionally he returned to Athens from Crete on the 7th of Pyanepsion the religious rites of that day were all explained by legendary episodes in his home-coming. The ceremonies of the *Pyanepsia* were represented as the fulfilment of vows to Apollo made by Theseus and his companions, who had put in at Delos and promised the god that if they returned home safely they would make these offerings in his honour. On landing in Attica 'they mixed together what was left of their provisions and put it into one common pot. When it was boiled they held a combined feast and ate it up together.' This evidently reproduces the effect of the feast at the *Pyanepsia* when the vegetable ingredients were all boiled up together and shared by those participating in the festival. Also it is implied that a share of the pot was offered to Apollo.[79]

The origin of the rite is probably to be sought in the season of the year. At the time of sowing a general mixture of all the edible plants to be sown was cooked and offered to the deity, and his worshippers also partook of it, while praying for a renewal of these different crops next year. One may question whether Apollo in particular had been the original god to receive the offering. He was not usually a god of fertility. But he may have attracted the festival to himself, as the 7th of the month – his special day – was a convenient occasion for it.

The festival of the *Pyanepsia* was also associated with a special practice which again though linked to Apollo was perhaps not originally his. This was known as the *Eiresione*. The name was applied to a bough of olive wreathed with wool which was carried about on this day. Such boughs were traditionally used as the sign of the suppliant on other occasions, but at this time the significance of the *eiresione* was emphasized by attaching all sorts of other objects to it. Models of a harp, a cup and a vine-branch made of pastry as well as other shapes were tied to the bough. Also all sorts of actual fruits were strung on. The result must have been as fanciful a piece of decoration as a Christmas tree. The fully equipped boughs were carried round by a group of boys who called at the doors of houses singing: 'The *eiresione* bears figs and rich cakes and honey in a jar and olive oil to anoint yourself with and a cup of mellow wine that you may drink and fall asleep.' This was one of the begging songs meant to be accompanied by an appeal for a gift to the singers. The bough itself with its various attachments was an obvious symbol of fruitfulness and when brought to a house conveyed a blessing with it. But also this blessing had to be earned by giving some present to those who brought it. In the Athenian custom the bough was actually left at the house to which it was brought. It was set up at the door and allowed to exercise its beneficial influence for the year. (Plate 32) As such it appears a couple of times in Aristophanes' plays. In *The Knights* Demos, hearing cries at the front door, comes out accusing the intruders of having torn down his *eiresione*, and in the *Ecclesiazousai* a withered old woman is rudely compared to such a branch when it is faded.[80]

Again, as with the mixed broth of the *Pyanepsia*, one feels that the custom may well be older than its association with Apollo in particular. Deubner compares it with the May bough set up on doors in Germany, and suggests that the practice started from its use as a blessing attached to houses and only developed the ritual of the song as a later accretion. Ancient scholars felt that the connection with Apollo needed some further explanation. So they vaguely suggested that the *Eiresione* was instituted originally to appeal to the god for relief from a plague. This was to equate it with such objects as the suppliant boughs borne by the Thebans in the opening scene of Sophocles' *Oedipus Tyrannus*. As we have already suggested, both kinds of decorated branches were intended to have a special potency, but the one is not directly derived from the other. It may, however, have been the association of suppliant boughs with Apollo which also suggested the appropriateness of assigning the *Eiresione* to his honour.[81]

This feast of the *Pyanepsia*, judging by the references in Attic literature, was a popular occasion in which many took part. Also on the same day there was performed a much more complicated and curious ceremony which was also explained by reference to the myth of Theseus. This was the *Oschophoria*. The main feature was a procession, which went from a sanctuary of Dionysus in Athens to the shrine of Athena Skiras at Phaleron. (We are not told from what Dionysiac temple it started, but as the ceremony was evidently ancient, it is reasonable to suppose that it was the sanctuary in Limnai, not the theatre of Dionysus Eleuthereus whose cult was a sixth-century BC importation.) The objects conveyed in the procession gave its name to the ceremony. These were vine-branches with their bunches of grapes still growing on them. They were called *oschoi* and so the name of the ceremony meant 'the carrying of the bunches of grapes on their branches'. The bearers were 'two young men chosen from those outstanding in birth and wealth'. For the occasion they were got up in female robes. They headed the procession and were followed by a choir singing special hymns known as 'those of the *Oschophoria*'. Unfortunately, unlike the *eiresione* song, no specimen verses are preserved.[82]

There were also a number of other peculiar features about the sacrifice at Phaleron and the subsequent banquet which were all appropriately provided with explanations linked to the legend of Theseus. For instance the herald who accompanied the procession did not wear a garland, which was the usual decoration assumed by those taking part in festivals. Instead he put the garland round his herald's staff. Again at the conclusion of the ceremony, when the libations had been poured, those present shouted 'Eleleu, Iou, Iou.' It was not unusual for the congregation to be required to shout or sing a hymn at some point in the procedure of sacrifice. But this particular combination of cries seemed to the Greeks odd. 'Eleleu' suggested a shout of encouragement or triumph, while 'Iou Iou' indicated amazement and confusion. Again a mythological explanation was produced.[83] (Plate 33)

Finally as a peculiarity one may mention that a number of women took part in the procession who were called the 'Dinner Carriers' *Deipnophoroi*. They carried with them the other food needed for the

meal in addition to the sacrificial meat, and after the victims were killed
they shared in the banquet. Whether they waited on the male banqueters as well is not clear from our authorities. It was not customary
in Athens for wives to accompany their husbands when going out to
dinner. So, the presence of these women sharing in a public feast must
have verged on the improper if it had not been justified by religious
convention.

We need not picture the banquet itself as anything but solemn and
dignified on this occasion. One special feature which was unusual is
recorded: it was customary for legends to be told during the meal.
What legends is not explained. One naturally conjectures those connected with Theseus; for the special features of the *Oschophoria* were
all explained in connection with the tale of his sailing to Crete to face
the Minotaur and his triumphant return.

For instance the Dinner Carriers were said to imitate the mothers of
the Twice Seven – the youths and maidens sent as tribute to Minos.
After they had been chosen by lot, their mothers came to them at
Phaleron before the ship set sail for Crete bringing them bread and
meat, and to cheer them told them tales. These features then were
reproduced in the Dinner Carriers walking in procession with food,
and the legends told at the banquet.[84]

The two young men dressed as girls – the Oschophoroi, who headed
the procession bearing branches with grapes – were said to recall a trick
which Theseus had successfully played on Minos. Instead of bringing
seven maidens he had only taken five and had made up the number
required 'by choosing two young men of his companions who had
fresh and girlish faces, but manly and eager spirits'. As Plutarch tells,
'he changed their outward appearance completely by giving them
warm baths and making them live in the shade, and by arranging their
hair and smoothing their skin and applying cosmetics to it. He also
taught them to resemble girls as much as possible in speech and gesture
and gait.' The deception was not discovered in Crete where one is to
suppose that two additional men proved their worth when Theseus
made his escape with the Twice Seven. On returning to Athens he put
these two young men, dressed as maidens at the head of the procession.
Some said that they bore the vine-branches in gratitude to Dionysus
and Ariadne for their part in the tale of Theseus. But others said it was
simply because the return of Theseus coincided in time with the
vintage.[85]

The unusual way in which the herald carried his garland, and the peculiar mixture of cries uttered at the sacrifice were legendarily connected with the death of Theseus' father. According to the traditional story, when Theseus forgot to hoist white sails on his return, King Aegeus watching from the edge of the Acropolis, at the sight of the black sails believed that his son had been killed and threw himself to his death from the cliff. So when the herald sent by Theseus to announce his safe return arrived at Athens he found the people plunged in sudden mourning for their king. But on hearing the good news of Theseus' arrival they made to crown the herald. However, although he accepted the garlands, he would not wear them as he had to return to Theseus with the sad news of his father's death. Instead he wound the garlands round his staff, and the practice was imitated thereafter by the herald at the *Oschophoria*. Similarly the mixture of cries at the libations reflected the mingled feelings of the Athenians in Theseus' day, half rejoicing at the safe return of the Twice Seven, half struck with horror and grief at the death of King Aegeus.[86]

These complicated mythological explanations are highly typical of the Greek love for accounting for abnormalities in ritual by such aetiological legends. Even if one were to suppose some kind of historic fact lay behind the legend of Theseus, these particular episodes were simply invented to fit pre-existing religious practices. What their real origins were can scarcely ever be conjectured. At any rate it is not to be supposed that they all sprang from one motive or one period of development. The young men masquerading in female costume reproduce a cult practice of transvestism which occurs elsewhere in Greek religion as well as pretty universally. The other customs are less characteristic or easy to identify. Until 1938 scholars used to devote much space to arguing whether the ceremony of the *Oschophoria* was consecrated to Dionysus or Athena, and Deubner came down decidedly in favour of Dionysus. He was right in arguing that in essence it was a vintage celebration, falling at the right time of the year and involving the carrying of boughs with grapes at its central ceremony, but he was wrong in refusing to associate these features primarily with Athena Skiras, as was proved by the long inscription found in the Athenian Agora and published in 1938. This concerned a dispute between the two branches of an Attic clan known as the Salaminians over their mutual rights in managing the festival of Athena Skiras, and proved conclusively that that particular shrine of the goddess and also the ceremony of the *Oschophoria* were in origin cults of this one clan which had become accepted as a general state cult.[87]

The Salaminians, as their name indicates, had originally lived on the island off Attica and in those days had worshipped a goddess, Skiras, whose concerns included the grape harvest. At some uncertain date, probably after the struggle between Athens and Megara for possession of Salamis had ended in Athens gaining control in the late seventh or early sixth century B C, the Salaminians had been transferred to Attica, settling in two groups, one near Sunion, the other at Phaleron. They brought with them the cult of their goddess who was conveniently connected with the goddess of Athens by the use of the combined name, Athena Skiras. On Salamis they may have practised a form of *Oschophoria*. On transplantation to Attica it was appropriately linked with the local cult of a wine-god by making the procession start from his shrine. An arrangement like this showed the acceptance by the Athenians of Athena Skiras as a goddess recognized by the state. Mythologically the linking of the *Oschophoria* with the legend of Theseus, the great Attic hero, completed the process. In the early sixth century the legend of Theseus was just developing into its canonical form, a process not completed till the end of the century. Its core lay in a hero who slew a bull-headed monster in Crete. So the Salaminians were just in time to gain a footing in the developed legend. The tales told at their banquet may have contributed not a little to its growth. For instance, they must be responsible for the statement that in Theseus' time the Athenians did not pay attention to seafaring, and so he had to get his helmsman and boatswain from Salamis.[88]

The two religious ceremonies of the 7th of Pyanepsion present a charming contrast. The *Pyanepsia* proper and the *Eiresione* are by their nature very primitive cult practices suitable to seed-time. In some such form they may have been observed by the Athenians for many centuries without any very specific deity as patron, but by the sixth century B C Apollo on whose sacred day they were held had acquired them, and a rather vague legendary connection had been achieved by attributing them to vows made by Theseus. The practices of the *Oschophoria*, much more sophisticated and complicated, were inherently the ritual of a fairly small clan and were run by its aristocracy. This continued to be true down to the fourth century B C, when, as the inscription shows, the rules governing this festival were defined by an arbitration between the two branches of the Salaminians. It appears as if the victims for the *Oschophoria* were supplied by the Oschophoroi and Deipnophoroi: otherwise, were provided by their families in their name. The Oschophoroi according to the literary sources were supposed to be chosen from the well-born and, as the inscription shows, were appointed by an official nominated by the Salaminians. So they were probably chosen from their members, those having the means to pay for the necessary victims undertaking this 'liturgy' in turn. The expense was not wasted on the general public. For the inscription lays down that the two branches of the Salaminians were to receive equal halves of the meat and carry it away raw. The god's portion will have been burnt in honour of Apollo, and after a banquet was held the remainder of the meat was divided up among the families and taken home for their private dinners.

We have seen how much the legend of Theseus was linked with the festivals of the 7th of Pyanepsion to explain their ritual peculiarities. It was appropriate that the annual festival of Theseus himself, the *Theseia*, fell on the following day – the 8th of Pyanepsion. That date of the month was traditionally linked with Poseidon, just as the 7th was proper to Apollo and the 6th to Artemis. As Theseus was the son of Poseidon the date was also appropriate to his celebration. In fact Plutarch says that he was also honoured on other eighths of the month. As a festival of the Athenian state the *Theseia* was instituted in 475 B C. In one of his earliest expeditions in command of the new fleet of the Athenian league Cimon captured the pirate stronghold of Scyros. Legend had told that Theseus died on the island and partly to justify this attack Cimon was equipped with a Delphic oracle which commanded him to find and remove Theseus' bones to Athens, where they were to be honoured with a cult. Of course the Delphic oracle was fulfilled by the finding of the relics, which were ceremonially brought to Athens and deposited in a shrine in the centre of the city near the Agora.[89]

Probably this place had been the site of some minor worship of Theseus before 475 B C which may have been the private privilege of a family called the Phytalidai. If so, at this point it was taken over by the Athenian state, backed by the authority of the Pythian Apollo. No temple was built there, but a major sacred area was laid out with suitable buildings and the *Theseia* was established as a chief state festival. References in inscriptions show that there was a procession and a sacrifice and an athletic contest. The accounts from the late fourth century show that the victims offered must have been many, and we can picture a generous distribution of meat to the populace. The feast was also the occasion for a special type of porridge made with milk, called *athara*. It may have been partly an outcome of this general banquet that from the fifth century one can trace a popular belief that Theseus when alive had been a friend of the people and had established a democratic government in his combined state of Athens. To escape the obvious inconsistancy with the accepted fact that democracy had been founded by Solon or Cleisthenes it had to be assumed that after Theseus' death his popular government had been subverted for many centuries. Theseus the democratic hero was strangely at variance with the fact that there were few shrines dedicated to him in Attica – Philochorus only knew of four – and the cult before Cimon's political move had probably been in the hands of a few aristocratic families who claimed descent from those who had accompanied Theseus to Crete or other contemporary figures of legend.[90]

A detailed record from about 160 BC lists the victors in the different events of the Theseian games. The competitors seem to have been confined to Athenians except in a few events where resident aliens also could compete. The whole programme though generally resembling that of the *Panathenaia* had a somewhat military flavour. This may perhaps be because by the second century BC the ordinary citizen did not engage in this kind of contest. There were prizes for trumpeters as well as heralds. There were teams in Manly Excellence, but also in Good Military Equipment. There were three classes of torch-race, but not as in the *Panathenaia* for single runners. The boys, adolescents (Epheboi) and young men (Neaniskoi) ran as teams and the names of their trainers are recorded. There were also the usual track and field events in various age groups and races in armour and horse-races. Unfortunately the kind of prizes awarded and their value were not included in the list. But though it would be unsafe to assume that all these details applied also to the *Theseia* from its foundation, we can justifiably assume that it was an important and popular occasion.[91]

Already in this month we have seen two festivals – the *Proerosia* and the *Pyanepsia* – connected with seed-time. A third such festival of much greater importance and extent filled the middle of the month. This was the *Thesmophoria*, dedicated to Demeter. It does not occur only in the Athenian calender, like the *Proerosia* and the *Pyanepsia*, but was observed in almost every part of the Greek world. One can therefore conjecture that it went back to very primitive origins, and this belief is confirmed by the character of the rites so far as they are known.

The *Thesmophoria* was a festival reserved for women. This form of sexual taboo was not common in Greek religion generally. Gods usually had men as their priests and goddesses had priestesses, but the worshippers might be of either sex. In a few cults, such as that of Heracles, women might be excluded from worship. The opposite pattern of the exclusion of men was practically confined to some fertility rituals of which the *Thesmophoria* is an example. In this respect it resembles the rites of the Bona Dea at Rome and like them the main ceremonies were held in the autumn. The name *Thesmophoria* and the title Thesmophoros applied to Demeter present a philological problem. *Thesmos* is an archaic Greek word for a 'law' or an 'ordinance', and superficially the festival and the goddess would seem to be associated therefore with 'carrying ordinances'. But in Greek, unlike English, the verb 'carry' is not normally used in such a connection. Also Demeter does not properly appear to be concerned with legislation. Hence, starting with Frazer, some modern scholars had proposed that, on the analogy of the many Greek names of festivals ending in *-phoria* (e.g. *Oschophoria*), the *thesmoi* must be some material objects which could be physically carried. Here there is a possible object which is known from descriptions of the ritual of the *Thesmophoria*. The only difficulty is that there are few examples to suggest how the word *thesmoi* acquired this meaning.

The ritual performed at the *Thesmophoria* was connected with that practised at another festival in the summer of the same year (apparently the *Skira*.) On that occasion the women concerned with the ceremony threw into caverns in the ground various offerings. The chief objects were sacrificed piglets, and also there were models of snakes and male genital organs shaped out of dough. The meaning behind these offerings placed in the depth of the earth was evidently connected with fertility. Pigs were usually offered to Demeter, and the reason for the choice was seen to be the fecundity of the animal. Snakes are associated with Demeter and with all forms of chthonic cult in Greece. The male organs again suggest fertility. These objects were thrown into the caverns just before midsummer, and it was a central activity of the *Thesmophoria* three and a half months later, to recover the decayed remains. Chosen for this function was a group of women who were called the Antletriai ('Balers'). Their task was to haul up, presumably in buckets, the contents of the caverns, which were then placed on the altars in the Thesmophoreion. The mixture of pigs' bones, decayed flesh and dough sounds most unsavoury, but it was regarded as consecrated. Hence the Antletriai were required to observe a state of purity, including no doubt abstinence from sexual intercourse, for three days before they undertook their duty. It was believed that the material placed on the altars had special powers. When sprinkled with seed in the fields it was supposed to promote fertility of crops.

A further detail about the activity of the Antletriai is recorded. It was said that there were snakes which haunted the caverns and ate much of what was thrown into them. So the Antletriai to frighten the snakes, which they regarded as the guardians of the caverns, used to make clapping sounds as they hauled on their burdens. It is hard to tell how much this is a mixture of fact and of fancy. Snakes at Eleusis and elsewhere were associated in ritual with Demeter, but also it would not be surprising if the caverns with their edible contents were the homes of actual serpents, who acquired a spiritual aura from their presence on this sacred spot.

If the title Thesmophoros and the name of the festival *Thesmophoria* are derived from the physical carrying of some objects, the reasonable supposition is that the *thesmoi* were the miscellaneous contents of the caverns, which were carried to the altars. Philologically it is possible to produce a derivation to suit, and it is probable that this is the correct explanation of the names.[92]

While the carrying of the *thesmoi* was the central act and origin of the festival, it had a great deal more to it. But our literary sources do not go into descriptive detail as the ceremonies were strictly a 'mystery' confined to women. Herodotus refers to them in connection with his theories that Greek religion was derived from Egypt, but is careful to declare that he is observing a pious reticence. Again, Aristophanes chose the festival as the setting for one of his comedies in which he played on the motive that the women of Athens combined in hatred of Euripides as the enemy of their sex. It provided the comedian with a convenient excuse for assembling a body of women, but he carefully avoids anything resembling a serious reference to ritual. Instead he makes play with such stock jokes as the slander that all women were secret tipplers or even topers. For example when Mnesilochos disguised as a woman has been caught and is being investigated to test his genuineness, one woman offers to interrogate him on the previous day's rites. After removing a man out of earshot, she asks:

'Tell me, what of the holy things was first shown to us?'

> Mnesilochos: Well now, what indeed was the first? We had a drink.
> Woman: What followed after that?
> Mn.: We drank toasts.
> Woman: You have heard this from someone. What then came third?
> Mn.: Xenylla called for a basin. For there was no chamber-pot.

This ribald picture of a religious festival was meant to raise a laugh in the male audience at the *Dionysia*. It is typical of the easy flippancy with which Aristophanes and the other comedians could make use of holy subjects for their jokes. At the same time it is plain to see that because of the extreme absurdity of the references to the showing of the 'Holy Things', no one could well lay a charge against the comic writer of impiety in revealing mysteries. In *The Women at the Thesmophoria* Aristophanes succeeds in working in bits of local colour and typical allusion, but carefully manages to avoid anything like serious religion, except for a pair of beautiful lyrics written in the form of hymns. The one invokes Artemis, Hera, Hermes, Pan and the Nymphs and Dionysus; the other Athena and the Two Goddesses Thesmophoroi (Demeter and Persephone). This easy-going polytheism avoided any concentrating on divine mysteries, though by ending with the Two Goddesses Aristophanes rightly pointed to the inner aspects of the festival.[93]

As the interrogation of Mnesilochos indicated, it lasted over several days. The first day, on the 11th of Pyanepsion, was called the 'Road Up', which seems to refer literally to the assembling at the Thesmophorion for the festival. The actual site of the Thesmophorion is not proved, but Homer A. Thompson has made a plausible case for identifying it with an area which he excavated just south of the Pnyx. The remains and the local finds were all consistent with this identification. It must have been an extensive open space which was surrounded by some wall or fence so that it could be shut to unauthorized male intruders. The large area was needed because once the festival began the women taking part camped there for three days and two nights. They set up booths or shelters in rows with gangways between them and slept in groups in these huts. Hence again in Aristophanes we find that Mnesilochos is asked: 'Have you come up here before?' Mn. 'Yes, of course, every year.' 'And who is your hut-mate?' Mn. 'Thingumbob'. There are references to a procession at the *Thesmophoria*. So the 'Road up' may have been formally organized with a meeting-place in Athens from which the cavalcade set out. With the prospect of camping three days in the open one can picture it as including carts to carry the bedding, the cooking vessels and the materials with which to construct the booths. The procession and the laying-out of the encampment must have involved a good deal of organization and even at times the use of some degree of authority. Hence it is not surprising that in the case of the local *Thesmophoria* of Attica there are references to two women

elected each year to act as 'officials' (Archousai). No doubt for the state
Thesmophoria two similar officials were appointed under whose direction
the procession would go up to the Thesmophorion.[94]

The departure of a large number of women from their homes for
three days would clearly disrupt the ordinary life of the male citizens.
Hence we find that Aristophanes mentions that on the middle day of
the festival there were no law courts held and no meeting of the city
council. The second day was known as the Fast. On it the women ab-
stained from solid food and sat on the ground. No doubt the huts had
the minimum of furniture, but this was meant to be an act of humility
and mourning. The origin of the custom could probably be explained
by a ritual act intended to conserve the energy which must be transferred instead into the seeds of the future crops. But by the classical
period it was probably thought of in terms of the legend of Demeter.
Just as when mourning for her absent daughter Persephone she fasted,
and refused to sit on a chair in the palace at Eleusis, so her worshippers
fasted and sat on the ground. Our literary authorities do not draw the
parallel, but here they are evidently exercising the reticence appropriate
to the subject of a religious mystery. The one point where the association with Demeter's mourning is admitted concerns the practice of
uttering abuse at each other. The women were said to indulge in this
at the *Thesmophoria* and even to strike each other with a scourge plaited
out of bark called a *morotton*. We have already come across verbal abuse
as sanctioned by a festival of Demeter in the *gephyrismos* of the Mysteries,
and flagellation is known in fertility cults. In the *Thesmophoria* the
explanation of the use of insulting language was found in the legend of
Iambe. She appears in the *Homeric Hymn to Demeter* as a servant in the
palace at Eleusis who first induces the goddess to be seated by offering
her a chair on which she had spread a sheepskin. When Demeter remained silently seated, Iambe at length induced her to smile by 'making
many mocking remarks'.[95]

It is clear that in this myth Iambe is simply the personification of the
abuse uttered by the women worshippers. Her name Iambe is derived
from the word for the metre which was traditionally supposed to suit
mockery. Perhaps the women were actually expected to speak the
taunts in impromptu verse. The authors who refer to the practice in
the *Thesmophoria* do not make it clear when exactly this part of the
ritual took place, but if as in the analogy of the goddess' conduct it
ended the day of sitting fasting it may have been in practice a very
satisfying release of the pent-up irritation brought on by hunger. One

of the Christian Fathers recorded that he found himself constrained to give up fasting because it made him so bad tempered. One will not be surprised if the women of Athens were relieved to end their ritual fast in an uninhibited outburst of vexation.[96]

The scene of the *Thesmophoriazousai* of Aristophanes, to which we have already referred, was supposed to take place on the day of fasting of the festival. Perhaps he chose that particular day because actually it was spent inactively, but he could therefore the more appropriately make his women take part in their plots to revenge themselves on Euripides without implying that his comic picture had any relation to their actual doings. Instead he makes the women convene their meeting as if it were a gathering of the political assembly of the Athenian male citizens (the Ecclesia), and develops the theme as a parody of the procedure of such a meeting. No guidance about the actual doings of the *Thesmophoria* can be extracted from this comic episode, and in view of the conventions of religious silence we should not expect it. The only feature which may be authentic is the reference here and elsewhere in the comedy to torches. They were much associated with Demeter and Persephone. Also it would be likely that some of the ritual took place at night by torch-light.[97]

What this ritual contained ancient authors do not tell us. Only one scrap of information survives which by its very obscurity shows how little was revealed. The late writers of dictionaries refer to 'a sacrifice performed at Athens by the women in secret at the *Thesmophoria*', which had the extraordinary name of 'Chalcidian pursuit' (*Chalcidicon Diogma*). Some explanatory myth told that in time of war the women had prayed, and the enemy had fled and had been pursued to Chalcis. No proper historical context is given for this event, and it is probably not worth while to conjecture, as it is much more likely that the myth is a pure fiction made to explain a name which was otherwise unintelligible, and which may itself have been corrupted in the course of centuries.[98]

As we have seen, the first day of what was originally a three-day festival was the 'Road Up', and the second day was the 'Fast'. The third day bore the title *Kalligeneia* which meant day of fair offspring. Sometimes Kalligeneia was described as an attendant goddess of Demeter, evidently derived from this day of the festival. This time the reference is not to agriculture or even to animal husbandry. The Greeks typically associated together all natural birth, and Demeter though chiefly goddess of the corn-crop also presided over human fertility. It is not surprising that when the women of Athens met together in seed-time the climax of their thoughts and interest was the bearing of fine children. After the grimness and mourning of the fast they will on this day have both celebrated the gift of children and prayed for a blessing on them and on any future family. Details of the secret ceremonies are entirely lacking.

These three days made up the *Thesmophoria* proper. But two days before it on the 9th of Pyanepsion there was another women's festival, the *Stenia*. By the classical period it was largely overshadowed by the *Thesmophoria*, and nothing of its rites is recorded, except that late lexicographers attribute also to it the practice of abusing each other which is assigned to the *Thesmophoria*. That it was a day dedicated to Demeter and Persephone is proved by the fact that the committee of the state council of Athens offered a sacrifice to those two goddesses on that day on behalf of the council and the people.[99]

The pattern of having festivals celebrated by women on the 9th, 11th, 12th, and 13th of the month had its inevitable effect. A further festival was found to fill in the 10th, and provide five continuous holidays. This was not held in Athens, but was a local *Thesmophoria* at Halimus on Cape Colias, the southern horn of the bay of Phaleron. We are told that already as early as the time of Solon the leading ladies of Athenian society went there to offer sacrifice and to dance. It may not be accidental that the story which Plutarch tells in this connection implies the aristocratic standing of the participants. The distance of some eight miles from Athens must have been easy to the wealthy who could afford a vehicle, but difficult for the ordinary housewife.[100]

The basic motive underlying these mysteries was evidently to ensure the fertility of the cereal crops sown at this time of the year. The exclusion of men from the rites may be derived ultimately from a time when the duty of the men of the tribe was to hunt and fish while the women tended the fields. By the classical period it will have become more a great occasion for social festivities and for the women to get together in a way which the rather confined life in the female quarters of the home did not otherwise encourage.

The other great festival of the month Pyanepsion, lasting at least three days, was the *Apaturia*. It differs from all those which we have already discussed in that it does not seem to have had a fixed date in the month. The explanation of this is because, though the *Apaturia* was recognized by the state as a public festival, its celebration was not in the hands of the central officials. It was a feast based on the separate communities linked by birth which were the basic foundation of primitive Greek society. These associations were called the *Phratriai* (i.e. Brotherhoods), and in theory all male members were descended from a common male ancestor. The *Apaturia* was essentially the festival of the *Phratriai*, which they all observed, but presumably it was left to the convenience or tradition of each *Phratria* to hold its own *Apaturia* on its appropriate dates in the month, provided they were within Pyanepsion. The festival had three regular days: the first was the *Dorpia* (The Supper Eve) on which one is to suppose the members foregathered for a meal together. As the *Phratriai* were hereditary groups, they had each a traditional locality with which they were connected, but individual members might live scattered throughout Attica. So one can picture that the first day was in the nature of a reunion. The second day was the Sacrificing (*Anarrhysis*) named after the action of drawing back the neck of the victim to cut its throat. The third day (*Koureotis*), the Day of Youths (but it could also imply the day of hair-cutting), was the official occasion when new members were introduced to the *Phratria*. This was done in the case of boys when they were still infants. In fact the male children of members born since the previous *Apaturia* would be registered at the next festival. As it was connected with a religious celebration, this has often been compared with the baptismal registration in Christian communities. The official state registration for secular purposes did not take place till the boy was approaching manhood. Then his registration with his *Phratria* as an infant could be cited as evidence of birth and paternity, if necessary. It would appear also that at puberty the boy was introduced a second time to the *Phratria* on the occasion of his admission to full membership. On each of these occasions the father was expected to provide a victim for sacrifice. The tariff of the victims required has been preserved in an inscription concerning one *Phratria*, the Demotionidai of Decelea. For the infant the sacrifice was 'the Lesser' (*Meion*) and the priest was entitled to receive from it a thigh, a side and an ear, with a fee of half a drachma. From the sacrifice for a full-grown son, he received again a thigh, a side and an ear, and in addition a flat cake made with a measure of flour, half a measure of wine, and a fee of a silver drachma. Presumably the father and his family and friends had the remainder of each victim for a feast with such further cakes and wine as the father could afford. It is not clear that female offspring needed to be registered and celebrated in the same way, but on marriage members of some *Phratriai* at least were expected to mark the occasion by a victim at a feast at the next *Apaturia*.

Considering the usual Greek social customs we must not suppose that
the young bride was brought to the banquet in her honour. The
feastings of the *Phratriai* will have been male junketings.[101]

The deities to whom the sacrifices were offered were Zeus Phratrios
and Athena Phratria who presided in common over all the activities of
the *Phratriai*. They were specialized aspects of the supreme god of the
Greeks and the chief goddess of Athens. But also in a way that is not
explained Dionysus had succeeded in winning a footing in the festival.
Its name *Apaturia* means – probably by derivation – 'the feast of common fatherhood', though some technical objections have been raised to
this etymology. To the Greeks it suggested the word for 'deceiving'
(*apate*). So a typical myth was invented to explain it.[102]

The Athenians and Boeotians were at war over a border district, and
the Athenian general Melanthus challenged the Boeotian King Xanthus
to single combat. When they fought, Melanthus saw a figure wearing a
black goatskin appear behind Xanthus. He called out that it is not fair to
come two against one. Xanthus taken off his guard looked round to
identify his unkown supporter, and Melanthus seized the opportunity
and stabbed him to death. Afterwards it was explained that the appari-
tion had been the god Dionysus and from this epiphany he acquired the
epithet Melanaigis ('of the Black Goat's Skin'). Also, in view of the
deception which had won Xanthus the victory, the festival of the
Apaturia was instituted. As an explanation of the festival this myth is
quite absurd. Even if the *Apaturia* was derived from a word meaning
'deceit', it was not only an Athenian festival instituted to celebrate the
local victory; it was commonly held in all the cities of Ionian origin.
In fact Herodotus uses its occurrence in a city as a test of pure Ionian
derivation. The plausible explanation is that some time in the mid-
sixth century when Dionysus the Wine God in the form worshipped
on the North Attic border was, as we shall later see, winning a pre-
dominance in Attic cult, he must have succeeded in securing acceptance
in the worship of some at least of the *Phratriai*. One can imagine that
the celebrations and toasts which made up no small part in the activities
of the *Apaturia* would readily suggest libations in honour of the Wine
God. The step from this practice to the creating of a myth linking him
with the festival by means of a popular derivation would be easy. The
story of the single combat, as has been noted, has curious undertones
suggesting the folk-tale motive behind such combats as St George and
the Saracen. For the name of the Athenian general means 'Dark
Coloured' and the name of the Boeotian king 'Fair'.[103]

As has been pointed out above, the name of the third day of the festival – *Koureotis* – could by its derivation suggest two ideas, 'Young Man' and 'Hair', and these were probably connected in its ritual. For it was traditional from the time of the epic to consecrate locks of hair to the gods and offer them on the successful attainment of manhood. The celebration on reaching puberty took place on the third day of the *Apaturia* and probably included this piece of ritual. Much of the festival, then, was occupied with these family occasions – birth, manhood, marriage. Also it would provide the opportunity for the annual general meeting of members who for the rest of the year might be scattered in different parts of Attica or the city of Athens.[104]

The decree of the Demotionidai which we have already cited was passed eight years after the end of the Peloponnesian War and illustrates graphically the problems which it must have caused to those celebrating the *Apaturia*. The altar of the *Phratria* was at Decelea, which was their original centre. This was the very place occupied by the Spartans as a military base in Attica. So for some ten years at least the Demotionidai must have been compelled to meet away from their proper sanctuary. The decree quaintly makes provision to cover this contingency in future. It requires the sacrifices for infants and adult children to be made on the altar at Decelea with a severe fine of 50 drachmas for infringement. But a saving clause is added 'unless there shall be a plague or a war. If any of these prevents it, they are to bring the sacrifices where the priest advertises in advance. He is to advertise five days before the *Dorpia* [i.e. the first day of the festival] in writing on a whitened tablet not smaller than a span in size where the Deceleans are to foregather in the city of Athens.' Evidently the decree was drafted so as to guarantee proper notice of the meeting and to ensure that members would not fail to attend through not having read the small print.

Curiously a passage in the contemporary orator Lysias casts some light on the meeting-places of countrymen in Athens. The speaker was investigating the defendant's claim to belong to Decelea and tells the jury that he 'went to the barber's beside the Hermai where the men from Decelea foregather', using the same verb as in the decree. So we can picture that local inhabitants from Decelea regularly met in town at a well-known hairdresser's in the Agora beside the statues of Hermes – a famous land-mark. Such a meeting place would have done for secular purposes. As, however, the priest of the Demotionidai had also to arrange for an altar on which sacrifices could be offered, the barber's shop, if used, could only have been a preliminary rendezvous.[105]

The family occasions for celebration must have given the *Apaturia* a lively and informal character, and it was only to be expected that the revelry lasted long on the third day. Hence the next day was sometimes counted as part of the festival under the name *Epibda* (meaning 'the Following'). Also *Epibda* had the associated meaning of a day of reckoning, what is now implied by 'the morning after'; evidently the day following the *Apaturia* was notorious for the hang-over which it left. This may have been another reason why it was convenient to let the *Phratriai* celebrate their *Apaturia* on different dates. The spreading of the festival assured that the public life of Attica was not completely interrupted on any one day.[106]

One may ask why this month in autumn was chosen for the *Apaturia*. For it fell about the same time or a month later in the calendars of other Ionic cities. Can it possibly be connected with the popular tradition in Greece for marriages in the spring? We shall see later that the seventh Attic month was actually named the Month of Weddings (Gamelion). Pyanepsion, then, the month in which the *Apaturia* fell, was the tenth month thereafter, counting inclusively. It may therefore have been expected that the male children would be just in time to be registered with the *Phratriai* of their fathers. This hypothesis cannot be proved by any statistic showing the distribution of births throughout the Attic year, but it is worth mentioning as a conjecture.

There was one more festival in Pyanepsion on the last day of the month – the *Chalkeia*. The name suggests the feast of the metalworkers and is derived from the Greek word for copper (*chalkos*) in the same way as the Greek word for smith (*chalkeis*). This implies an origin reaching back into the Bronze Age. In the classical period the festival was associated both with Hephaestus the god of smiths and with Athena, and modern scholars have argued at length over the question to which deity it was dedicated. In a polytheistic culture this is scarcely relevant. Evidence on the whole suggests that Hephaestus was introduced as a god from Asia Minor where his cult was widespread. Except at Athens he was little worshipped on the Greek mainland. But in Athens he was closely associated with Athena in primitive legends and in art. For instance they sit next to one another in the groups of the Twelve Gods on the Parthenon frieze. In the mid-fifth century the beautiful temple (miscalled the Theseion) was built in honour of Hephaestus on this hill overlooking the Agora. Its dominant position indicates his importance as a god of craftsmen. Already by 343 BC at latest a statue of Athena Hephaistia was set up in the shrine next to the cult statue of the god.

The use of the epithet implied the special association of Athena in this aspect with the god of the smiths. But it was not only under this aspect that Athena was worshipped on this day. In 277/6 BC we find the city council arranging for a vote of the people to pay out of state funds (actually the budget of the military treasury) for a sacrifice at the *Chalkeia* to Athena the founding goddess (Archegetis). Again a fragment of a lost play of Sophocles is preserved in which a chorus of workers at the *Chalkeia* is addressed with the words: 'Step into the road then all the host of handicraftsmen who in honour of the grim-eyed daughter of Zeus, the goddess of labour (Ergane), attend with standing corn-baskets and by the anvil with weighty hammer . . .' Here Athena is invoked as the goddess of all handicraft.[107] (Plate 34)

There is no evidence for any special features of cult at the *Chalkeia*. Evidently there were sacrifices, and Sophocles seems to suggest a procession of workers with baskets full of corn to be set up as offerings. No doubt there was a holiday from toil in the workshops and a feast at night on the sacrificial meat.

Also as we have already noted, the *Chalkeia* was the occasion of a piece of ritual connected with Athena personally. On the Acropolis the priestess of the goddess and the Arrephoroi set up the loom on which the *peplos* to be presented at the *Panathenaia* was woven. The date may have been determined by a mixture of considerations. There must have been the practical need to allow sufficient time for the elaborate piece of tapestry to be produced. The choice of the last day of Pyanepsion allowed just short of nine months. But also the festival of handicrafts in which Athena had a considerable interest provided an auspicious date. Perhaps, too, the choice may have been influenced by the fact that with Pyanepsion the fine-weather period of the year could be expected to end. From that date indoor activity such as weaving would be specially appropriate.

If we look back on Pyanepsion it is noteworthy that as a month the emphasis of its festivals rested on the act of sowing in the agricultural year. This was at the core of the *Proerosia*, the *Pyanepsia* and the *Thesmophoria* – all taking place in the first half of the month. On the other hand the *Oschophoria* was related to the wine-harvest. But as we have seen, it was a rather specialized and aristocratic festival ultimately derived from the cult practices of one small clan hailing from Salamis. Generally speaking the Athenians did little to celebrate the wine-harvest at the time when the grapes were plucked in September and October (Boedromion and Pyanepsion). This may have been partly because of the relative unimportance of viticulture compared, for instance, with the cultivation of the olive in Attica. Cereals, of course, were essential even if in the fifth and fourth century the Athenians depended more on the import of grain than on the local harvest. But Attic wines were of no repute in the ancient world, as is shown by their absence from Pliny the Elder's detailed survey of the subject.

5 MAIMAKTERION

With Pyanepsion the months of the summer season were over and the winter season began with the next month MAIMAKTERION. Also an extraordinary change comes over the Attic calendar. In Pyanepsion, if the *Apaturia* did not coincide with any of the major festivals, there could have been as many as thirteen holidays out of a month of thirty days for men and women. Maimakterion in contrast contained no popular feast day at all. Similarly, the next two months, Poseideon and Gamelion, contained less than the average number of festivals. The basic reason for this change was probably the practical one that these were months of bad weather with little occasion to go out in the open air. Activity on the farms fell off until the return of spring. Seafaring was stopped or reduced to the minimum. Gatherings in the open air ran a risk of being spoiled by rain, and most major Greek festivals involved processions and sacrifices which could not be held indoors. Even the name of the month is significant. It was derived from an epithet of Zeus as the god of the sky and of weather and meant 'Blustering'. The month belonged to him as the god of storms, and its name implies that there was a festival in the month in which prayers were addressed to him to be kind to men in his control of the wind's violence. The literal and physical side of this appeal belonged more to primitive times when storm damage could have been more serious to buildings. Crops at this season would not be greatly exposed to it. But it is not surprising if in the classical period most Athenians had ceased to feel very concerned in the object of this festival.[108]

There remained another aspect of Zeus which some ancient scholars correctly saw as correlative. This was represented by the epithet Meilichios – 'kindly' or 'open to propitiation'. It was applied to Zeus also in a later festival, the *Diasia*, as we shall see. In Maimakterion in the last third of the month there took place a procession which was dedicated to Zeus Meilichios and was of a purificatory and propitiatory intention. Its central feature was an object called the Sheepskin of Zeus (*Dion Koidion*) which figures elsewhere in purificatory rites in Attica. (The subject was such a large and complicated one that Polemon of Ilion, the famous Hellenistic antiquary, dedicated one whole treatise to it.) From him we learn that a sheep was sacrificed to Zeus and its fleece was removed and kept for magic purposes. Those who were being purified were required to stand on it with their left foot. This implies that it was regarded in some way as capable of absorbing and retaining the guilty infection. The Daiduchos at Eleusis is mentioned in this connection, and it is possible that the Eleusinian priesthood used this method to purify before admission to the Mysteries any would-be initiate whose conscience was particularly charged with a sense of guilt. In one well-known representation such an initiate is shown seated on a sheepskin, and Demeter herself is described in the *Homeric Hymn* as accepting such a chair after her wanderings. In this case one may suspect that the sheep-skin really had no connection with Zeus originally, but was associated with him by a process of assimilation. In Maimakterion when probably the sheep was sacrificed, the skin was carried round in a procession which gave the name *Pompaia* (procession) to the ceremony. In this rite it was also accompanied by a *caduceus*, the rod with entwined snakes which was the special badge of Hermes. But in this context one may doubt whether Hermes as deity was originally concerned in the festival. The whole procedure suggests apotropaic magic which may have had no primitive link with the person of any deity, but simply have been directed at controlling the unindividualized forces of nature. With the onset of winter and the darker time of the year the need was felt to exorcize evil and protect the community. The Fleece was felt to have such a power and the *caduceus* was a magic wand whose potency could ward off evil. Hence the procession of the *Pompaia* with these powerful symbols. Unfortunately our ancient authorities do not describe the route which it took. One would con-·ecture a circuit of the city.[109] (Plate 26)

When the month Maimakterion became associated with Zeus, the god of weather, as its patron deity, it was natural to link the *Pompaia* with him and assign it to his aspect as a god of atonement. Nilsson has pointed out how examples can be found of the use of fleeces to influence the weather. So this would assist the assimilation, though we need not suppose that the *Maimakteria* and the *Pompaia* took place on the same day. Neither festival is mentioned in popular literature, though the *Pompaia* of Zeus provided a picturesque verb with the meaning 'to exorcize'. The ordinary Athenian played no part in these ceremonies which were the responsibility of the priestly officials whose duty was to maintain the supernatural safety of the community by such magic rites.

Shrine of
ronos; view
om the
lympieion,
oking towards
e Ilissos

Calendar of
crifices.
scription from
e Agora giving
rt of
icomachus'
vision of Solon's
de; this portion
als with the
noikia

3 Eirene and Ploutos. Roman copy of the cult statue in the Agora carved by Cephisodotus

4 The Burgon Amphora; one of the earliest of the Panathenaic vases, showing the conventional figure of Athena and the inscription 'From the games at Athens'

5 Panathenaic vase, showing four events of the Pentathlon: from l. to r. discus-throwing, running, jumping, javelin-throwing

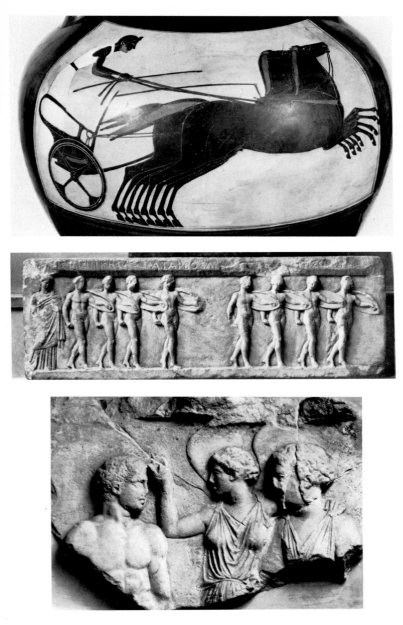

6 Panathenaic vase, showing quadriga–racing

7 Marble relief from the Acropolis, showing two groups of four nude men with shields; probably performing the Pyrrhic dance

8 Athena and Nike crowning a victorious athlete – relief from the Acropolis

9 Part of the balustrade surrounding the shrine of Athena and Nike, showing two Nikai, one of them with a cow for sacrifice

10 Athena in the procession of deities on the François Vase. She is shown without armour and wearing a *peplos*

11 Scene of a procession to Apollo on a vase from Spina. The leading figure is a Kanephoros, richly robed and bearing an elaborate basket

12 Parthenon frieze: central group showing the receiving of the *peplos*

13 Parthenon frieze: maidens at the head of the processions – probably the Ergastinai

14 Parthenon frieze: southeast group of men

15 Parthenon frieze: northeast group of men

16 Parthenon frieze: maidens carrying an incense-burner, jugs and bowls for the sacrifice

17 Parthenon frieze: charioteer with *apobates* and a marshal

18 Parthenon frieze: handsome older men

19 Parthenon frieze: young men carrying jars

20 Temple of Artemis Agrotera, seen from the southwest, and to the right the Ilissos bridge in front of the Stadium. Drawn by Stuart and Revett 1751–1753

21 The Panathenaic Way above the Agora, where it passes the Eleusinion, looking towards the Acropolis

22 *Kernoi*, from the Eleusinion at Athens

23 Relief from Eleusis:
Persephone purifying a
Mystes by pouring water
over him

24 Tablet from Eleusis, dedicated by Ninion: Mysta
carrying torches and staves are led to Demeter and
Persephone. In foreground, two crossed *bacchoi*

25 Marble statuette of sacrificial pig from Eleusis

26 Relief on the Lovatelli urn: to right an
Eleusinian priest purifying a sacrificial pig held by
Heracles: in centre a veiled figure (Heracles) seated
with bare feet on a ram's skin and being purified by
the sacred *liknon*

27 The western end of the Telesterion at Eleusis, looking east

28 Mid fifth-century red-figure stamnos (Eleusis) showing a procession led by a man who by his head-band, beard and robe is to be identified as a Daiduchos: possibly Callias Lakkoploutos

29 Relief from the Asklepieion; Persephone, Demeter, Asklepius and worshippers

30 *Skyphos* by Makron; Triptolemus being sent off by the Eleusinian goddesses in his winged chariot bearing to mankind the first ears of wheat (detail)

Late fifth-century red-figure amphora showing Demeter, Persephone, Triptolemus, Heracles and the Dioscuri, who are to be taken as initiates, as they carry *bacchoi*

Frieze from Hagios Eleutherios with figures representing the Calendar: Pyanepsion, including a boy with the *eiresione*

33 François Vase: Theseus' companions in a ritual dance (detail)

34 The Hephaisteion: a view of the east end from the Agora

35 Amphora with
woman preparing a
wine-offering, and
flute-player. By the
Villa Giulia Painter

36 Priestess mixing wine before image of Dionysus: maenads in frenzy. By the
Dinos Painter

37 Funeral relief of young boy, recording that death took him just before he was old enough for the *Choes*

38 Small *chous* with scene of two children playing

6 POSEIDEON

The sixth month, POSEIDEON, was dedicated to Poseidon, and once more its name implies the existence of a festival, *Poseidea*, not known to any great extent from our sources. Traditionally the 8th of the month was the date appropriate to Poseidon, just as the 7th belonged to Apollo and the 6th to Artemis. So one would expect that to be the day of Poseideon on which the god's festival was held, but curiously the only evidence for it is in the sacrificial calendars of a local district and of a private guild. The month seems a strange choice in which to honour the god of the sea. For as it corresponded approximately with December, it must have fallen in the time of year in which there was least navigation. We do know from literary sources that there was a festival once every fifth year at Sunium in honour of Poseidon – evidently, then, a major event. But as it included a regatta one may seriously doubt the suggestion, accepted by Deubner, that it took place in this month. The organizers would have been asking to have their programme cancelled because of bad weather.[110]

The choice of December for worshipping the god of the sea suggests either some paradox of offering to him when he most showed his formidable power or else its origins go back to a time when Poseidon was a deity of much wider province. Modern research has shown much evidence to support the view that in the Mycenaean period Poseidon may have been, as his name seems to mean, 'the lord of the earth' or 'the husband of the earth goddess'. The local Attic legend of his contest with Athena for the sovereignty of the land points to a time when he was a dominant god in Athens, and throughout the Ionian world a month Poseideon and a festival *Poseidea* in his honour were commonly found. Whether elsewhere also it was always in winter would be less easy to prove.[111] One general point may be noted. Just as the Attic year with its preponderance of months named after festivals of Apollo and of Artemis was probably arranged under the influence of the cult of Apollo, these months run in a continuous series from Elaphebolion (March) to Pyanepsion (October) with the one doubtful exception of Skiraphorion (June). The months which are not associated with Apollo form another block from Maimakterion (November) to Anthesterion

(February) inclusive. Also, as we shall see, they seem to have been dedicated each to a festival of one of the other major gods, as though to guarantee them some recognition. We have already seen Maimakterion for Zeus, and Poseideon for Poseidon; of the two following, Gamelion was dedicated to Hera and Anthesterion to Dionysus. This distribution of the year into two blocks of months, one Apolline and one for the rest, corresponds to the belief that Apollo was absent in the land of the Hyperboreans for the winter months and returned in the spring. This left only such a month as December open to be assigned to Poseidon.

Towards the end of the month, on the 26th, there took place the festival of the *Haloa*. The name obviously suggested that it was connected with the threshing-floor (*halos*) – the circular area covered with cobblestones such as is still to be seen near Greek villages. But this raised a difficulty to ancient scholars because clearly December was not the month for threshing, which ought to follow directly on the harvest in the hot dry months of high summer. So they spent much effort in providing alternative derivations, such as that the name was derived from the word for gathering and referred to the people who assembled for the festival, or else if the derivation from 'threshing-floor' was retained it was explained that the festivities took place at that site. None of this is very convincing, and the efforts of modern scholars such as Solmsen and Nilsson to derive the name from roots meaning 'cultivated field' and so to connect it with agricultural fertility are not much more successful. The name is best left as unexplained.[112]

Most ancient references are so concerned with the derivation that they do not tell much about the festival itself except that it was held in honour of Demeter and Dionysus. The only description occurs in a rather muddled commentary on Lucian where we are told that a secret rite confined to women was held at Eleusis. The magistrates prepared a feast which consisted of every sort of food, except those forbidden in the Mysteries – pomegranates, apples, eggs and fowls and certain specified kinds of fish. When the banquet was ready the magistrates departed leaving it to the women. The scholiast explained the rich feast as demonstrating that it was in Eleusis that mankind had learned humane eating. The conduct of the women, however, introduced quite another element into the rite. They carried models of male and female genital organs and indulged in uninhibited obscenity of language and abuse of the kind which we have already seen attributed to other festivals confined to women. Even the priestesses went about whispering to the

wives that they should take lovers, as a piece of secret advice. Also on
the tables were cakes in the shape of phalli and pudenda, and much wine
was consumed. The description of this obscene banquet might be
regarded as exaggerated if it was not for the fact that it is possible to
illustrate it from various pictures on Greek vases. These are unfortunately not labelled with ancient inscriptions to identify the happenings,
but some correspond closely to what is described by the scholiast. So
it can be taken that the account is correct enough.[113]

Our ancient evidence usually mentions Eleusis as the scene of the
Haloa, and one is perhaps right in supposing that it only took place
there. Evidently it was in origin a fertility festival connected with the
Eleusinian claim to be the source of corn for mankind. The purpose
would be to stimulate the growth of the corn from seed. In this connection A. B. Cook and Deubner have called attention to a red-figure
vase in the British Museum which probably illustrates some part of the
attendant ritual. 'A girl leans forward to the right and sprinkles something from a rectangular box held in her left arm. Before her on the
ground stand four phalli with round their bases the leaves of corn
springing.' The phalli are presumably clay models such as we are told
women carried at the *Haloa*. The girl has brought them to a field and
set them up in a row amid the first shoots of the new season's growth.
She is sprinkling the place with something meant together with the
presence of the phalli to stimulate their growth.[114]

If this is correctly identified with the practices of the *Haloa*, one may
suppose that what began as a phallic rite practised by women to promote the growth of wheat ended by becoming an all-night orgy of
banqueting in an atmosphere of indecency. It is therefore not surprising
that the allusions to the festival in Greek authors from the fourth century BC onwards tend to connect it with courtesans. These ladies of
easy virtue were not concerned greatly with the fertility of crops, but
the tone of the banquet will have suited them perfectly. An episode in
one of Demosthenes' speeches illustrates the connection of a courtesan
with the festival. Archias the hierophant of the Mysteries in the mid-
fourth century BC was convicted of impiety for offences committed in
connection with his office. (There are strong grounds for believing that
the real motive of the prosecution was political: Archias had been in
close relations with the oligarchic government of Thebes and had tried
to warn them before their overthrow by Pelopidas.) The validity of the
charge is less significant than the fact that it was made. It alleged that he
had offered a sacrifice at the hearth in the courtyard at Eleusis during

the *Haloa* – for Sinope the courtesan – though it was not lawful to offer sacrifices on that day, and the sacrifice did not concern him, but the priestess of Demeter. The grounds of this charge are impossible for us to check. But one notes that the account of the festival in the *scholia* mentioned the part played by the priestesses, and men were excluded from the banquet. Late grammarians write as though the offerings made to Demeter were first-fruits of grain, and though this seems to be connected with their belief that the name of the festival was derived from the threshing floor, it is likely that it was not an occasion for blood sacrifices. Besides it is plausible enough to find a prominent courtesan, perhaps with a view to notoriety, persuading the hierophant to perform an offering for her in the most conspicuous place at Eleusis on this popular occasion.[115]

Besides the worship of Demeter the *Haloa* is described as being dedicated to Dionysus. It is probable that he is intrusive into what was originally a festival of corn. The phallic element would fit with Dionysiac rites and prepare the way for his introduction. Also, as we shall see, the other festival held in the month Poseideon was Bacchic and may well, as Deubner suggests, have influenced the development of the *Haloa*. In addition there is reference to a procession in honour of Poseidon. As it was his month this is reasonable enough. Perhaps also the men, excluded from the banquet to Demeter, found a way to assert themselves in worship of a male deity. One inscription from Eleusis which honours a general called Aristophanes because he 'had invited all the citizens to the festival thinking they ought to have a share in the good things provided in the sanctuary', points to a separate banquet for the men being served on at least one occasion.[116]

The latter part of Poseideon was also the occasion for a popular festival held in various localities all over Attica. This was the *Country Dionysia* which like the *Apaturia* was not tied to a single date in the month, but was celebrated according to the choice of each neighbourhood. It was the religious ceremony from which the great Athenian festivals of the *Lenaia* and the *City Dionysia* were derived. But it survived as a local festival in various places throughout Attica, to some extent retaining the primitive character of the original ritual, but in many parts influenced by the development of the city festivals and tending to imitate them on a more modest scale.

Plutarch gives a rather sentimentally wistful picture of the primitive form of the ceremony.

The patriarchal rite of the *Dionysia* consisted in a procession in the old days organized in a popular and cheerful style: a jar of wine and a vine, then someone dragging a he-goat, another followed carrying a wicker basket of raisins, and to crown it all the phallus. But now these things are ignored and eclipsed when gold vessels are borne along and expensive costumes and teams of horses driven and masks. Thus the modest minimum of wealth and usefulness is overwhelmed by the useless and excessive.

Plutarch is writing of the extravagant splendour of processions in the days of Roman imperialism, but the picture which he draws in contrast to primitive simplicity, even if we cannot be sure that he was thinking of Attica, was true enough for it.[117]

This fact is demonstrated by Aristophanes writing more than five hundred years earlier. In the *Acharnians*, so as to rouse in his audience the regrets for the peaceful days before the Peloponnesian War, his hero Dikaiopolis, as soon as he has opted out by a separate peace, announces that he will celebrate a *Country Dionysia*. The parody of a procession is produced by his daughter acting as basket-bearer (Kanephoros), the slave Xanthias bearing the phallus, perhaps assisted by a second slave, and Dikaiopolis himself leading the he-goat. The scene must have given plenty of scope for comic business, and Aristophanes mixes in ribald jokes with the ritual, but the picture of the ceremony was basically realistic and meant to remind his audience of the joys of peace in the country.

> Dikaiopolis: Keep holy silence! Keep holy silence!
>
> Chorus: Quiet everyone. Didn't you hear the man call silence. This is the one we are looking for. But all of you stand clear. For the fellow seems to be coming out to sacrifice.
>
> Dikaiopolis: Keep holy silence! Keep holy silence! Let her go ahead a little, you the Basket-bearer. Xanthias, set the phallus upright. Put down the basket, daughter, that we may perform the consecration.
>
> Daughter: Mother, give me here the soup-ladle so that I can pour some soup over this flat-cake. [This was a parody of consecrating the victim – which should have been a he-goat – by sprinkling sanctified corn over it.]
>
> Dikaiopolis: Well, that is right enough. O Dionysus, Lord, in thankfulness may it please you that I lead this procession and offer

sacrifice together with my slaves and celebrate successfully the
Country Dionysia . . . Come, daughter, see that you carry the basket
nicely and put on a vinegar expression. [At this point there will have
been some business parodying the manner of an aristocratic maiden
acting as Kanephoros.] Xanthias, you two have to keep the phallus
upright behind the Basket-bearer while I shall follow and sing the
Phallic song. Wife, look at the spectacle of the procession from the
roof. Forward! [Then Dikaiopolis sings a Phallic song full of
obscenities.][118]

The Athenian audience in 425 BC will have found much to laugh at
in this parody, but also many of them, refugees in Athens owing to the
Spartan invasions, will have felt at heart a longing for the country
festivals. To the modern reader, even those parts that are not indecent
waken no chords of religious sympathy. But we must recognize that
to the contemporary Athenian it must have had a sentimental appeal
comparable to that which Dickens evokes by a family Christmas party
in *A Christmas Carol*.

Like Christmas festivities, it was shared by all, even the slaves, and
for this fact we do not depend only on Aristophanes' comic version.
Also like Christmas it was the occasion for traditional games. A
goatskin was blown up and greased, the contest consisting in jumping
on top of it and trying to stand there. This was called *askoliasmos*. But
the word properly meant standing on one leg, and there were various
trials of skill based on that handicap: a contest to hop the longest
distance, or a form of tig in which the player had to hop on one leg and
try and touch the other players with the leg which he held off the
ground. Or all hopped together counting the jumps and the one who
reached the highest number was the winner.[119]

These games suggest what Plutarch called 'the popular and cheerful
style' of the original festival. But under the influence of the greater
Athenian occasions the local townships developed theirs. For instance
local theatres were constructed on the lines of the Dionysiac theatre
at Athens and evidently tragedies and comedies were performed just
as in the capital. When Demosthenes wishes to pour scorn on the
career of his opponent, Aeschines, who had been earlier in life a tragic
actor, he refers to the performances in which he had taken part at the
Country Dionysia. He had been third actor in a team led by Simykas
and Socrates who were known as the Deep-Groaners ('Barnstormers'?).
One is to picture a touring company, playing to audiences at the local

festivals and specializing in heavy emotional roles. It may have been convenient in this connection that there was no single fixed date for these *Dionysia*, since this would allow the possibility of organizing a tour through the Attic townships.[120]

One local festival stood out beyond the others and was not a country celebration. This was held in the Peiraeus, in the theatre which still survives. The official (Demarchos) responsible for organizing it was not left to local choice, but was allotted from a short list by the central government. There was the traditional procession, and tragedies and comedies were performed. The standard of these must have been acceptable to the sophisticated, for we find that when Athens in the Hellenistic period was visited by an embassy from Colophon renewing the traditional links between the two cities, the ambassadors were invited to a performance in the Dionysiac theatre in the Peiraeus, which must have coincided with their visit.[121]

The festivals most prominent in Poseideon – the *Haloa* and the *Country Dionysia* – were evidently in origins fertility festivals. The *Haloa* may originally have been designed to encourage the growth of the seedling corn. The *Dionysia* shows little sign of being directly concerned with the vine, which would not be growing in December. Both festivals were predominantly phallic in emphasis. They fell round the period of the shortest and darkest days of the year. So they may have had some connection with that season. The Greeks, unlike the pagans of northern Europe, show no consciousness in their ritual that the sun is at its lowest point and may need strengthening and encouragement. Instead the need may have been a human one, to cheer oneself up at the most depressing season by games and feasts. Apollo had vanished, and Dionysus had taken his place at Delphi, and in Attica Poseideon and the two months that follow are notable for Dionysiac Festivals.

7 GAMELION

The following month, GAMELION, meant 'the month of marriage'. On the human level this was because it was the favourite season for weddings: on the divine level it was also the month of a marriage festival – the Sacred Marriage of Zeus and Hera which was celebrated on the 26th of the month as the anniversary. It is hard to tell which of these events came first. Whether the prevalence of weddings in Gamelion made it seem the appropriate month to celebrate the marriage of the king and queen of the gods, or the occurrence of the festival at this traditional date induced folk to choose then as an auspicious time for marriage. Behind both aspects may have lain the feeling that now life was about to come with the spring, and marriage and conception could suitably be linked to it. No details of the festival of the *Hieros Gamos* (Sacred Wedding) or the *Gamelia* are preserved.[122]

The only other festival in Gamelion was the *Lenaia*, dedicated to Dionysus. It took place on the 12th and even about it comparatively little is known. The dictionary of Hesychius on the phrase from Aristophanes 'the contest at the *Lenaia*' explained that the Lenaion was 'a place in the city of Athens with an extensive enclosure and in it the sanctuary of Dionysus Lenaios in which the dramatic contests of the *Lenaia* were held before the (Dionysiac) theatre was built'. This explanation is generally to be accepted in the sense that there was within the walls of Athens an extensive area called the Lenaion consecrated to Dionysus. This had been a primitive centre of his cult, perhaps the earliest, and certainly had preceded the introduction of Dionysus Eleuthereus in the mid-sixth century and the establishment of the *City Dionysia*. In that sense dramatic contests had originally been performed there in whatever rudimentary form one is to picture them before the establishment of the Theatre of Dionysus. In fact it would probably be correct to regard the *Lenaia* as in origin the primitive *Dionysia* of Athens corresponding to the *Country Dionysia* which we have been discussing. In the classical period the *City Dionysia* had taken much of the prestige from the *Lenaia*. But the latter still had a procession and tragedies and comedies which will have lasted several days starting from the 12th. The *Acharnians* of Aristophanes was performed there and the poet reminds his audience that no foreigners are present, when he criticizes the Athenian war-policy; in fact even the resident aliens (the Metoikoi) were excluded from this more native and intimate occasion.[123]

There is no precise information about the procession, although some ancient commentaries refer to people riding on carts and singing abusive songs. But this feature is so typical of these festivals that it cannot be regarded as giving it any special character.[124]

The primitive origin of the festival is indicated by the fact that it was organized by the Basileus (the King), the original authority for religious as well as civil administration. By the fourth century at least he was joined in organizing the procession by the overseers of the Eleusinian Mysteries. This may have been originally an administrative development to assist the Basileus, particularly when in the fifth century he was chosen by lot from a lower social class than the aristocracy. But it appears as if the effect may have been to allow the Eleusinian priesthood to get a footing in a festival with which they cannot have had any basic connection. This is illustrated by the solitary statement which we have about the ritual. 'In the theatrical contests at the Lenaion the Daiduchos ("Torch-bearer") holding a torch says, "Call on the god," and the audience shout, "Son of Semele, Iacchos, giver of wealth." ' This cannot have been an early piece of ritual. For as we have already seen in discussing the Mysteries, Iacchos was a deity invented originally to personify the triumphant shout of the initiates in the procession to Eleusis. He had early become equated with Bacchus, probably because of the resemblance of the two names. In this invocation the identification is complete. He is addressed as son of Semele, the Theban mother of Dionysus. On the other hand the address 'giver of wealth' has Eleusinian connections as it was also an epithet of Demeter. This small bit of liturgy is a good example of the way in which in polytheistic Athens one popular cult could inter-penetrate another.[125]

Deubner has tried to conjecture further details of the *Lenaia*, which our literary sources do not describe. The name itself could be derived from the word for a wine-vat (*lenos*) which would be appropriate to a Dionysiac festival, except that January would not be the month for treading the grapes. Some modern scholars have agreed to derive the name from Lenai, sometimes applied to the maenads or infatuated female worshippers of Dionysus. It would be quite appropriate to attribute a festival in the depth of winter to them, as other examples prove. For instance we read in Plutarch that the Delphic women devoted to Dionysus, called the Thyiades, had gone up into Parnassus in winter and been caught in a snow blizzard, and how an expedition had to be sent up to rescue them. The Athenian guild of women used to go to Delphi every second year for a combined festival with those of Delphi. So one can accept it that maenads existed as an organized group at Athens and held their ecstatic dances in winter. In drawings on red-figure vases from about 480 B C, instead of the archaic design of maenads and satyrs a new type of more realistic Bacchic dancers appear. These are girls fully clothed in Greek dress, with castanets or the thyrsus dancing together with no male companions, human or satyr. On some vases the god's image is also shown as a pillar with a human head, draped in male costume. In one particularly beautiful vase in Naples a priestess with a garland is measuring out cups of wine from a jar which stands on a table before the image. Her careful attention to her work is charmingly contrasted with the two lines of excited dancers who approach the altar from either side. Besides the thyrsus some of them carry tambourines or a double flute and lit torches, which show that the ceremony is one of those all-night revels associated with Dionysus. These scenes give the clear impression that they are not more or less imaginary like the maenad and satyr orgies, but are an artistic transcription of some actual festival. Various other occasions have been suggested, such as the *Anthesteria* and the *Skira-phoria*, both of which we shall later discuss. But the best identification is that proposed originally by Frickenhaus and adopted by Deubner that these are scenes from the *Lenaia*. If so, we would have to suppose that part of the festival was a midnight revel of women devoted to Dionysus. By the fifth century this continued, but was overshadowed by the procession and the plays[126] so that it found no place in our literary tradition, but some red-figure painters saw in it a convenient subject with which to decorate cups and wine-jars which may have been intended for use at the festival. (Plates 35, 36)

8 ANTHESTERION

In the next month, ANTHESTERION, occurred a great festival of Dionysus, the *Anthesteria*, which gave its name to the month. It is derived from the Greek word for flowers and corresponded to the time of year when the first shoots of blossom begin to show themselves. But there also was a particular use of flowers, which may have led to the title of the feast. It was an Athenian custom on this day to crown with flowers children who were three years old. In fact the *Anthesteria* in one of its many aspects was a festival for children. They were given as presents little miniature wine-jars with appropriate scenes painted on them. For, as we shall see, a particular type of jar played a special part in the festival. That in later periods it was the traditional date on which schoolmasters were paid their annual fee with such additional gifts as the parent chose to bestow may have derived from this connection of the *Anthesteria* with childhood. In return, the teachers were expected to invite their pupils to a reception. This link of the *Anthesteria* with flowers and with the young may have resulted from Dionysus being in some aspects not only the god of the vine, but of all birth and growth. However, the festival mainly concerned itself with the two themes of wine and of the spirits of the unseen world. Wine was appropriate to the occasion when the new wine was sampled. Why the unseen powers should also have been associated with the *Anthesteria* is not so clear.[127] (Plates 37, 38)

The festival lasted three days, the 11th, 12th and 13th of the month. The first day was the *Pithoigia*, 'the jar-opening' when the new wine was tasted. As we have seen, the Athenians had no great festival for the grape harvest in late summer. The *Anthesteria* instead was the occasion to celebrate the fruit of the vine. When the grapes had been gathered and pressed, the juice was stored to ferment in *pithoi* – large earthenware jars; the Greeks did not use wooden casks. The contents were left untouched till the *Pithoigia*, when the jars were opened, and samples of the new sweet wine were taken out and carried to the shrine of Dionysus in the Marshes where the main ceremonies of the *Anthesteria* were held.[128]

This sanctuary is mentioned by Thucydides as the most ancient site

of the worship of Dionysus, in contrast to the shrine of Dionysus
Eleuthereus. He implies that it was on the southward side of the
Acropolis approximately, but unfortunately does not give any clearer
indications. Dörpfeld in the last years of the nineteenth century
excavated a site of a sanctuary of Dionysus in the little valley below the
Areiopagus about due west of the Acropolis. This is the only site
within the city walls which has a good case to be identified with the
sanctuary in the Marshes, as Dörpfeld claimed. But even against it two
arguments can be brought: that it lay less far south of the Acropolis
than Thucydides suggests, and that although there is some local water
in the neighbourhood it scarcely seems enough to justify the description
'in the Marshes'. Even in the fifth century the marshes must have been
a reality. For, as we shall see, it is in them that Aristophanes imagines
his chorus of frogs as singing. So the site of the shrine of Dionysus in
the Marshes is best regarded as still uncertain of identification.[129]

On the *Pithoigia* the samples of new wine were brought to the shrine
and there mixed with water in the right proportion. To the ancient
Greek, wine was not something which should be taken neat and
Dionysus was credited with having taught men how to dilute wine
correctly. In honour of this gift and of the new vintage the first mixed
wine was offered to the god, and afterwards the male worshippers
could drink their first tastes of the season's wine. But before they did
so they prayed with their libation that their partaking of this potion
would be harmless and actually beneficial to them. No doubt the
prayer was meant to cover all the future use of that vintage and the
phrase uttered implies that wine had a potent, even a magical, power
which only Dionysus could control. Once the new wine had been
sampled the rest of the day may have been given over to drinking. At
least no further activities are assigned to it. (Plates 39, 40)

The 12th of *Anthesterion* was the Feast of the *Choes* – the Wine-jugs –
and the central day of the festival. The shape of the pottery which gave
its name to the occasion can be safely recognized in a type with 'a
generously curving belly, a short neck that merges into the body and a
trefoil mouth'. Numbers of these survive in a miniature form because
it was evidently usual to give them to children as presents during the
Anthesteria, so they were produced in large numbers and decorated
with scenes usually showing chubby little boys engaged in play or some
appropriate activity. Deductions with regard to the festival itself can
sometimes be drawn from these pictures. But the real *chous* was a full-
scale vessel which actually represented a standard measure. It was

supposed to contain twelve cups (*kotylai*) each nearly equal to half a pint and so it contained somewhat under three quarts.[130]

A large number of references survive to events which took place during the *Anthesteria*, but some doubts remain on which day they occurred. However, it is likely that the chief features occupied the middle date of the festival. There was, for instance, a procession, and we hear about it again that those riding in the carts engaged in abuse and mocking of people they met in the roadway. This time the ribaldry was delivered by men, not women.

The chief feature of the procession was the god Dionysus himself who came riding in a ship mounted on wheels. There is no reference to this in Attic literature, but representations on Attic vases from the black-figure period of the later sixth century prove its existence by that date at least and the whole character of the ceremony is basically primitive. We cannot be sure to what Attic festival the ship-chariot belonged, but clear descriptions of a similar rite at Smyrna where it occurred in their local month, Anthesterion, make it reasonably certain that the festival of the *Choes* was the occasion in Athens. Again, we are not told what was the route of the procession, but as the vehicle represented a boat it must be assumed that Dionysus was represented as though he arrived by sea. This could well be a primitive feature, for as references in Homer and the *Homeric Hymns* show, to the Ionians, at least, Dionysus was associated with the sea and seafaring. The god was probably personified in the procession by an actor wearing a mask and was accompanied in the chariot by others representing satyrs and playing double flutes. But the procession had also, judging by the representations, the more conventional items of Kanephoroi, sacrificial victims, and young men carrying the utensils needed for the service. If the god was shown as arriving in Athens by sea, the natural supposition is that he was making his way to his temple, which for the purpose of this festival was the shrine in the Marshes. The whole occasion, however, was evidently less taken to have a theological purpose than to provide an opportunity for joyful and uninhibited celebration at the end of winter and the arrival of spring. Unlike the *Country Dionysia* the phallic aspects are not prominent, and the emphasis seems to rest on wine and merriment. [131] (Plates 41, 42)

It is perhaps natural, though somewhat misleading, that this part of the *Anthesteria* has suggested analogies with the carnival which in the modern world takes place about the same time of the year. In fact by a false, but attractive, etymology the word carnival itself has been derived from the *carrus navalis* – the ship-chariot of the god. But the derivation is wrong, and though the cars and masked figures and the invitation to celebrate with intoxicating drink all are common to both occasions, there the parallel ceases. The Greeks were not having a last fling before a period of fasting, though, as we shall see, the day that followed the Feast of the Wine-jars presented a solemn and melancholy contrast.

But even on the day of the *Choes* itself much more serious ritual was performed. Our evidence on this comes from a speech attributed to Demosthenes in which the prosecutor sets out to create prejudice in the minds of the jury against the defendant, Neaira, by attacking her daughter. He had already alleged that Neaira was a foreigner and a courtesan and so was legally precluded from contracting a legitimate marriage with a citizen, but in spite of this prohibition she had done so and her daughter had been treated as an Athenian and had married a citizen who had even been elected Basileus. As we have seen, the Basileus (King Archon) retained the responsibility for many of the older religious ceremonies of the city throughout his year of office and by old tradition he shared some of these rites with his wife. On account of this, as the prosecutor explains, it was an ancient law that the Basileus must be married and that his wife, known as the Basilinna, must have come to him as a virgin and not after a previous marriage. The particular ceremonies incumbent on the Basilinna which the prosecutor chose to emphasize were those connected with the *Anthesteria*. [132]

The prosecutor explained that the law governing the qualifications of the Basilinna was inscribed on a stone *stele* set up by the altar in the sanctuary of Dionysus in the Marshes, and described how this was the most ancient and most holy sanctuary of the god, which was opened only once a year on the 12th of Anthesterion, otherwise the Feast of the Wine-jars. (This was not in itself a peculiar arrangement for an ancient holy place. These precincts or buildings were intended to be used for specific official rites and not for casual worship. As mentioned earlier, the idea of leaving a temple open, like a Christian church, for the use of worshippers attending for private devotions would have seemed entirely strange to both Greeks and Romans.) The statement that the sanctuary was only open for the one day (the 12th of Anthesterion) has given some difficulty to scholars because, as we have seen, at the *Pithoigia* offerings of wine were brought to the shrine in the Marshes, apparently on the previous day, the 11th. If the statement of the orator is to be taken strictly and literally, there may be a way out of the problem by noting that to the Greeks, as to the Jews, the day began at sunset. So the new *pithoi* may have been opened in the course of the day and the samples of their contents may have been brought to the shrine in the Marshes in time for it to be unlocked at sunset and for the drinking to begin.

But the prosecutor in the case against Neaira stressed the duties of the Basilinna on the day of the 12th. 'She offered secret offerings on behalf of the city, and saw what no foreigner could fittingly see, and entered whither no other Athenian, of all the many there are, enters except the wife of the Basileus.' These allusions indicate that when the sanctuary was open, the Basilinna went through some sacred ritual of the sort which we have seen already was often kept secret in connection with fertility rites performed by women. There is no statement that there was a temple at the Marshes; instead the references are to a sacred precinct and an altar. But perhaps one is to picture the precinct as containing not a temple, but a small sacristy, which held the 'Holy Things' and the apparatus used in the annual ceremonies and which was reserved for the use of the Basilinna only.

Her other function was to exact an oath from 'the Gerarai who serve the sacred rites'. These were fourteen women who were required to perform ritual functions under the direction of the Basilinna. They were equal in number to the altars in the sanctuary, and evidently we are to suppose that they made simultaneous offerings at each of these altars. What they offered we are not told. It might have been animals such as goats – the particular victim of Dionysus – or it might simply have been libations of wine. But it was probably part of the mystery with which this ceremony is surrounded that we are told no more. The Gerarai were appointed for each occasion by the Basileus and under the guidance of the Basilinna went through a ritual formula before starting on their duties. The purpose of this administration of an oath was to guarantee that they were pure and suitable for their office. So as to impress the jury, the prosecutor of Neaira summoned as a witness 'the Sacred Herald who acts as servant to the wife of the Basileus when she administers the oath to the Gerarai at the baskets beside the altar'. The formula as quoted, if authentic, ran: 'I sanctify myself and am pure and holy, from all things which are not purifying and particularly from intercourse with a man, and I shall act as Gerara at the *Theoinia* and the *Iobaccheia* in the ancestral fashion and at the appropriate times.' The references to purity are of a usual type; particularly it was typical to regard sexual intercourse as involving a mild degree of impurity. The only surprising feature is that the oath did not specify how long an interval should have elapsed as is usual in such formulae. The references to the *Theoinia* and the *Iobaccheia* are quite obscure. That these were some rites devoted to Dionysus under these titles is indicated by a few other references, but what they were and when they took place is lost to us. If the whole formula of the oath is not a fiction inserted in the text of the Demosthenic speeches, one may suppose that it is given in an abbreviated form and originally dated from some archaic period where these rites were of greater importance. The title Gerarai by derivation meant 'reverend' and implied the respect due to the office held by the fourteen women. Certainly one is not led to picture them as maenads indulging in some licentious ritual. Instead it suggests solemn and elderly priestesses, and the little we know of their duties accords with this view.[133] (Plate 43)

When the inauguration of the Gerarai and their offering to Dionysus took place is not stated. If we were right in picturing the day of the Wine-jars as starting with a procession bringing the god to his shrine in the Marshes, then the middle of the day may have been occupied with making offerings to him. The Basilinna, however, had still one important function to perform. She had to be married to Dionysus and be united with him. No details of the ceremonial are recorded, as no doubt it was regarded as a sacred mystery. Only it is stated that the marriage ceremony and the union with the god took place not in his shrine at the Marshes, but in a building called the Boukoleion beside the Prytaneion in the civic centre of Athens.[134] So one must suppose that the day's ritual at the shrine in the Marshes ended with a wedding procession in which the priestess accompanied by the god was escorted to the civic centre where their marriage was celebrated. In ordinary Greek marriages in the same way the bridegroom at nightfall escorted the bride to her new home as the climax of the ceremony. Aristotle, who knew of this ritual at the *Anthesteria*, deduced from it that the Boukoleion was originally the official building of the Basileus. Modern scholars would prefer to associate the early Attic kings with a palace on the Acropolis. But there may be some truth behind Aristotle's sugges-tion. As Deubner has pointed out, if one is to suppose that some actual union took place as the central act of this ceremony, the easiest sup-position is that the Basileus himself acted the part of Dionysus through-out. As we have seen, our evidence points to someone impersonating the god in the procession. If so, it could appropriately be the Basileus, and again robed and masked to impersonate the god he will have emerged for the wedding procession and for the final intimacies of the Boukoleion. (Plate 44)

A *Hieros Gamos* (a Holy Marriage) of this sort is not elsewhere found in Athenian ritual, and is rare in Greek religion. The idea that the priestess was the consort of a male god, as Herodotus recognized, was an oriental practice. How it came to Athens and was accepted as part of the cult of Dionysus remains unexplained. It might be possible to account for the ritual as meant to induce fertility in the vine, though it was very early in the year to picture this happening in the form of the new shoots budding. Alternatively we might suppose that by the ceremonial wedding Dionysus who had arrived by sea was accepted into the community and united with it in a visible manifestation. In any case one can agree that the festival and its ritual are primitive and date from some early period.

What we have just discussed may well have been the core of the festival of the *Anthesteria*. But though when carefully expounded it might be used to thrill an Athenian jury, it is safe to assume that the ordinary citizen's mind on the 12th of Anthesterion was not still on the ritual at the shrine in the Marshes or on the mystery at the Boukoleion, but on the celebrations which closed the day. As its name of Wine-jars implied, this was an occasion for drinking on a large scale, following appropriately on the opening of the wine stored up since the vintage. However, the festivities were conducted according to rules which to the Athenians seemed peculiar enough to need explaining by an elaborate legend. The evening of the 12th was a traditional occasion to invite friends to a party, but the host only provided garlands, perfumes and dessert. The guests each brought their own food and still more significantly their own drink in the form of a wine-jar and a cup each. These practices were quite at variance with the usual Greek party at which the host provided the meal and the wine. Still more it was the normal practice for the wine for all the guests to be mixed in a large mixing-bowl (*crater*) and ladled out from the common supply to each of the guests. The community spirit of the party was particularly expressed by this social practice. Hence the idea of each guest bringing his own stock of wine and drinking from it privately was the negation of traditional good fellowship. But the peculiar customs of the Feast of the Wine-jars were carried even one stage further. It was apparently the tradition that each drinker consumed his share in silence. This was the complete antithesis of the symposium with its sharing of talk or song.[135]

The strange practice adds additional point to the story which Plutarch tells of Timon the misanthrope. Once he and his friend Adeimantus were drinking together without further company on the Feast of the Wine-jars. At the end of their silent drinking Adeimantus said to Timon, 'What a fine party we make !' 'Yes', replied the misanthrope, 'if only you were not present.'[136]

The legend provided an appropriate explanation for these peculiar customs: Orestes, infected with blood-guilt through the murder of his mother Clytemnestra had taken refuge in Athens. As he had not yet been tried and acquitted by the Areiopagus, he would be regarded as contaminating with his guilt anyone with whom he had social contact. He had arrived at the feast of the *Anthesteria*, which we must suppose before his day was conducted like any ordinary Greek banquet. The king did not wish to be so inhospitable as to exclude Orestes from the celebration, but had to protect his citizens from the deadly curse of blood-guilt. So he commanded that all the temples be closed and that each guest be furnished with a jar of wine to drink from. By this method it was guaranteed that Orestes could not enter consecrated ground and defile it, nor could he share in the drink of the Athenians and contaminate them by his contact. Hence the guests and the hosts drank separately in silence. The legend implies then, that ever after the same rules were applied to the festival.[137]

Tradition also attributed to the king the institution of a contest in drinking. Whoever drained his jar first was awarded a cake as a prize. This practice had its counterpart in the fifth century, just like all the other features which we have mentioned. Presumably private parties ran their own contests in drinking, but also there was a state banquet to which guests were invited by the priest of Dionysus. The whole scene is comically and brilliantly represented in the *Acharnians* of Aristophanes. As we have seen, that very Dionysiac play in its earlier part gave a presentation of a country *Dionysia*. It was actually produced at the *Lenaia* of 425 BC and (with comic licence) it ends as though the date was the 12th of *Anthesterion*. Its hero, Dikaiopolis, who has managed to opt out of the Peloponnesian War, is contrasted with Lamachus, who by name and character represents the militant Athenian. So on the stage in parallel action Dikaiopolis prepares to indulge in the Feast of the Wine-jars while Lamachus is called up to lead the resistance to a sudden Boeotian raid on Attica.[138]

A herald announces that in accordance with the ancestral practice the Feast of the Wine-jars will be held. Whoever drinks up the contents of his jar first is to win the prize of a wine-skin. (Here Aristophanes seems to differ from the practice as described by ancient commentators who wrote of the prize as a cake. Perhaps both were right, but at private parties a cake was enough, at the public banquet a whole leather bottle of wine was the rule. As we shall see, the amount of the prize was later inflated.) The start of the contest was signalled by the sounding of a trumpet, so that all the contestants could begin simultaneously. Dikaiopolis takes with him a basket with the food for his banquet. The delicacies which he chooses are contrasted with the coarse rations of the soldier, Lamachus, and he is assured that the priest of Dionysus has everything prepared on his side: '. . . couches, tables, cushions, rugs, garlands, scent, sweetmeats, cakes – and beautiful flute-players'. After an interval occupied by a choric ode the contrasting pair return. Lamachus on his night expedition has fallen in a ditch and sprained his ankle and cracked his head. Dikaiopolis of course has won the contest in drinking and comes back singing a traditional song of victory and bearing his prize, the wine-skin.

Aristophanes has cleverly stylized his scene to point the moral of the difference between war and peace, but there is no doubt that he founded it on the actual practices of the Feast of the Wine-jars. In the fourth century the competition could take on a more elaborate style. Timaeus, the third-century BC historian, describes how a century previously Dionysius the elder, the famous tyrant of Syracuse, had on the occasion of the Feast of the Wine-jars paid for a specially expensive celebration. A hundred guests were invited and the servants brought in a hundred jugs of gold filled with wine and put one by each drinker. The prize was a beautiful garland made of gold which was placed on a tripod in the middle of the gathering. The winner was Xenocrates, the philosopher, who must at the time have been quite a young man, but in 339 was to succeed to the headship of Plato's Academy. To the wonder and admiration of everyone instead of keeping possession of the garland he did exactly what he used to do daily with garlands of flowers. He hung it on the image of Hermes at the entrance to his house, giving it as an offering to the god of good luck. The story was remembered as a moral tale illustrating the true philosopher's scorn of riches. [139]

The ordinary garlands at the Feast of the Wine-jars were also the object of a special ritual. It was usual for banqueters at any festival to wear garlands, and as we have seen, the host provided them on this occasion, but instead of offering them in the usual way to shrines at the

end of the feast each banqueter put his garland round his empty jug
and carried it to the shrine of Dionysus in the Marshes where it was
handed over to the priestess. Tradition attributed this practice, too, to
Demophon the king of Athens in Orestes' time and saw in it a special
way of getting rid of garlands that had been under the same roof with
the murderer. It is probably to this custom also that Aristophanes makes
his chorus of frogs refer when they say: 'Let us utter the shout – which
in honour of Dionysus, son of Zeus, of Nysa we cried in the Marshes
when on the holy day of the Pots the revelling crowd with the hang-
over makes its way by my territory.' The Pots was the day after the
Feast of the Wine-jars and the belated revellers suffering from the
effects of their heavy potations were pictured as staggering after sunset
past the Marshes on the way to the priestess accompanied by a chorus
of croaking frogs. They might well have shown the effects of their
carousing if they had each drunk the entire contents of a jug (*chous*)
which would be just under three quarts. But we must allow for a
certain proportion of water in the mixture.[140]

The third day of the *Anthesteria*, the day of the Pots (*Chytrai*) was
entirely different in character from the celebration which preceded it.
It took its name from the cooking utensil in which a mixture of all
kinds of vegetables was boiled in daytime. This was not meant to be a
meal for the living. Instead it was offered to Hermes of the Underworld
on behalf of the dead, and no members of the household took part in
this meal which was meant to placate the hostility of the departed.
With this as its main ceremony it is not surprising to find that it was
reckoned the day of ill omen. On it the spirits of the dead were free
to come up to the land of the living and roam about. So householders
took precautions. They smeared their doorways with pitch from a
naïve belief that this would hinder the entrance of the ghosts, and they
themselves chewed buckthorn from daybreak as it was supposed to
have protective qualities. Clearly it was for this reason also that the
sanctuaries of Athens were closed, and not in memory of some pre-
caution against Orestes' blood-guilt. The spirits must not be allowed
free access to the holy places.[141]

Then when the day was over the spirits could safely be sent packing.
This was done by the householder going round shouting: 'Get out,
Goblins (*Keres*), the *Anthesteria* is over!' The line makes an iambic verse
of the sort usual in Greek popular sayings. There is no reason to doubt
its original meaning and serious purpose. But it is interesting to note
that in more sophisticated and sceptical periods some Athenians found

a method of explaining it away. In the original saying the spirits were addressed as *Keres*, a word applicable to spirits which could work harm. This meaning is well in harmony with the general character of the festival, which obviously was not concerned with the sentimental tendance of the spirits of deceased ancestors, but with the controlling and appeasing of vaguer and less personalized ghosts. However, later commentators changed the word from *Keres* to *Kares* ('Carians') and explained that it was used as a typical description for slaves in general. During the *Anthesteria* slaves were allowed to join with the free members of the household in enjoying themselves. So the master's warning that the *Anthesteria* was over was interpreted as bidding the slaves return to their usual tasks. This is certainly wrong as an explanation and would not account for the first part of the phrase which in Greek tells those addressed to go to the door. It only makes proper sense when driving someone from the house. But it is interesting to see how less superstitious ages were unwilling to accept the original simple meaning of the rite.

The notion that there is some time of the year when ghosts are free to wander is primitive and common to many races. Northern Europe has mostly chosen Hallow-e'en. The Romans observed the *Lemuria* for three days – the 9th, 10th and 11th of May – and had their own peculiar methods of appeasing the ghosts with gifts of beans and expelling them when their time was over.[142]

The ritual so far described was the concern of the individual householder. But the state also had its special ritual on the 12th of *Anthesteria*. This was connected with a site near the Olympieion where according to Pausanias there was a chasm in the ground about a cubit wide. This was said to be the gap through which the waters had drained away at the end of Deucalion's Flood, and Pausanias records that annually there was thrown into it wheaten flour mixed with honey. This mixture would be a typical offering to the dead, and there can be no doubt that that was its original purpose. The chasm was originally identified as an entrance to the underworld and it was regarded as a convenient place to offer a general atonement to the spirits. The association with the Flood probably came later when sophisticated interpreters had got to work. Evidently as well as wheaten flour and honey, water was poured into the gap. For we hear of the Water-carrying Festival (*Hydrophoria*) 'a feast of mourning at Athens for those who were killed in the Flood, as explained by Apollonius of Acharnai'. Again, libations of water are a usual offering to the dead.[143]

The legendary notion of the Flood probably came to Greece from the East, but never took much hold on the popular imagination. It was only adopted in some places in northern Greece and also in Attica. The strange procedure of cooking the meal in the pot and leaving it untasted was worked into the legend by the Athenians. They explained that those who had escaped the Flood at first were in panic and the 14th of Anthesterion was the day on which they first plucked up enough courage to put a pot on a fire and throw into it anything that came to hand. One other Dionysiac legend was also connected with this day and served to account for yet another ritual practice. The story was linked with Icaria, a *deme* in Attica. When Dionysus came there he was welcomed by Icarius, the eponymous chieftain to whom he gave in gratitude the gift of wine. But when those to whom Icarius first handed on the wine collapsed overcome by the new drink, their relations took Icarius for a poisoner and slew him. His dog guided his daughter, Erigone, to the tree beneath which her father lay, and at the sight of his body she hanged herself in grief. Attica was consequently struck with a plague till the Delphic oracle was consulted. The Pythia warned the Athenians of their impiety towards Dionysus and instructed them to worship him and associate with him in their cult Icarius, Erigone and the dog. As a special charm they were to hang up figures and masks to swing in trees, and also their maidens were to swing.

The literary evidence for this legend and for the practice of swinging is rather slight and confused, but a beautiful representation on a mid-fifth-century Attic vase shows a teenage girl sitting on a swing and being pushed by a satyr who wears a garland. The presence of the satyr proves beyond doubt that this is not just a scene of youthful play, but is connected symbolically with a Dionysiac festival. That it was the *Anthesteria* is strongly suggested by a reference in Callimachus. Hence Deubner was probably right in supposing that the scene on the other side of the red-figure wine-cup (*skyphos*) was also connected with the *Anthesteria*. It shows a young matron stepping forward in a very dignified and modest pose while a satyr walking behind holds over her head some kind of sunshade. The satyr himself is wearing an elaborate crown. Deubner's interpretation is that the lady is the Basilinna walking in procession to her wedding with Dionysus. The satyr guarantees that Dionysiac ritual is shown, and the pose and manner of the lady suit well the traditional representation of the bride. The only objection one might make is that brides were escorted in chariots not on foot to their weddings. Also, if the sunshade is of practical significance, one might object that February was not a month in which it would be needed. But perhaps it must be taken as a purely symbolic gesture of honour to the Basilinna. The identification of this scene, then, remains at least doubtful.[144] (Plates 45, 46)

The three days of the *Anthesteria* suggest a curious mixture of ceremonies. The ritual opening of the wine-jars and the ceremonial drinking were appropriate to the inception of the new vintage. Also in so far as Dionysus was particularly a god of wine this day might be regarded as specially appropriate for receiving him annually afresh into the community. But the ritual of appeasing possibly malevolent spirits and the banishment of the wandering ghosts again to their own domain has no evident connection with the god of wine. Some scholars have attempted to show that Dionysus could be concerned with the dead, and in the somewhat fluid theology of Greek paganism scarcely any deity is without a chthonic aspect. But there is no evidence that the ritual at the chasm near the Olympieon was connected with Dionysus, and the food cooked on the Day of the Pots was not offered to him, but to Hermes. So it is probably best to suppose that the conjunction of the two festivals was originally accidental, but that in the course of a long period they became to some extent interpenetrated. For example Deubner calls attention to the abundant anthropological evidence which Frazer collected to show that swinging as a practice was meant to produce purification. The rushing through the air was felt to drive away any impurities. If so, the original purpose of swinging at the time of the *Anthesteria* may have been connected with ridding the community of evil spirits. The legend connecting the practice with Dionysus and Erigone looks as if it was simply a late fiction produced to account for this custom at what was thought of as the wine-god's festival. This also may explain the curious rules governing the wine-drinking on the night of the Feast of the Wine-jars. The legend connecting the customs with Orestes is fictitious, but it rightly hints that the underlying motive is that each individual separated himself from contact with his neighbour in what was a communal feast. The reasons may be that the eve of the festival of the ghosts was an unholy time when it was as well not to lay oneself open to any dangerous outside influences.

In putting forward these possible explanations of the various aspects of the festival of the *Anthesteria*, one must not suggest that to the ordinary Athenian any ideas of the sort were clearly and analytically present. To him the occasion must have felt like Hallow-e'en – an occasion mainly for jolly parties with perhaps at times a somewhat eerie atmosphere to it and certain odd traditional games all of which simply added spice to the occasion.

Ten days after the *Anthesteria* there was another religious occasion, the *Diasia*, which like the Feast of Pots had a feeling of appeasement connected with it. It was dedicated to Zeus under his title of Meilichios – 'kindly' or 'open to propitiation' – which we have already encountered in the month of Maimakterion when the procession of the Sheep-skin of Zeus was held. That earlier holy day had been a quasi-magical piece of ritual performed by state officials. The *Diasia* was instead a great popular festival in which all the citizens took part. It was a very primitive institution of which we first hear in connection with the attempt of Cylon to seize by force the position of tyrant in Athens in 632 B C. He had won distinction in Greece as an Olympic champion and had married the daughter of the tyrant of the neighbouring state of Megara. When he conceived the idea of seizing political power in Athens he first consulted the Delphic oracle and was advised to occupy the Acropolis on the greatest feast of Zeus. So with the help of forces supplied by his father-in-law he took control of the Acropolis on the occasion of the Olympic games, thinking that this was the greatest feast of Zeus and one specially appropriate to himself. But the attempt ended disastrously as the people of Attica rose and besieged Cylon and his supporters.

It was at this period an unquestioned principle that the Delphic oracle did not err. So the only explanation of Cylon's failure which contemporaries would have accepted was that he had been mistaken in his interpretation of the response and that it must therefore have referred to a different feast of Zeus. Thucydides, who tells the story, reproduces what was evidently the traditional explanation, that Cylon should not have chosen the Olympic games as the date of his attack, but the greatest Attic festival: the *Diasia*. The reason why this choice would have been tactically wiser emerges from Thucydides' description. 'The *Diasia* is the name of the greatest feast of Zeus Meilichios held outside the town. On it the whole populace make offerings to him, not sacrifices, but bloodless offerings of a native kind.' The implication is that, if Cylon had chosen this festival he would have found Athens deserted as the populace would have mostly gone outside to take part in the rite of Zeus Meilichios. The site of his sanctuary was probably on the banks of the Ilissos near the place where Peisistratus was to found his temple of the Olympian Zeus. In the seventh century this would have lain well outside the town, and being in the opposite direction to the approach to the Acropolis would have been conveniently out of sight of Cylon's operation.[145] (Plates 47, 48)

The description which Thucydides gives of the people's offerings was explained by the ancient commentators as referring to cakes made in the shape of animals. The reason was that each family was expected to make an offering to Zeus, but only the wealthy could afford to sacrifice an animal as a victim, particularly as this was meant as an atonement and so must be made a whole burnt-offering. Any Athenian might stretch his resources occasionally to pay for a sheep or a pig if the flesh could mostly be consumed by the family. But a whole burnt-offering was sheer monetary loss, whatever its spiritual value, and one can understand why instead a substitute could be burnt in the shape of a sheep or a pig of pastry.[146]

We have, however, from Xenophon's *Anabasis* an interesting testimony which shows that some Athenian families did go to the full length of offering to Zeus Meilichios whole burnt-offerings of animals. Xenophon came of a wealthy Athenian family which could afford to be generous in their piety, and he himself was devoted to the worship of the gods. He describes how when the remnant of the Ten Thousand under his personal leadership had at last got back safely as far as the Troad, he was so short of money that he had to sell his horse. Shortly afterwards he was making an offering to Apollo when Eucleides of Phlyus, a prophet, was in attendance. On examining the sacrifice, the prophet said that he was satisfied by the signs that Xenophon was short of money, but he would get some in the future, except that Zeus Meilichios was an obstacle. He therefore asked Xenophon if he still sacrificed to the god and made whole burnt-offerings as he had to do at home. Xenophon admitted that he had made no sacrifices to the god since he had gone abroad. So the prophet advised him to resume his usual customs and it would turn out better for him. Next day the pious Xenophon put the advice into practice by making 'a sacrifice and whole burnt-offering of some pigs in the ancestral manner'. The omen turned out well at the ceremony, and on that very same day two friends arrived with money for the soldiers and also Xenophon's horse which they had bought back for him and for which they refused to be paid in return. Xenophon who was sincerely convinced of the power of sacrifice to achieve results tells the story without further comment as a clear lesson to those who believed in piety. He does not actually say that his family's custom had been to offer the whole burnt-offerings of pigs at the *Diasia*, and it might have been possible that they chose some other date in the calendar, but as it was the greatest festival of Zeus in Athens the occasion is the most probable.[147]

The general tone of a festival of appeasement and whole burnt-offerings is not likely to have been very cheerful. But Strepsiades, the indulgent father and typical man of the people, in Aristophanes' the *Clouds* twice mentions the *Diasia* in contexts which suggest a popular holiday. He reminds his son how when he was only six years old and lisped in his speech he had asked his father for a toy cart, and he had bought it for him at the *Diasia* with the first fee which he had earned on a jury. Again, when Socrates has explained to Strepsiades that the origin of thunder and lightning is in clouds blown up to bursting point, he upsets the scientific exposition by a vulgar analogy.

'Good heavens, I had just the same experience once at the *Diasia*, when I was cooking a haggis for my relations, and I had carelessly failed to lance it. So it blew up and burst with a crash and spattered both my eyes and burned my face.'

The picture evidently is that the *Diasia* was a holiday, and even if its religious significance was solemn and depressing, it was an occasion for families to get together for a meal. But since the festival was one for whole burnt-offerings, no good joints were readily available. The best that an ordinary family could do was to purchase offal such as the maw of a sheep and make a party-dish out of it. With this kind of entertainment and presents for the children the grim ceremonies of the *Diasia* will have ended in a cheerful spirit.[148]

In the same direction near the Ilissus where was the shrine of Zeus Meilichios, there also took place in the month of Anthesterion the rites of the Lesser Mysteries. The suburb was known as Agrai: so the mysteries themselves were called the Mysteries at Agrai. As we have already seen, in the classical period they were linked with the Eleusinian Mysteries in a subordinate position. Those who intended to be initiated at Eleusis were expected first to undergo the initiation at Agrai, which took place seven months earlier. How strictly this rule was applied it is impossible to prove. Ancient writers who mention the matter imply it was strictly obligatory, and we have seen that the preliminary stages of the Eleusinian initiation gave ample occasion to check the credentials of those registering for admission. So it is better to accept that those initiated at Eleusis had previously been initiated at Agrai. This would require the same numbers to assemble in February as in September.

Yet the paucity of the allusions to Agrai in ancient literature is hard to explain if it really took place annually on this scale. There is some evidence from Hellenistic times of the Mysteries at Agrai being celebrated twice in the year, which may have been a facility for foreigners and others who had missed the celebration in February. Alternatively would-be initiates may have been allowed to use the precedent of Asclepius, which we have already mentioned, and pass through all the preliminary proceedings on the fourth day of the Eleusinian festival.[149] But such exceptional treatment is not recorded. The only instance of an expedited initiation known is the glaring example of Demetrius Poliorcetes.

In 307 B C when he had freed Athens from the dominance of Cassander, Demetrius wrote asking that he be admitted to all the grades of initiation at once. The letter was received in the month of Munichion (i.e. about April). So, to please the monarch, a politician, Stratocles, proposed that the current month be named Anthesterion and the Lesser Mysteries held for Demetrius' benefit; then the name of the month was to be changed again to Boedromion, so that the Eleusinian Mysteries could be performed for his convenience, and he was to be allowed not only to be initiated, but to proceed immediately afterwards to the final stage of the *Epopteia*. At the time this was done in spite of the protest of Pythodorus the Torch-bearer (Daiduchos), and four centuries later Plutarch was duly shocked at the impious flattery.[150]

The content of the Mysteries at Agrai is never described. This reticence is only to be expected; although Agrai may not have been surrounded with the degree of religious awe which enveloped Eleusis, it will in principle have been under the same rule of secrecy. Legend explained that these Lesser Mysteries had been instituted first for the benefit of Heracles, who wished to be initiated at Eleusis but was inadmissible as a foreigner. The suggestion that the initiation at Agrai was not as old as that at Eleusis is no doubt wrong. Each was a local cult of the goddess of fertility and it was only after the political incorporation of Eleusis in Attica that its rites had to be combined with those of Agrai in one pattern. But the legend may stress correctly the relationship of the two festivals in this later period. The Lesser Mysteries as a preliminary to the Greater may well have emphasized the aspect of purification. One of our few literary references to them mentions the use of the Ilissos for ablutions. Heracles himself is represented in a couple of related carvings which show with some variations his purification from blood-guilt in company with Demeter and Persephone.

The figure of a ministrant in the ceremony is evidently the Daiduchos, and the use of a winnowing-fan again indicates a close connection with the Mysteries. But as Mylonas correctly argues, it would be unwise to identify the scene as showing some central act of the Mysteries at Agrai or Eleusis, both of which no doubt remained secret. We are simply shown some preliminary purification such as was specially required to cleanse the blood-guilt of Heracles. One late reference has been taken to indicate that the Lesser Mysteries included dramatic representations of the legend of the Two Goddesses, but the inference is unsafe. Agrai remains as obscure as Eleusis and less significant.[151] (Plate 26)

9 ELAPHEBOLION

The ninth month of the Attic year, ELAPHEBOLION, was named after a title of Artemis – the Shooter of the Deer (Elaphebolios). It corresponded to a festival dedicated to the goddess under this name which presumably took place on the 6th of the month, her usual day. But, like so many of the Attic months the festival after which it was named had dropped into unimportance. Elaphebolion was dominated instead by the *City Dionysia* which was held on the 9th and following dates. The title of Shooter of the Deer and the festival called after it were known elsewhere in Greece and it was an ancient tradition to represent Artemis with a captured stag. There had been a custom at Athens of sacrificing stags to the goddess on this day, but in the classical period substitutes were offered instead – cakes called 'stags' (*elaphoi*) moulded out of dough, honey and sesame-seeds. One may surmise that the use of pastry models in substitution was not so much, as at the *Diasia*, because the poorer families could not afford a victim. The cult of Artemis Elaphebolios is not likely to have been at all widespread in the community. But by the fourth century it was probably rather difficult for anyone to ensure the provision of a fresh stag on the date. When the cult had been started in some primitive period, deer would be available to the hunter in the hills immediately outside Athens itself and many Athenians will have supplemented the larder by hunting under the blessing of Artemis. But though our evidence is lacking, the spread of building and farming will have driven the deer back to the mountainous regions of Attica, and the worship of Artemis under this title will have been the concern of few.[152] (Plate 49)

As the old local festival declined in significance in the mid-sixth century a new Dionysiac festival was introduced, which rose to great importance, and also near the end of the fifth century a new cult of a god of healing, Asclepius, was brought to Athens and acquired a holy day in this month. The introduction of Asclepius in 429 BC is chronologically certain; the advent of the cult of Dionysus in its new form is much more difficult to date. It came from Eleutherai, a small community on the border between Athens and Boeotia. The god therefore bore the epithet Eleuthereus, and was represented by a primitive wooden image. Pausanias, probably correctly, described the transfer of this figure to Athens as taking place at the time when the inhabitants of Eleutherai voluntarily acceded to the state of Athens so as to escape from their other neighbours, the Boeotians, whom they hated. This event cannot be dated precisely, but is likely to have occurred in the mid-sixth century under Peisistratus. This would fit with the archaeological remains at the Dionysiac theatre in Athens where the earliest temple seems to be of approximately this date. Tradition also preserved the name of a certain Pegasos of Eleutherai as the man responsible for the transfer of the cult and this may be correct. Pausanias adds that he was supported in this move by a response of the Delphic oracle which reminded the Athenians of the visit to Icaria which Dionysus had made in legendary times. It is unfortunate that the text of this reply of Apollo is not preserved verbatim, as it might well have been produced in the mid-sixth century in this form and, if extant, would give strong evidence for or against the date.[153]

Besides, the tradition which Pausanias reproduced there was evidently another legendary version in which Pegasos and the coming of the god were transferred to mythological periods. This was given material embodiment in a building which Pausanias himself saw in the Kerameikos. It contained terracotta statues showing Amphictyon, one of the earliest mythical kings of Attica, entertaining to a banquet Dionysus and other gods while Pegasos of Eleutherai was among the guests. It is to be supposed that the historical circumstances of the transfer of the cult of Dionysus Eleuthereus were embroidered so as to make it take on a venerable antiquity. Also the usual kind of myth was attached to it: that the Athenians had not received the god with proper honour. Hence his wrath was manifested in a disease attacking the genital organs of the men. On appealing to the oracle they were advised to pay Dionysus due worship and particularly to hold a procession with a phallus in his honour. On doing this the sickness was cured. The myth of Dionysus being repulsed and then enforcing recognition of his cult is universal throughout Greece. In this instance it was also adapted to explain and justify phallic processions and, as we shall see, this was a feature of the *City Dionysia* in historic times.[154]

In one curious ceremony the coming from Eleutherai was perpetuated annually. Some days before the *Dionysia* the old wooden statue was removed from the temple in the city and taken to a small shrine in the gymnasium – sanctuary of the Academy. This was situated outside the city walls on the road to Boeotia, and would have been the last convenient stopping-place on the route from Eleutherai. The statue was housed in this shrine for some days, and was the object of sacrifices. Then probably on the evening of the 8th or the 9th of the month it was brought back with an appropriate escort to its temple beside the Dionysiac theatre in time to be used in the festival of the *Dionysia*.[155] (Plate 50)

The escorting of the statue from the Academy was known as the 'Bringing in from the sacrificial hearth', and appears to be quite distinct from the main procession which was the central rite of the *Dionysia*. This probably took place on the 10th of the month and consisted essentially in bringing victims – bulls were the traditional animal – for sacrifice in the sanctuary in the city. Also it was the occasion for carrying phalli in procession. The whole affair was evidently, in general importance though on a smaller scale, quite comparable to the Panathenaic procession. This is illustrated by a provision in the foundation charter of the Athenian colony of Brea (*c.* 445 BC), requiring the colonists to send a cow and a panoply to the *Great Panathenaia* and a phallus to the *Dionysia*. Also as at the festival of Athena, the different classes of the inhabitants of Athens were represented in appropriate groups and functions. 'The resident aliens (Metoikoi) put on purple robes and carried trays of offerings (*skaphia*.) Hence they were called "tray-bearers" (*Skaphephoroi*). The citizens wore what clothes they pleased and carried leather bottles (*askoi*) on their shoulders: hence they were called "bottle-carriers" (Askophoroi).' One is to picture the bottles as loaded with wine to offer to the god the first-fruits of his bounty. One high-born maiden was chosen as the Kanephoros to walk in procession carrying a golden basket full of first-fruits, presumably grapes. But the products of the vine were not the only food offered to Dionysus. We hear of special loaves of bread called *obeliai* ('like spits') which we can picture as long thin rods. For they, just as the leather bottles, are described as being carried on the shoulders. The route of the procession is unknown, but it passed by various shrines or other stopping-places where it paused for the performance of dances in honour of the gods.[156] The climax came with the arrival at the altar near the Dionysiac theatre and the slaughter of victims. Ferguson has calculated from the financial accounts of 333 BC that in that year for example 240 bulls were offered. So, as after the *Panathenaia*, those taking part in the ceremony and many other citizens besides must have had a good dinner of beef that night. In addition they probably washed it down with abundant wine as would be appropriate to a feast of

Dionysus, but also because the final event of the day was a revel (*Komos*). This was an occasion for somewhat formalized licence. After dark, men escorted by torches and accompanied with the music of flutes and harps went out singing and dancing in the streets. This kind of revelry is frequently represented on Athenian pottery, especially on the vessels and cups intended for wine-drinking. It is impossible to tell whether the artist is consistently picturing the *Komos* of the *City Dionysia* or whether he is merely showing an informal revel. For it was usual enough for a men's wine-party to end informally in this kind of an uninhibited performance, as is shown by such descriptions as the entrance of Alcibiades in the *Symposium* of Plato.[157] (Plates 51–53)

The procession in the day and the *Komos* in the following night were the core of the Dionysiac festival and so long as it had consisted only of these elements it did not exhibit a character superior to the other festivals of Dionysus. But already in the sixth century there began to develop a connection between the *City Dionysia* and the performances of dramas. The origins of Greek tragedy and comedy are very obscure and not fully relevant to this general description of Athenian festivals. It is sufficient to state here that the earliest element was a chorus of men who sang and danced, and this performance, not only in Attica, but also in Sicyon in the northern Peloponnese and probably elsewhere, was linked with the worship of Dionysus. In the fifth and fourth centuries plays were performed not only at the *Dionysia* in Elaphebolion, but also, as we have seen, at the *Lenaia* and the rural *Dionysia* earlier in the year. Evidence suggests that these other performances were derived from those at the *City Dionysia*. Choric singing and dancing may have been a common feature of all three festivals, but it was in the worship of Dionysus of Eleutherai that this was originally evolved into a dramatic performance. The traditional date of the first performance of a tragedy was 534 BC under the leadership of Thespis, and it is likely that this is approximately accurate. The introduction of Dionysus of Eleutherai had probably taken place under Peisistratus and was partly occasioned by the political development of the incorporation of the people of Eleutherai into Attica. But also it was the period where there was a tendency to introduce into the city the prominent cults of local districts. We shall see another such example in the admission of Artemis of Brauron to the Athenian Acropolis. This was all part of the broadening of the basis of the Athenian state which was typical of the policy of Peisistratus and it is likely that he took positive steps to introduce and develop the cult of Dionysus – a deity

39 *Skyphos* with scene of man pouring libation on an altar in presence of a priestess and maenads: perhaps at the *Anthesteria* (detail)

40 *Chous* with scene of Dionysus as drunken reveller at the *Anthesteria*

41 Dionysus at sea: kylix painted by Exekias

42 *Skyphos* showing ship-car carrying Dionysus and satyrs

43 Women preparing oxen for sacrificing: perhaps Gerarai

44 Scene on a small *chous*: children enacting the Basilinna's marriage procession

45 *Skyphos*: young girl in swing pushed by satyr

46 Matron walking under sunshade held by satyr, on reverse of vase shown in Ill. 45

47 The Olympieion: view looking northwest in direction of the Acropolis

48 Relief of Zeus Meilichios: family offering a pig

49 Melian vase showing Artemis as huntress of deer, seventh century B C
(detail)

50 Seat of the priest of Dionysus Eleuthereus in the Dionysiac Theatre

51, 52 Komos scenes on a kylix by the Brygos Painter

53 The Morning After: from the interior of the kylix by the Brygos
Painter (cf. Plates 51, 52)

54 View of the Asclepieion under the south wall of the Acropolis

55 Sanctuary of Artemis at Brauron

56 The Artemis of Gabii: probably a copy of the cult-statue from the temple of Artemis Brauronia on the Acropolis

57 Stone figure of a bear from the Acropolis

58 Balustrade with frieze of Erotes from the shrine of Eros and Aphrodite below the Acropolis

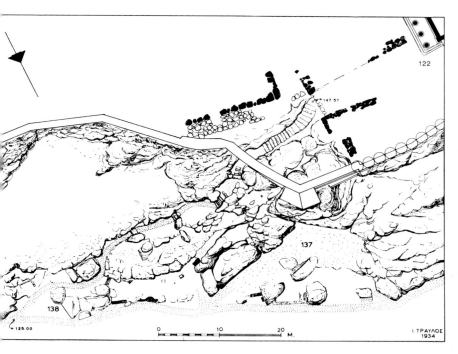

59 Plan of the sanctuary of Eros and Aphrodite, showing its relation
to the Acropolis. 122. Northeast corner of the Erechtheion. 137. Shrine
of Aphrodite and Eros. 138. Mycenaean path to the Acropolis.

60 Vase painting: Aphrodite and Eros with attendants; the small figure
may represent an Arrephoros

61 Relief from the fill of the Themistoclean wall: a team playing a form of hockey

62 Relief showing a horseman riding towards a prize tripod: from the base of a dedication made by a winning team in the *Anthippasia*. The statue was carved by Bryaxis

63 Seated Athena with burning altar and ox standing before a shrine. This may have some reference to the *Bouphonia*

64 Team after a torch-race: fifth-century red-figure kylix

65 Inscription from the *deme* Ercheia; the *Greater Demarchia*

66 The Berlin Goddess: a larger than life-size statue exemplifying a cult image from Attica

67 A sacrifice to Athena Polias on a black-figure amphora

68 Relief showing Athena and family making offering

of popular appeal whose festivals were of the kind which tyrants encouraged in their movement away from the rites and privileges of the aristocracy. (It is significant in this connection that the official responsible for all the organization of the *City Dionysia* was not the Basileus, the old religious official of the community, but the archon, the political leader whose secular importance had tended to increase during the sixth century. Peisistratus took care to control the nominations to magistracies. So we can be sure that the official controlling the new festival was under his direct influence.)[158]

The first step in the development of drama by Thespis was that he engaged in dialogue with the chorus and dressed himself up in a mask and robes so that he could impersonate different characters. The creation of the actor as an individual led gradually to the development of two and three actors on the stage at one time. But other forms of drama besides tragedy were added. By the end of the sixth century tragedies were performed in groups of three successive plays, followed by a satyr play, in which the chorus instead of impersonating men or women appeared dressed as the half-animal creatures who were the mythical companions of Dionysus. Possibly the satyr play was less a new invention than the production in fixed form of something which had been a primitive popular masquerade. Finally in 486 BC comedies with a comic chorus and actors were added to the dramatic programme of the *City Dionysia*. Already about 509 choral singing of dithyrambs, odes in honour of Dionysus, first invented in Corinth, had been officially included in the festival.

Thus by the early years of the fifth century the feast of Dionysus of Eleutherai had become the centre of an elaborate series of public performances which gave it a popular interest far exceeding the other *Dionysia* of Attica or of elsewhere in Greece. The site of the shrine at the foot of the southern slope below the Acropolis gave an ideal situation for a crowd seated above to observe the action of a drama taking place on a levelled space beneath them. Gradually the natural setting was developed until about 330 BC the statesman Lycurgus was responsible for the first complete stone-built theatre. It was usual in literature to refer to the audience as if it was the whole population of Athens and apply to it the conventional estimate of 30,000. But modern calculations suggest that the seating capacity was not more than some 17,000. Even so this represented a very considerable fraction of the population. But besides citizens the resident aliens (Metoikoi) were allowed to attend and even foreigners could obtain tickets of admission.

In this respect the *City Dionysia* was different from the *Lenaia* which was only open to citizens. Actually the date of this later festival was more suitable for visitors since it fell about mid-March which was the traditional time for the opening of the sailing season. So visitors from the Aegean islands and the coast of Asia Minor could be expected to be present to see what was one of the greatest manifestations of Athenian culture.

It is a more difficult question to answer whether women were admitted to see the tragedies and comedies. Some references seem to imply that they were present at the tragedies. For instance a description (admittedly written long after the event) states that the entrance of the Furies in the *Oresteia* of Aeschylus was so horrific that it caused some women spectators to miscarry. Also Aristophanes' humorous picture of the women of Athens as enraged against Euripides because of his presentation of their sex in his plays is much more plausible and effective if they could actually have seen these tragedies. To suppose that they simply knew of them from male gossip or from the rare facility of written texts would have been much less convincing. On the other hand there are several passages in Aristophanes' comedies which seem to enumerate the age groups of the audience only in terms of males or otherwise imply that no women are in the theatre. Perhaps in the fifth century at least the distinction may have existed that women could attend the tragedies, but not the comedies.[159]

Admission was obtained by purchasing a ticket costing two obols. This was comparable to a minimum day's wage in the fifth century. So it would have excluded many of the poorer citizens. But Pericles is credited with founding the Theoric fund which paid out this amount per head to the citizens and so enabled anyone who wanted to attend the theatre. Front seats were reserved for the magistrates and other chief officials and also for the various priests of the gods and goddesses, while distinguished visitors from overseas might also be honoured by special accommodation. The presiding person was the priest of Dionysus, and some references in the comedies suggest that the old wooden statue of the god was also brought out to attend the spectacle.[160]

As the tickets did not give admission to particular seats, the ordinary citizen who had no official position or priesthood must have joined in a stream making their way to the theatre at some early hour. It was usual to equip oneself with a cushion to make the seat more comfortable. Theophrastus pictures the Flatterer as seizing his cushion from the slave who had accompanied him so as to prop the man whom he is

flattering. Again Aeschines attacked Demosthenes because he had
provided Philip's ambassadors with front seats and had placed cushions
for them and spread purple rugs round them. [161]

The spectators had need to make themselves comfortable for they
were booked for a long day's entertainment. The usual pattern in the
fifth century at least seems to have been a group of three tragedies in
the morning followed by a satyr play: then after a considerable
interval in the late afternoon, a comedy. Philochorus writing in the
third century B C gives a picturesque account:

> The Athenians on the occasion of the Dionysiac plays used to walk
> to the theatre after having broken their fast and having had a drink.
> Throughout the whole performance wine was poured for them and
> sweetmeats were handed round. As the chorus entered they filled
> their cups to drink and when the play was over while the chorus were
> leaving they filled up again.

It is not clear whether the wine and savouries were brought by the
spectators or were dispensed by sellers standing in the gangways.
Perhaps both practices were the custom. The savouries or sweetmeats
were evidently a familiar feature. For Aristotle in the *Nicomachean
Ethics*, when he wishes to illustrate the psychological proposition that
pleasures tend to monopolize attention when they are intense, quotes
as an opposite example: 'In the theatre, those who are eating sweetmeats engage in this activity most when the actors are bad.' During the
performance of comedies it was even a well-known practice to make
occasion for someone from the stage to throw nuts and raisins to the
audience. As is rather typical, Aristophanes at one time decries the
device and adopts it on another occasion. The whole question of
managing to spend a day in the theatre must have presented problems
to the spectators, and in the *Birds* the comedian in typical Aristophanic
manner suggests to the audience all the advantages which they would
have if only they could acquire wings.[162]

The whole-day performances lasted normally for four days in the
fifth century, though for economy as a war-measure they were cut
down to three during the Peloponnesian War. But in the Hellenistic
period they may even have been extended by additional days. The
organizing of the programme was an elaborate business, and it was
based on the principle of competition. The archon chose three wealthy
individuals every year, one from each of three different tribes, to act as

choregos for the tragedies, and also five for the comedies, when five were produced. *Choregoi* were also appointed for the dithyrambs, three for those sung by men and three for those sung by boys. The choosing of the members of the choruses, their training, and finally their fitting-out with costumes were the most time-consuming and expensive part of the production for the *choregoi*. Each *choregos* also had actors assigned to him up to the maximum of three, and each had a poet assigned to him. It was the responsibility of the archon to choose the panel of poets, and he could interview them and require them to submit specimens of their work. For the purpose of the competition at the festival there had also to be a panel of judges, which was appointed by an elaborate method typical of the Athenian democracy in its efforts to exclude the possibilities of bribery or favouritism. The names of candidates to act as judges were put into ten jars which were sealed and deposited on the Acropolis. Then at the start of the festival, the jars were produced and ten names were drawn, one from each jar, to act as judges. At the end of the contest they wrote out the names of the poets in order of merit and once more the archon drew five of the written verdicts from a jar. The majority decision of these five was accepted.[163]

This procedure guaranteed that no one could know in advance what men to bribe so as to ensure a majority in his interest, unless he took the extravagant and improbable step of bribing every potential judge. Also the risk of favouritism was somewhat reduced by leaving to chance whether any of the judges belonged to the same tribe as the competing *choregoi*. The *choregos* himself had to bear a heavy expense. It was left to his judgement how much he undertook, but obviously a stingy man who skimped the cost of dressing the chorus or failed to provide adequate fees for a good trainer would prejudice his chances of winning a prize for himself and his tribe. On the other hand the *choregos* of abundant means was prepared to spend lavishly to make it a great occasion for presenting himself in an impressive way to the Athenian public. Demosthenes when *choregos* for a dithyrambic chorus provided all fifty of them with golden crowns and himself with a gold crown and gold-embroidered robe. As a shrewd politician he must have reckoned that the propaganda value of all this expenditure would repay itself later in his career.[164]

The competition also showed itself in a curious ceremony known as the Preliminary to the Contest (*Proagon*) which took place on the 9th of Elaphebolion, the day before the *Pompe*. The *choregoi* together with their teams were paraded before the public on a platform which from the mid-fifth century was set up in Pericles' new Odeion. This it seems was simply intended to give everyone a preliminary notice of what the festival itself would contain. The actors for instance appeared in their ordinary clothes without any masks or costumes. This publicity was probably needed. We have no evidence that placards were set up to announce what plays were being produced, nor that programmes were available in the theatre telling the names of the casts. Since chorus and actors all wore masks they would not be identified by their appearance. Hence a previous exhibition of the various teams with an announcement of the poet and the titles of his plays would satisfy an obvious need.[165] In the *City Dionysia* in the fifth century the tragedies were always newly written for the occasion. But they could be revived for production in the *Country Dionysia* in subsequent years. During the fourth century the revival of earlier tragedies was even allowed in the *City Dionysia*, and at last it was systematically arranged that a certain proportion of the festival would be devoted to 'old tragedies' which were chosen from the writings of the canonically approved poets – Aeschylus, Sophocles and Euripides. This development showed the shift of popular interest. In the fifth century it had been concentrated mainly on the playwright and his new production. In the fourth century by a familiar change of taste the interest concentrated more on the famous actors of the day and there was a natural wish to see them in the classic roles of the past. But, whether in the fifth or the fourth century, the Athenian public and the visitors from abroad found in the theatrical productions of the *City Dionysia* one of the great events of the year.

As it was the time when more Athenians and foreigners were gathered together in Athens than on any other occasion it was made the opportunity for various other exhibitions. The *City Dionysia* as the opening of the sailing season was the date when the tribute of the empire was due to be delivered in Athens. This was divided into portions of a talent and carried in sacks of coins into the dancing-floor of the theatre to be exhibited before the assembled audience. Thus the Athenian state proudly displayed the fruits of empire. But also with a grim realism the one spectacle was balanced by another. The orphan sons of those killed in war were maintained by the democracy till they came of age. Then annually at the *City Dionysia* they had a kind of passing-out parade. They marched on to the dancing-floor dressed in full hoplite armour while a herald proclaimed that these were the sons of those who had died heroically in battle; now the Athenian state having reared them and equipped them with arms sent them out into life, and for this occasion invited them to front seats in the theatre.[166]

The pride in tribute and in war was typical of the fifth century. The fourth century did not give Athens scope for these displays. Instead the practice developed of voting a golden crown to politicians or other benefactors of the city and proclaiming the award through the mouth of a herald at the new tragedies. This was the subject of Aeschines' famous attack on Demosthenes, when he prosecuted the proposer, Ctesiphon, on the ground that it was an unconstitutional procedure. Even Aeschines however had to admit that, whether legal or not, it was not the first time by any means when this had been done. In fact he even told the jury how at one time with no legal justification Athenians used to hire heralds to proclaim before the audience all sorts of lesser honours, both crowns given by tribes and *demes* to their members and foreign distinctions such as *proxeniai* – the equivalent of an honorary vice-consulship. He even mentions a more curious form of publicity for which the occasion of the *Dionysia* was employed. An owner who wished to free his slave would arrange to have the fact broadcast to the audience. This instance was less designed to shed glory on the slave-owner than to protect the rights of the new freedman. For in Athens, unlike in Rome, the freeing of a slave was not a matter of public law performed before a magistrate. There was no state record of slaves freed. So the best security for a freed slave was to be able to call on a sufficient number of witnesses that the act of liberation had really taken place.[167]

It was typical of the curiously easy-going attitude of the Athenians to religious festivals that on the one hand the Dionysiac theatre as a holy precinct was consecrated to the worship of the god and the tragedies themselves were not a secular entertainment, but a religious rite. Yet these considerations did not on the other hand prevent the intrusion of such mundane affairs as we have mentioned into what we might expect to be a solemn and dedicated occasion. Similarly, when the plays were performed the audience felt itself at liberty to behave with at least as great freedom in expressing its feelings as the traditional occupants of the gallery of a modern theatre. There was no ban on applause such as we might expect at a miracle play acted in a cathedral. But more often we hear of the opposite kind of demonstration. Hissing was the most common, but also some kind of hooting, was used and one writer refers to banging one's heels against the back of the seats, though this was presumably only effective so long as some of the audience sat on rows of wooden benches and not in the stone theatres of the late fourth and Hellenistic periods.[168]

The importance of the Dionysiac festival in the public eye and also the possibility of unsuitable events occurring at a great popular gathering was recognized by the arrangement that on one of the days immediately after the *Dionysia* a meeting of the people was held in the Dionysiac theatre presided over in the usual way by the Council of the Five Hundred at which an open inquest was held into the conduct of the festival. This could end highly satisfactorily in the council proposing a vote of a crown to the archon in recognition of his conduct of the matter. But also it was open to any member of the public to come forward and lodge a complaint. When one considers the character of the Athenian democracy and their claim to freedom of speech it is unlikely that some individuals were not found each year to avail themselves of this privilege.[169]

In a curious way one other religious festival managed to intrude itself into the *Dionysia*. As we have seen already, in 420 BC the Athenians welcomed to their city the god of healing, Asclepius, from Epidaurus. He was housed in a sanctuary above the Dionysiac theatre on the higher slopes of the Acropolis under the cliff wall. The annual festival of his arrival in Athens was celebrated at the time of the Eleusinian Mysteries. His other festival called the *Asclepieia* was held on the day of the Preliminary to the Contest. No details of the ceremony are known except that there was a considerable sacrifice, probably followed by a common meal which was usual in the worship of Asclepius. It is somewhat remarkable that this intrusive cult managed to stake a claim within the feast days of two such cults as the Eleusinian Demeter and Dionysus Eleuthereus. As we have seen Asclepius' arrival seems to be linked with Eleusis which may therefore have given him admittance there. There is no usual connection between him and Dionysus, but it may be more than a coincidence that one of the Athenians most prominent in introducing this new god was Sophocles. By 420 BC he was in his early sixties and was a well established playwright with strong political associations. Was it through his effort that the site assigned to Asclepius adjoined the precinct of Dionysus where Sophocles must have had great influence and can he also have arranged for the local festival to take place on a date covered to some extent by Dionysiac patronage?[170] (Plate 54)

One more festival in the month of Elaphebolion is worth mention, though very little is known about it. This was the *Pandia*, a festival of Zeus of which the exact date is uncertain, but it evidently was held almost immediately after the *City Dionysia* for the day following the *Pandia* was the one set aside, as we have seen, for the meeting at which an inquest on the *Dionysia* was held. Otherwise almost nothing is known about it. The ancient commentators who mention it are only concerned with the derivation, which gave them trouble. On the analogy of the *Panathenaia*, it should mean a festival of Zeus in which all combined, and therefore one is inclined to think that it must have involved all the communities of Attica. But there is nothing to show this. Only one district (Plotheia) is known to have celebrated it.

The other connection of the festival should be with Pandion, one of the mythical kings of Attica who was also the eponymous hero of one of the ten tribes. Pandion should derive his name from the festival and be the founder of it. But if so, the myth has vanished. Deubner has conjectured that the tribe Pandionis had some special link with the festival and this is possible as we find the assembly of the tribe passing a decree in honour of one of its members, Demon, a cousin of Demosthenes and a priest, for his services at the festival. But in that form it can only date from the establishment of the ten tribes by Cleisthenes in the late sixth century. What cult the hero Pandion had before then and how it was connected with the *Pandia* is quite unknown. Nothing suggests that the festival was a popular occasion. It was probably a survival from the archaic past which had become fossilized.[171]

10 MUNICHION

The tenth month of the Attic year, MUNICHION, like the month Elaphebolion was named after a festival of Artemis. In fact the month contained two days at least with special dedications to that goddess. On the 6th of Munichion there was a procession of the maidens of Athens to the Delphinion, the shrine on the bank of the Ilissos near the Olympieion, where both Apollo and Artemis were worshipped. The girls went to make supplication and so carried boughs of the sacred Athenian olive bound with white wool. Plutarch who is the only source of our information about this ceremony explained its origin by connecting it with Theseus. The 6th of Munichion was the day on which he sailed for Crete with his fellow-victims to meet the Minotaur, and before he sailed he had dedicated a suppliant bough like this to Apollo at the Delphinion. As we have already seen, Theseus in legend was closely connected with the cult of Apollo, but though Plutarch is not explicit on the point it is much more probable that this ceremony was really directed to Artemis rather than to her brother. A procession of girls would be inappropriate to the god and still more significantly the 6th of the month was the traditional date for festivals of Artemis, while the 7th was the day for Apollo. No doubt the original ceremony had nothing whatever to do with Theseus, but was simply a general supplication on behalf of the community and as it was held on the 6th and conducted by women it was probably intended to appeal to Artemis as particularly the goddess of the female sex for protection on their behalf.[172]

The better known festival of Artemis was that which gave its name to the month, the *Munichia*. The previous month, Elaphebolion, was named after a festival of Artemis which practically vanished from popular recognition, but the *Munichia* though never of great importance maintained a position of some standing. This was probably because it was dedicated to Artemis as the presiding goddess of the steep hill of Munichia which lay just inland from the Peiraeus. From the founding of the Peiraeus as the naval base of Athena in 492 BC, the port and the town surrounding it grew greatly in population and wealth. So the local cults acquired much greater significance than they had originally possessed.

The tradition of the foundation of the cult was quite colourless, simply stating that the sanctuary was established by Munichos, the hero who gave his name to the place. One piece of its ritual, however, had a special legend attached to it. This was the sacrifice of a she-goat to Artemis, presumably on the day of the festival. The story ran that a she-bear had entered the shrine where it was killed by the Athenians. This act roused the wrath of the goddess, who brought a plague on them as a punishment. The oracle was consulted and declared that the remedy would be found if someone sacrificed his daughter to Artemis. This response naturally created a reluctance to comply, until a man named Embaros volunteered to satisfy the oracle, if he and his family were awarded the priesthood of the goddess for life. He solved the problem of the sacrifice by a naïvely simple trick. For he brought his daughter to the shrine as though to offer her and hid her in the inner-most sanctuary. He then produced a she-goat dressed up like his daughter and sacrificed it.[173]

One may wonder whether this story of substitution points directly to a primitive time when originally a human sacrifice of a girl was made to Artemis. In legend she is often associated with this kind of offering. Also it would be interesting to know whether, in classical times, the she-goat was actually draped in some garment or decorated with some items of female jewellery. The form of the legend seems to require some such detail to explain its origin. For she-goats were so commonly the victims offered to Artemis that of themselves they scarcely seem to need a legend to explain them.

The goat and the she-bear point to the side of Artemis as the mistress of beasts and goddess of the wild, but another element in the festival shows her as moon-goddess. Special cakes called *amphiphontes* ('shining all round') were carried in the procession on the 16th of Munichion. They had lighted candles stuck in a circle, and ancient commentators were probably right in seeing in this some reference to the circle of the moon. Besides their use in the public procession they were also brought privately as offerings to the goddess. A fragment of the comedy *The Poor Girl* or *The Girl from Rhodes* by Philemon shows a woman praying: 'Artemis, dear mistress, to you I carry, lady, this cake shining all around and what is to serve as a drink-offering.'[174]

By the Hellenistic period the festival had evidently become a general celebration in the Peiraeus. The Epheboi (the young men on military training) held a regatta culminating in a race at sea round the promontory from the harbour of the Peiraeus to the harbour of Munichia.

This had little to do with Artemis who unlike Apollo was not greatly concerned with the sea. The Epheboi, as we shall see, had similar events later in the year on the *Diisoteria*. It seems simply to be that they found a couple of holidays which made convenient dates for these sporting exercises which were part of the young men's training course.[175]

The other curious feature in the story of Munichia is the motive of the she-bear as the occasion of the goddess's anger. Evidently as numbers of legends show, Artemis was associated with this animal and may herself in primitive times have been imagined in its form. The place most connected with this aspect was not Munichia, but Brauron in east Attica, where Artemis was the great local goddess with an important temple. Her cult was accepted by the Athenian state, and by the late sixth century Artemia Brauronia was even allowed to occupy a branch establishment on the Acropolis. There was an annual festival in east Attica called the *Brauronia* which like the *Panathenaia* was celebrated with special splendour every fourth year when it was organized not by local officials, but by the same Athenian commission of ten Hieropoioi (Performers of Sacred Rites) who were responsible for the *Panathenaia*.[176] (Plates 55-57)

However, it was not the festival itself which was the most notable feature of the ritual at Brauron. It was the practice of 'acting the she-bear' (*arkteuein*). This was supposed to be a ritual of appeasement to Artemis performed by little girls who must be not older than ten or younger than five. They were dressed in long yellowish coloured robes and probably mimed the actions of a bear walking on its hind legs. An explanatory myth was told which was a more convincing variant of part of the myth about Artemis of Munichia. It went as follows: a she-bear frequented the neighbourhood and was tamed and lived in the sanctuary. A young girl who was playing with it teased it so that in its rage it tore out one of her eyes. Her brothers in revenge killed it. But the goddess's anger had been roused and a plague followed. When the oracle was consulted for a remedy, the Athenians were told to make their daughters act the she-bear as an atonement. So the Athenians voted that a maiden might not be wedded before she had performed this ritual.[177]

The myth is only a rationalizing explanation of the requirement for little girls to spend a period of their youth at Brauron serving the goddess in the guise of bears. This must have been a primitive custom dating from the days when Artemis was herself thought of as a she-bear who must have she-bears as her attendants. Possibly the local women of Brauron had then all been required to perform this service before marriage. But by the time that the cult had been recognized as part of the Athenian state religion, the practice of acting the she-bear was the duty and privilege of a limited number of the aristocrats. This is beautifully illustrated by Aristophanes in his comedy *Lysistrata* where the chorus of women list the various sacral duties which they have performed and describe how they have been luxuriously maintained while they did them.

> At the age of seven at once I carried the secret objects. Then I was a corn-grinder (*aletris*). At ten for the presiding goddess I was a bear shedding the saffron-robe at the *Brauronia*, and some time I carried in a basket a bunch of dried figs when I was a fine young girl.[178]

This list of four stages in her growth is an interesting illustration of the part which a young woman played in religious festivals. The last of these, when the girl was well grown, and acted as a basket-carrier (Kanephoros) we have seen in various religious processions. The immediately preceding stage was the she-bear at Brauron which stopped at the age of ten. What her duties were there can be illustrated from the little pottery jars lately found in the excavations of the sanctuary. They show 'young girls running or dancing, sometimes holding torches or wreaths at a place recognizable as a sanctuary by the presence of an altar and as an Artemis sanctuary by the presence of a palm-tree'. Some of the girls are shown wearing a short *chiton* – presumably the yellow robe – but on others the girls are naked. Presumably this was part of the ritual, and it is possible that Aristophanes' reference to shedding the robe alludes to this fact, that in some part of the ceremonies the girls dropped their clothes and performed the rites in the nude.[179]

The two earlier functions mentioned by the chorus are each also worth a separate discussion. The corn-grinders are rarely mentioned. They ground the meal for the sacred cakes to be offered to Athena. Presumably they used hand-mills of a light kind and the quantity of meal needed for such ritual offerings will have been small. Otherwise it would have been a heavy task for little girls and could only be performed by a token service. The scholiast commenting on Aristophanes assures us that they were members of high-born families and that it was an honourable function. In ordinary circumstances to condemn a slave to the mill was to reduce him to hard labour. The purpose of the task was to provide Athena, the virgin goddess, with domestic servants of suitable dignity and purity.

The first function – 'to carry the unspoken things – [*arrephorein*]' – is often mentioned in Athenian inscriptions and in the ancient dictionaries. The Arrephoroi were girls between seven and eleven of whom four were chosen each year according to their aristocratic birth by the Basileus, and his nominations were confirmed by a vote of the people. As we have already seen, two of them took part in the ritual ceremony of starting the weaving of Athena's robe on the feast of Hephaestus. But this was not the function from which they derived their title. This is described by Pausanias, who evidently believed he was recording something unfamiliar.

What follows has caused me much surprise, and it is not known to everyone, but I am writing what actually occurs. Two maidens have a residence not far from the temple of Athena Polias (on the Acropolis) and are called 'the Carriers of the Unspoken Things' by the Athenians. They spend a certain time living beside the goddess and when the feast comes round by night they do as follows: They put on their heads what the priestess of Athena gives them to carry, but neither she who gives them knows what she gives nor do those who carry it understand. There is an enclosure on the Acropolis dedicated to Aphrodite called 'Her in the Gardens' and there is a natural underground way down to it. The girls go down by this way and leave below what they were carrying and take something else wrapped up and fetch it from there. Then they release these girls and bring others to the Acropolis to take their place.[180] (Plate 60)

Though Pausanias is an accurate authority on religious practices, his account might have been regarded as rather far-fetched, if it had not been largely confirmed by the explorations of Broneer. He found in the northern cliff of the Acropolis a subterranean passage which led below between the rocks to an open-air sanctuary with inscriptions indicating that it was dedicated to Aphrodite and Eros. This was evidently the route which the Arrephoroi travelled at night on their mysterious mission. The whole procedure indicates that it was a magical fertility ritual: the secrecy, the performance by night and the fact that it was done only by women all point that way. The choice of little girls rather than adults was probably determined, as often in magic rites, by the belief that young children were ritually pure and so less liable than their elders to upset the efficacy of the ceremony by some ritual impurity. The procedure must date from some primitive period when Athena was more generally the community's goddess for all functions and so was as much concerned with the fertility of plants as with war or handicrafts. In fact the original predecessors of the Arrephoroi may well have been the daughters of the ancient kings of Athens or other young female relations, who descended from the palace on the Acropolis to perform this secret ritual. On the fall of the kingship the post of Arrephoros was thrown open to the daughters of the noble families, but they were still selected by the Basileus, the annual king who had taken the place of the hereditary monarch for religious purposes. Also they were still expected to live on the Acropolis in close proximity to the city-goddess whom they served. The ritual linked Athena and her servants on the Acropolis with Aphrodite whose sanctuary lay immediately below the cliffs. She was a female deity of fertility, whether human or vegetable. Broneer found evidence of phallic symbols in the sanctuary, but the fact that it was called 'the gardens' suggests that it was also cultivated and was associated with the growth of plants. The notion of women secretly descending with some mysterious objects and returning with others suggests a parallelism with the *Thesmophoria*. Nilsson would believe that the cults became confused, but more likely they represent distinct developments of the same primitive ritual.[181] (Plates 58, 59)

The date on which the ceremony took place is not at all clear. Pausanias gives no indication of this. A late lexicon states that the *Arrephoria* was a feast to Athena performed in the month Skiraphorion, the last of the Attic year, and the height of summer. But the difficulty about using this as evidence for the date is that in the same entry the lexicographer records an alternative spelling with an E: *Errephoria* or *Ersephoria*. This word certainly also existed with the meaning 'Dew-carrying'. It was a festival connected with Erse, the minor goddess of the dew, who was identified in legend as a daughter of King Cecrops of Athens. Both words occur in Attic inscriptions and it appears as if they originally were quite separate, but by the Hellenistic period were frequently confused. The two meanings become so muddled in the later literature that it is impossible for instance to decide whether the festival in Skirophorion was the carrying of mysterious objects to the sanctuary of Aphrodite or a procession in honour of Erse. If the date in midsummer has any special significance it may have been the ceremony

connected with dew, in principle an appeal to the goddess to grant
life-giving moisture to the thirsty parched soil. If so, the night ritual of
the Arrephoroi may have taken place at any other time of the year, but
would be more probably at seed time or in some period of early
growth.[182]

Before we leave the Arrephoroi several other quaint details about
them are worth mention. They wore white robes, and if they put on
gold ornaments, these became consecrated. The meaning of this last
custom is not clear. Was it that the mystic potency of the Arrephoroi
was such that objects with which they had been in contact could
ostensibly not thereafter be used for secular purposes? Or may one
wonder more cynically whether it was an indirect method of discouraging doting relatives from decking the little girls in fancy jewellery? If
they did so, the pieces remained the property of Athena. Again we
hear of a special kind of light bread called *anastatos* which was given to
the Arrephoroi. Finally, it is interesting to notice that the little girls
had a special ball-alley named after them on the Acropolis. So presumably they were allowed to play games like other children when
they were not wanted for sacred duties. The reference to the place
comes from an account of the life of the orator Isocrates which tells
that there was a bronze statue of him as a boy in this ball-alley on the
Acropolis, showing him as a hockey-player. One might perhaps be
sceptical about the identification, but the statement is good evidence
for the existence of the ball-alley and also for a bronze statue of a boy
hockey-player at the place. Was the ground used by boys as well as
girls, or was there mixed hockey? These questions remain un-
answered.[183] (Plate 61)

Broneer discovered in the sanctuary of Aphrodite in the gardens an
inscription dating from the mid-fifth century which is evidence for a
festival in honour of Eros not otherwise recorded. It simply states that
the feast to Eros took place on the 4th of Munichion, which is the
month we are discussing. The 4th day of the month was the traditional
one dedicated to Aphrodite, and so was appropriate too for the festival
of Eros, who was also worshipped at other shrines in Athens. As there
are no other references to this particular feast, there are no details of
the ritual available, nor is it explained why the inscription was set up
at this particular date in the mid-fifth century, but it points to the cult
of Eros either having been established at this date in the sanctuary,
previously dedicated to Aphrodite, or else having been revived at this
period.[184]

There was one other festival in Munichion. On the 19th of the month the *Olympieia* was held. It was in honour of the Olympian Zeus and was probably instituted by Peisistratus in the latter half of the sixth century when he laid the foundations of the colossal temple near the Ilissos. It was designed in the Ionic style and planned to imitate in scale the great temples of Ephesus, Samos and Miletus which were built at this period. The work was suspended on the fall of the tyranny and the building remained incomplete till the emperor Hadrian finished it. But the festival continued to be celebrated on the date which was probably the anniversary of the foundation. It appears to have been mainly an occasion for the Athenian cavalry. Plutarch describes with irony and pathos the scene at the execution by drinking hemlock of Phocion, the fourth-century BC politician. Public feeling was outraged that the sentence was carried out on a public festival consecrated to Zeus. By the date which he quotes Plutarch evidently meant the *Olympieia* and he describes how the cavalry who were taking part in the procession rode past the prison where the execution was taking place. 'Some of them removed the garlands which they were wearing to celebrate the occasion, while others with tears in their eyes gazed at the doors of the prison.'[185]

In the Hellenistic period, if not before, the festival included cavalry exercises in the Hippodrome. The most important was a competition known as the 'Riding opposite' [*Anthippasia*]. Xenophon in the fourth century describes such an occasion with the enthusiasm of a professional cavalryman.

Whenever there is the display in the Hippodrome . . . it is a beautiful thing when the tribal contingents in the 'Riding opposite' flee from and pursue each other in turn. In this spectacle the riding against each other is grim, the riding through and then halting opposite each other is impressive, and at the trumpet signal the riding at each other faster the second time is beautiful. After halting again a third time at the trumpet signal they must ride at each other at the fastest speed and after riding through, when they have brought their horses to a halt (at the dismissing point) in line, they ride to face the city council.

The lively description gives a general notion at least of the complicated evolutions, but in his enthusiasm Xenophon does not explain how the competition was run. It was evidently not a mere race, but a series of operations worthy of a military tattoo, and in fact it was meant to provide training in horsemanship of a kind which would be of practical use in battle. Presumably, then, there were judges who either awarded points for proficiency or deducted them for faults. The importance of the occasion was marked by the presence of the city council who were seated in some sort of grandstand.

These great exertions were accompanied by a sacrifice on a very large scale. In 334/3 BC for instance the official record shows that 671 drachmas was earned from the sale of the hides of the victims. The proper offering to Zeus would be a bull. So one may picture the day as ending in a large number of dinners of beef.[186] (Plate 62)

11 THARGELION

The eleventh Attic month was called THARGELION after the important festival of Apollo which took place in it. Like other major Apolline festivals it was celebrated on the 7th of the month, but the previous day was also linked with it. The 6th was Artemis' day: in fact the Delians believed that she was actually born on the 6th of Thargelion and Apollo, her twin brother, on the 7th. So the two days made a combined festival, at which in Athens Apollo was the main deity honoured. Actually a *Thargelia* was celebrated in much the same general way in many of the cities of the Ionians, and we can take it that its practices represent something very basic to the worship of Apollo and not a special Attic development.[187]

The two days were very different. The 6th was a day of purification. This in itself had a proper connection with Apollo. In the *Iliad* (1,314) when the Greek camp has been smitten by a plague, it is attributed to the wrath of Apollo. The two remedies used are for the men to clean themselves and throw the off-scourings into the sea, and then to offer hecatombs of bulls and he-goats to the god. The *Thargelia* was arranged on exactly this pattern. The first day was devoted to purification, the second to offerings.

The form of purification used for public ritual in Athens and the other Ionian states consisted in what were known as Pharmakoi – persons whose title implied that they possessed magical properties. In Athens two men were chosen each year, the qualification being that they should be ugly and poor. We have already seen that in selecting the old men for the Panathenaic procession preference was given to good looks. This choice of the Pharmakos is the correlative to it. The Athenians in both instances showed themselves very conscious of the effect of physical beauty. Poverty was necessary so as to ensure the willingness of the victims. These Pharmakoi were fed for some time at the state's expense, and on the first day of the *Thargelia* they were led out to act as scapegoats for the people of Athens. One was taken to act as substitute for the men and wore a string of black figs round his neck: the other for the women, and wore a string of white figs. After they had been taken in a procession round the city, they were beaten with branches of figs and pelted with squills, and so driven out. Treatment of a similar kind was meted out to Pharmakoi in such places as Ephesus, where it is evidenced by extracts from the sixth-century satiric poet Hipponax.[188]

The purpose of the ritual was evidently to create scapegoats for the men and women of the community, and, as the ancient commentators recognized, the beating and pelting were a milder substitute for a much grimmer ceremony in which the victims were beaten with real rods and stoned to death. The choice of squills as missiles was because they were employed in purificatory rituals.[189]

The folk memory of the earlier stages had only dimly survived into the classical period. In fifth- and fourth-century Attic literature the Pharmakos only appears as a term of comic abuse. Probably the custom still lasted on in its modified form, becoming more and more a bit of vulgar horseplay, disregarded by the more serious-minded religious people.[190]

The main other activity of the *Thargelia*, which took place on the 7th of the month was to make the offering to Apollo which gave its name to the festival. This was a pot full of all kinds of corn and vegetables boiled together and offered as the first-fruits. The name for this offering was *thargelos*, but in spite of the efforts of modern philologists the origin of the word remains unsolved. Ancient scholars equated it with the word *thalusia*, which was used as early as the time of Homer for an offering of first-fruits made to the gods. Actually this was evidently the intention of the *thargelos*. The festival would fall about the beginning of May when in Attica the crops would be grown, but not yet fully ripe. So one can take it that the ritual was less a harvest festival when all was safely gathered than an anticipatory appeal to the gods – in this instance Apollo – to bless with ripeness the coming harvest. The resemblance with the ceremony of the *Pyanepsia* seven months previously is obvious. At each festival a mixture of all kinds of vegetables was cooked and given to the god. The *Pyanepsia* was linked with seed-time, the *Thargelia* with harvest and evidently Apollo was worshipped as a god of fertility of all kinds of vegetation.[191]

This aspect of Apollo is quite different from what usually appears in Greek, particularly Attic, literature. There he gives fertility to the flocks of King Admetus when he has to act as the royal shepherd. Otherwise he is associated with the growth of young men and this may be the reason why he is a patron of athletics. But agriculture and the cultivation of vegetables are not his concern; they belong to Demeter and the women who are her special worshippers. Here we see the effects of polytheism. One cannot doubt that Demeter was established as a cult in Attica from the most primitive times. Before she came to Athens, Athena herself may have fulfilled all necessary functions in providing her people with food. Apollo on the other hand is to be regarded as a new-comer compared with these, most likely arriving from Asia via Delos in the eighth century or so. In Asia he had probably fulfilled all the functions of a major god, and as god of fertility brought with him the rites of the *Pyanepsia* and *Thargelia* already practised in Ionia. Though the Athenians probably had already fertility cults such as the *Thesmophoria*, which the Ionians had taken with them to Asia, this did not prevent them from accepting the rituals of a new and powerful god.

However, it is not surprising that the *Thargelia* at Athens developed more sophisticated features suitable to a society which was not exclusively agricultural in interest and corresponding to the development of Apollo himself as a god of culture. In the fifth century the archon, who was responsible for organizing the dramatic and choral performances at the *City Dionysia*, also was required in a similar way to provide for choirs of men and boys to compete as two classes in singing hymns at the *Thargelia*. The choirs were recruited from the different tribes, but as ten units would have been too many for the competition, the tribes were grouped in pairs to form five choirs of men and five of boys, each containing fifty singers. The victors received a tripod as their award which was then dedicated to Apollo in the Pythion, his temple near the Ilissos.[192]

Also the *Phratriai*, the religious groupings of the Athenians, recognized the *Thargelia* as a day of sacrifice and festival. Apollo had managed to be accepted into the traditional pattern of Attic society under the title Patroös (Ancestral god). In mythology this was justified by making him the father of Ion, the eponymous ancestor of the Ionians. Thus he would be regarded as the founder of the race to which the Athenians belonged and could be treated as a general ancestor suitable to be worshipped by the family units of the *Phratriai*. A client in one of Isaeus' speeches recalls how he had been introduced to the *Phratria* at the *Thargelia* as a child adopted by his father. He explains that it was a custom of the *Phratria* that the father should present his child at the altar and pledge himself by the sacrifice that the boy whether sired by him or adopted was born of an Athenian woman who was herself a citizen. Then the tribesmen passed a vote accepting the new member.

This function was fully appropriate to the patronage of Apollo as protector of young boys.[193]

The first day of the *Thargelia* was also the date of another piece of ritual. A ram was offered on the Acropolis to Demeter Chloe. This title applied to her as the goddess of the green shoots, and Deubner is probably right in seeing this sacrifice as particularly directed to winning her blessing before the harvest. Ancient commentators were chiefly interested in it, because it was unusual to offer a male animal to a female deity. The cult itself may have been imported into Athens from Eleusis. For there the local community celebrated a whole festival with the title *Chloia*. It is described as a lively occasion taking place in spring. So probably it fell earlier than Thargelion.[194]

In connection with the *Thargelia* we have discussed Apollo as a god winning acceptance when an incomer to Athens. If this is correct, it must have been in the eighth century BC. But in the time of the Peloponnesian War we have a well authenticated instance of the introduction of a new deity to the Peiraeus with official approval. This was Bendis, a Thracian goddess, who was identified with Artemis. In the Peiraeus her festival occurred on the 19th of Thargelion and the night following.

The recognition of this foreign cult took place in 429 BC and had a political background. Thrace, the homeland of Bendis, was strategically of great importance to Athens at the time, and Sitalces, the king of the Thracian tribes, was treated as a friend and ally. There was evidently a colony of Thracians resident in the Peiraeus, who will have settled there as a result of trade between the two countries in recent years. Now the Athenian state in a manner quite unusual in Greece gave this foreign community the right to acquire possession of some Attic land and to found a sanctuary to Bendis. The place chosen was on the hill of Munichia near to the temple of Artemis and on the same road. This must have seemed appropriate, since, as we have said, Bendis was equated with Artemis in the typical Greek manner of identifying foreign deities approximately with Hellenic counterparts. In art she is shown with a Phrygian cap on her head and a cloak hanging from her shoulders over a short dress. She wears high boots with fur tops and carries a long spear in her right hand. This was the proper costume for the goddess as huntress. When the shrine was founded in 429 BC the cult was organized in two guilds, one of Thracians resident in Attica and the other of native Athenians who had become worshippers of the goddess. Also in a way fully in accordance with Greek custom the

Athenian state took care to receive oracular sanction for these innovations. The only difficulty in this matter was that Delphi was not available. Even before the Peloponnesian War the Pythian Apollo had shown himself hostile to Athens, and after the war broke out Delphi could not be reached conveniently by land or sea. So the Athenians, who were developing friendly relations with the oracle of Zeus at Dodona, consulted him instead and received a favourable response.[195]

The first occasion of the festival of the *Bendidia* is known through the fact that it was made the scene of one of the great books of European literature. The *Republic* of Plato commences with Socrates describing how he and Plato's brother, Adeimantus, the son of Ariston, had 'gone down to the Peiraeus the previous day to pray to the goddess and at the same time wishing to see in what way they keep the festival since they were holding it for the first time. And indeed the procession of the local people seemed to me to be fine and not less suitable seemed the procession which the Thracians arranged. So we said our prayers and saw the sights and were setting off to return to Athens,' when they were intercepted by Polemarchus whose father Cephalus, an old man, was a prosperous manufacturer, living as a resident alien (Metoikos) in the Peiraeus. Socrates and Adeimantus were invited to return and have dinner with Cephalus, as they had not yet seen a unique part of the ceremonies. It is introduced by this description in dialogue:

'Do you not know', said he, 'that there will be a torch race on horses in the evening in honour of the goddess'? 'On horses', said I, 'that is a novelty. Do they hold torches and pass them to each other while racing on horseback – or what do you mean'? 'Just that', said Polemarchus. 'Also besides they will hold an all-night festival which is worth seeing. We shall rise from the table after dinner and see the all-night festival. You can meet many of the young men there and have a talk.'

So the party go back to Cephalus' home, where after some introductory conversation with their venerable host, the dialogue with the young men begins and reaches through the ten books of the *Republic*. After the myth of Er at its close the subject of the torch-race and the all-night festival is allowed to drop. It had from Plato's point of view fulfilled its dramatic purpose by providing an interesting occasion to bring together the interlocuters, not in Athens, but in the house of Cephalus in the Peiraeus.[196]

The pattern of the festival which Plato sketches out is evidently correct. We hear elsewhere of the procession of the Athenians which actually started from Athens at the Prytaneion (the office of the presiding committee of the state) and went to the sanctuary in the Peiraeus. The procession of the Thracians, which as Plato indicates, was separately organized, may have started in the Peiraeus itself and been timed to link with the procession from the city at the approach to the sanctuary. The devotees of Bendis who had marched over six miles in procession from Athens deserved a good reception at the Peiraeus, and a regulation is extant which lays down that they were to be provided with sponges, basins and water and also with garlands. After a wash-up, they would be ready for the lunch which was to be served in the precinct. [197]

There would evidently be an interval, even time for a siesta, after lunch, and the equestrian torch relay-race took place after dusk. Plato recorded the first performance and treated it as a peculiar novelty, but it became an established institution. A beautiful marble relief from the Peiraeus dating from the mid-fourth century shows a winning team offering their thanks to Bendis. This dedicatory carving represents the goddess, larger than human size, in the costume which we have described. She is holding in her right hand a cup with which to greet her worshippers. In front of her stand in a row the team of eight young men and their two trainers who are older and bearded. The young men are all naked, which is how they will have been when riding. No horses are shown, as it is the artist's intention to depict not the race itself, but the later stage when the victorious team presented themselves to the goddess. The only indication of the method of the contest is that one of the trainers and the leading member of the team carry large torches held downwards. Though this was just a commercial piece of religious sculpture commissioned for dedication, it is infused with a charming spirit of natural observation, which puts life into the rather dull subject of eight young men standing in a line.

Such races were a special feature of Attic festivals, torch-races being otherwise run on foot. The Thracians must have been responsible for the innovation of racing on horse-back. They were well known as horsemen and lived in a country more suited to horse-breeding than Greece. Whether such races were held in Thrace is not known.

The all-night festival which followed the race is not described anywhere. Cotyto, the other Thracian goddess, who is often mentioned, was notorious for the wildly orgiastic character of her nocturnal rites.

But she was not accepted in Athens, though apparently in Corinth. We
need not suppose that the rites of Bendis differed greatly from the other
all-night festivals in Athens.[198]

What function Bendis was supposed to perform for her worshippers
is not explained. Probably she was simply looked to for general blessing and protection. But modern scholars who note that Herodotus
described the Thracian women as offering wheat to her (whom he calls
Artemis) have suggested with some plausibility that the choice of late
May for the festival was because it approximated to the Attic harvest.
Also one may add that Thrace was extremely important strategically
for the route by which the Athenian corn supplies were imported.

Toward the end of Thargelion two festivals which intimately concerned Athena herself took place: the *Kallynteria* and the *Plynteria*. The
exact dates are uncertain. If, as one late lexicon states, the *Kallynteria*
was held on the 19th, it coincided with the *Bendidia*, which is improbable. The same source states that the *Plynteria* took place on the
penultimate day of the month. But this is almost certainly wrong as a
better source gives the 25th as the date. So probably the *Kallynteria* took
place between the 20th and the 25th. The two festivals were concerned
with spring-cleaning Athena and her temple. The *Kallynteria* is scarcely
mentioned in our sources, but the name, meaning to beautify by
sweeping up and polishing, points clearly enough to it being the
occasion when the temple of Athena received a special annual clean-up.
This would be carried out under the direction of the priestess by the
women who, as we shall see, had other functions of cleansing to perform. Deubner also suggests with some plausibility that it was the date
of the year on which the famous ever-burning lamp of Athena Polias
was refilled with olive oil and relit. Presumably Athena had had a
lamp always kept burning in her shrine from primitive times, but
in the late fifth century when the Erechtheum was rebuilt in the
wonderful form in which it survives, Callimachus, a distinguished
Athenian sculptor and metalworker, made a gold lamp which was
regarded as specially noteworthy because it held enough oil to burn
day and night for twelve months without refilling. The oil was re-
plenished on the same day each year, and the occasion of the temple's
cleaning would be a sensible date to choose.[199]

The *Plynteria* (Festival of Washing) was the occasion for cleaning the
goddess herself. This must have been initiated in primitive times when
the statue of the goddess was made of wood, and was human-size or
less. The ceremony evidently continued into the fifth century even after

the colossal gold and ivory statue made by Pheidias had become the chief cult object on the Acropolis. The Praxiergidai, who were a family traditionally entrusted with robing the image, performed the ritual. For though the cleaning was a practical business, it also was treated by the women as a secret ceremony of great solemnity. This intimate contact with the goddess was not to be open to the casual male or the uninitiated female. The first procedure was to strip the image of its robes and ornaments. Then it was wrapped up, for it had to be taken out of the temple for its cleaning. All this one can picture as done early on the morning of the 25th with much special traditional ceremonial. Then the statue had to be carried in procession to the sea for a purificatory bath. To sponge it in the temple was evidently not regarded as sufficiently cleansing. The Greeks in this matter were very conscious of the purifying effects of running water. But in May it would have been hard to find more than a trickle in the Attic rivers, the Kephisos and Ilissos. Also, as we have seen in the case of the Mystai, the salt sea was the most purifying element. So, like the Mystai, and probably long before the Mysteries of Demeter came to Athens, the image of the city goddess had to go in procession to Phaleron. In the fourth century the goddess was escorted by the young men in military training (the Epheboi) to whom it was a ceremonial parade. In this the procession resembled the procession of the Mysteries, and as in it the sacred objects carried must not be seen by the public, so also on this occasion the image was wrapped up and carried in privacy. The journey probably had ritual stoppings and procedures. Certainly it was not without elaborate detail. For instance the procession was headed by a woman carrying a basket containing sweetmeats made out of figs. The myth alleging that it was in memory of the fact that figs were the first food cultivated by man was used to explain this. But it does not seem to have any relevance, and Deubner is probably right in suggesting instead that these were an offering to Athena who could be expected to need some refreshment on this picnic.[200]

On arrival at the sea the image was unrobed and washed by two young women called the Bathers or Washers. Also it may have been at the same time that Athena's robe was washed. There was a special priestess to whom was assigned the duty of laundress. Though we are not told when she performed her task, the best opportunity would seem to be when the goddess was already undressed for her bathe, and the *peplos* could be made clean to be put on the statue when its purification was finished.[201]

The procession returned by torchlight, the torches being held by the military escort. Then presumably the image was unwrapped by the Praxiergidai, robed once more, decorated with its jewellery and restored to its place in the shrine. This procedure may be the subject of a sadly fragmentary inscription which shows that at some date in the mid-fifth century the Delphic oracle had been consulted on the matter. The inscription recorded a decree of the people authorizing the putting into effect of Apollo's response. Money was to be provided from state funds for robing the image of Athena and this was to be done in accordance with ancestral custom and the oracle of the god. Apollo had replied that the image should be robed, and sacrifice as a preliminary should be made to the Fates, Zeus the leader of the Fates, the Earth Goddess – at this point the text breaks off. It could be referring to the robing of the statue annually at the time of the *Panathenaia*, but, if so, it is curious that there is no mention of the *Panathenaia* in the inscription even in its fragmentary state. Also it seems somewhat improbable that Apollo would have advised, and the Athenians accepted, the instructions for an elaborate series of preliminary sacrifices of the kind prescribed to be inserted in the great Athenian festival. Actually the selection of deities may show a certain local prejudice on the part of the Pythia. Of those mentioned Ge was worshipped within the precinct at Delphi; Zeus, Leader of the Fates, and two Fates (not the usual three) were actually worshipped within the temple itself. Probably the Pythia had asked to approve of some change in the ritual of the *Plynteria*, which was explained as a reinterpretation of ancestral custom, and had agreed, but had taken the opportunity to recommend some of the deities of Delphic cult.[202]

It was not surprising that the day of the *Plynteria* was treated as highly inauspicious. The fact that the goddess was otherwise preoccupied might be regarded as making it unwise to do anything which might need her attention. Indeed the character of the day was marked by the fact that the sanctuaries of the city generally were kept shut throughout it. A barrier of rope was put up across the entrances to prevent intrusion. Deubner calls attention to the similar practice at the time of the Festival of Pots in Anthesterion and suggests that as spirits of harm were then supposed to be about, so also on the *Plynteria* the purification of the goddess implied the presence of foul powers. In his view the washing of the image had become less a material act of hygiene than a spiritual act meant to reinforce the goddess's powers. But this view is probably overstressing the uncanny and magical aspects of the ritual. However, that the day was treated as inauspicious remains certain. In 408 B C when after seven years in exile Alcibiades at last ventured, as a victorious general, to return to his native city, he happened to arrive at the Peiraeus on the day of the *Plynteria*. Xenophon, who was probably a young soldier in Athens at the time, records that 'some people took it as an omen boding ill to him and the city both. For no Athenian would dare to touch any serious business on that day.' For the moment Alicibiades seemed on the crest of the wave, but within a few months his plans collapsed and he never recovered his position.[203]

12 SKIRAPHORION

The last month of the Attic year was called SKIRAPHORION after the chief festival to be held in it – the *Skiraphoria* or as it was more often called the *Skira*. It presents some of the most puzzling problems in the study of Athenian cults and has been the subject of a great deal of controversial writing in recent years. This was evidently also true in antiquity. For echoes of considerable disagreements about it and of conflicting theories are reproduced in a fragmentary way in the ancient lexica. Late Greek scholars were as keen as modern ones to classify the festivals of Athens tidily under the names of the gods and goddesses to whom they were dedicated. But the *Skira* resisted easy classification. Some scholars said it was a feast of Athena and others of Demeter: and the same disagreement reappears in modern works. Another problem concerned the meaning or derivation of *skiron* – the significant part of the festival's name. There was no agreement on the subject in antiquity. Five explanations were offered, two deriving it from the names of two quite different material objects. The other three, in a way typical of ancient scholarship, are based on the belief that it was derived from the name of a person: but again three different characters in mythology were suggested. Modern scholars while rejecting the derivations from mythology have produced further conjectures about the original meaning of the word to suit their particular views of the festival.[204]

It is quite usual, but unfortunate, that we have no comprehensive description of the *Skira*. Instead ancient authorities, such as Aristophanes, make casual allusions to it which imply that it was a women's festival. In the *Thesmophoriazousai* he makes a woman suggest that those of them who had served the Athenian state well should be given front seats at the *Stenia* and the *Skira*. The *Stenia* we have seen was a preliminary feast before the *Thesmophoria*, and it is clearly implicit that the *Skira*, like it, was a women's festival, where they should receive the kind of honour which important men had in the *City Dionysia*. Again, in the *Ecclesiazousai* a woman refers to the proposals which she and her friends had carried at the *Skira*, implying that it was a female festival where women could plot against the opposite sex. This picture of the

Skira as excluding men fits with those ancient scholars who said it was dedicated to Demeter and Persephone.[205]

On the other hand Harpocration, a careful and accurate dictionary writer, explains the word *skiron* as follows:

> *Skira* is a festival among the Athenians from which is derived also the month Skiraphorion. Those who have written on the months and festivals at Athens, one of whom is Lysimachides, say that the *skiron* is a large sunshade. When it is carried, there walk under it from the Acropolis to a place called Skiron the priestess of Athena, the priest of Poseidon and the priest of the Sun. The [clan of the] Eteobutadai convey it. It is a sign that one must build houses and make shelter, as that is the best time of the year for house-building.

Lysimachides was a fairly late writer, probably of the Augustan period, but he is a good authority for the actual practice, which itself is sufficiently remarkable for it to be unlikely that it is invented or misunderstood. So one feature of the *Skira* was a strange procession which set out from the Acropolis. The two chief officials of the two oldest cults practised there, that of Athena and that of Poseidon, associated with the Erechtheum, went on foot through the city of Athens, out at the Dipylon Gate, and along the road of Eleusis as far as a site just before the crossing of the river Kephisos. The distance must have been nearly three miles and on a date in June this would be a hot and sunny tramp unless it was started early in the morning. Hence the sunshade could have a practical purpose, even if it was developed into a dignified and impressive piece of ritual. From another source we learn that it was white in colour. As it had to cover at least three people, one is to picture it, with Deubner, as being like a canopy, and its supports were carried by at least four attendants. They were drawn from the ancient Attic clan of the Eteobutadai, the same family which supplied the priestess of Athena and the priest of Poseidon. So this procession seems to have its roots deep in the traditions of Athens. If it had been established in the period of the democracy, one could not imagine this function being assigned to a hereditary clan rather than to certain annual officials. The place called Skiron which was the goal of the procession was the site of some worship of Athena under the title Skiras. Though whether there was a temple there is not clearly stated.

So far, if we had only the description of the procession at the *Skira* to go on, we would see no reason to assign the festival to Demeter.

Everything would point to Athena the city Goddess (Polias) as the deity chiefly concerned. The association of Poseidon in view of his cult on the Acropolis is not surprising. The only element impossible to explain in Lysimachides' description is the priest of the Sun. The sun was not worshipped in archaic or classical Athens. Either Lysimachides was recording some very late innovation or he was describing Apollo by a paraphrase sometimes used in late authors. The explanation of the procession which Lysimachides offers – that it was a reminder of the need for shelter and house-building – is absurd.[206]

The situation with regard to the *Skira* then is somewhat similar to that of the *Pyanepsia*. In each instance two quite different deities with quite separate ceremonies happened to coincide on one day. In the *Pyanepsia* it was the Apolline festival with the *eiresione* and the special dish of vegetables, which was combined with the festival of Athena Skiras to whom the procession was sent to her temple at Phaleron. In the *Skira* the procession to Skiron which originally concerned Athena and her rival deity on the Acropolis coincided with some mystic ritual of Demeter confined to female participants. We have seen the most obvious external part of the ceremony concerning Athena – the picturesque procession under the canopy. What the priestess and the priest did when they reached Skiron we are not told, but there is reason to suppose that it had something to do with the fertility of crops. Plutarch records: 'The Athenians practise three sacred ploughings, firstly at Skiron, a reminder of the oldest of sowings, secondly in the Rarian plain, and thirdly under the Acropolis in the place called the Ox-yoking,' Plutarch's order need not be taken seriously. It was evidently determined by the relative importance of the ceremonies in his judgement, and he put that at Skiron first because (probably erroneously) he gave it the greatest antiquity. The ploughing of the Rarian plain near Eleusis was really an Eleusinian rite, and only became Athenian when Eleusis and its Mysteries were incorporated in the Athenian state. The other two sites of ploughing will at all times have lain within the territory of Athens. The site under the Acropolis sounds likely to be the most primitive and its name is clearly linked with one of the ancient aristocratic families of Athens – the Bouzygai – whose ancestor was said to have yoked the first oxen to the plough. The site at Skiron, though old, need not be so ancient. It was the scene of a ritual ploughing at some date in the Attic year not otherwise recorded. About the time of the *Thesmophoria* would be the correct season. If so, the *Skira* would correspond to the time of harvest. If there was a ploughing, presumably there was a sowing and the procession of the *Skira* will either have been to bless the ripening crops or to be present at the formal act of harvesting this sacred grain. When we look at it in this way the reason why the festivals of Athena and Demeter coincided on this date becomes more apparent. Both of them served the same general purpose of furthering fertility.[207]

The next problem is to ask what the women did in honour of Demeter on this day. Our evidence for this depends on one lengthy commentary on a passage in Lucian. The scholar who originally produced this note evidently had access to some good ancient source in which the three festivals of the *Thesmophoria*, the *Skira* and the *Arrephoria* were all compared as occasions of women's ritual. But unfortunately the description has been garbled through abridgement in transmission, so that it is not possible to see clearly what ritual he attributed to which festival. One festival was connected with the myth of the Rape of Persephone in a special form: 'When the Maiden was carried away by Pluto as she was gathering flowers, at that time in the same place a swineherd Eubouleus was grazing his pigs and they were swallowed up in the chasm with the Maiden. Therefore in honour of Eubouleus piglets are thrown into the chasms of Demeter and the Maiden. The decayed remains of those thrown in to the "chambers" are brought by the women called the Antletriai (the Balers).' (We have discussed these women before in connection with the *Thesmophoria*.)[208]

Obviously the myth of Eubouleus and his herd of swine swallowed in the ground were the rationalizing explanation produced to account for the ritual of killing piglets and throwing them into holes in the ground called 'chambers' in the Thesmophorion. Also the remains were extracted some considerable time later after they had decayed in the interval. Hence the attempts of modern scholars to have both the depositing of the piglets and their recovery take place in the same festival do not make sense. Clearly the throwing-in took place some months before the recovery, and the festivals concerned are the *Skira* and the *Thesmophoria*. It might be questioned at which festival each part of the ritual took place. But again it is clear that the *Thesmophoria* in October would be an impossible date for Persephone to be picking flowers. The *Skira* in late May or early June is rather too near the hot season for the typical growth of flowers in Greece, but at least it is still possible. So Deubner appears to be right in his interpretation of the evidence as pointing to a fertility ritual, whereby offerings of piglets were thrown into the earth at the *Skira* and recovered four months later to be used in making a fertilizing magic. The *Skira* would be at the time of harvest and the piglets may originally have been intended as much to be offerings of thanksgiving to the goddess of the corn. But if not originally, certainly later, the idea of the piglet – a typical sacrifice to Demeter and Persephone – as itself conveying fertility was important.

The festival of the *Skira* occupied only one day and, unlike the *Thesmophoria*, there was no need for the women taking part to leave their homes and encamp in the sanctuary. But at both festivals there evidently was a taboo on intercourse between the sexes. This was probably not mainly because such intercourse was generally regarded as making the parties temporarily unclean. In fertility rites throughout the world the temporary withholding of sexual activity was thought of as serving to strengthen fecundity when it was resumed. The abstinence over the time of these festivals was demonstrated by a curious practice on the part of the women. They ate garlic at the time of the *Skira* so as to discourage their husbands from being demanding on account of the strength of the smell, which took the place of their usual perfumes. Though the fact is not recorded in literature, garlic must have been used in the same way at the *Thesmophoria*, for in an account of expenses the impressive entry appears of two *staters'* weight of garlic for the use of the women of one district.[209]

Another ritual event may have taken place at the *Skira*. We have seen already that the *Oschophoria* consisted essentially in a procession led by two young men dressed as women who went from the sanctuary of Dionysus to the temple of Athena Skiras at Phaleron carrying boughs of vines with grapes. There is an account going back to a Hellenistic commentator of a race run over the same route by young men bearing vine-branches. The parallel between the two events is so close that it is not surprising that in later references they are sometimes confused with one another. But it is clear from a study of the sources that there was both a procession in Pyanepsion and a race which our earliest source dates to the *Skira*. The account of the race contains some special details which would make no sense if they were referred to the procession. The young men who took part were chosen from the tribes. Otherwise they were ten or teams in multiples of ten. The winner as a prize was given a drink called the 'Fivefold' (*pentaploa*), which had five ingredients: wine, honey, cheese, and a little corn and olive oil. Probably it was really a libation of all the fruits which the goddess, Athena Skiras, was asked to bless. The victor was the only person allowed to share it with the goddess. The procession of the *Oschophoria* in autumn appeared to be meant primarily to celebrate the vintage. The race at the *Skira* would correspond to the date when the grapes first set on the branches, but it may also have been extended to cover all the fruits of the earth and also the cheese which was similarly a seasonable food.[210]

Thus we are to picture the *Skira* as an occasion when three distinct pieces of ritual took place on the same day. A large number of women assembled separately at the Thesmophorion and went through their mystic ritual with the piglets. A solemn procession from the Acropolis to the suburbs was led under a canopy by some of the chief members of the city's priesthood. From the sanctuary of Dionysus to the temple in the Phaleron young men carrying vine branches were racing. A mystery, a procession and an athletic contest – three of the most typical rituals by which the Athenians worshipped their gods – all combined in the one festival of the *Skira*.

We may return briefly to discuss again the puzzling name of the festival. If Lysimachides was right and the name for the great white canopy carried on that day was *skiron*, then this would have supplied a plausible derivation and the longer form of the name would mean the festival of carrying the *skiron* (the canopy). One might only be a little uneasy over the shortened form *Skira*. The *Thesmophoria* is never shortened to the *Thesmoi*. But philologists have a more serious doubt whether Lysimachides is stating fact. Never elsewhere is a canopy or a parasol called *skiron*, though sunshades were used for individuals in other processions. Hence an uncomfortable doubt remains that Lysimachides may have applied the word *skiron* to the canopy as a means of explaining the name of the festival. This doubt is made all the stronger since there was another quite different derivation also recognized in antiquity. The ordinary meaning of the word *skiros* was 'hard white earth' or a 'hard white crust', such as the rind on cheese. It did not suggest a likely origin for the name of the festival, but legend achieved this by stating that Theseus when he returned from slaying the Minotaur made a figure of Athena out of white clay (*skiros*) and carried it in triumph. Hence the name Athena Skiras and the *Skiraphoria*. The chief objection to this myth is that it was obviously designed to suit the *Oschophoria* and the festival on the traditional date of Theseus' return from Crete. How could it then take in the *Skiraphoria*?[211]

The alternative style of explanation was the one that derived the title of the goddess from various male characters of approximately that name. The Megarians derived it from the Skiron who was the guardian of the Skironian rocks and whose overthrow was one of the heroic deeds of Theseus. To the Megarians Skiron was a revered ancestral figure; to the Athenians, their enemies, a villain whose killing was a service to humanity. Again, there was a traditional Skiros who was the first to settle Salamis. This would be the appropriate Salaminian derivation of the goddess's name. But the Athenians had yet a third personage to explain the title. They told the myth that in the time of King Erechtheus the Eleusinians had challenged them in war. They were supported by a prophet who had come from the famous oracle of Dodona. He fell in battle on the Eleusinian side and the Athenians when victorious buried him where he fell and named the place and the nearby stream after him. This was the legend to explain the name Skiron for the place outside Athens, to which the procession of the *Skirophoria* went. Evidently besides the sanctuary of Athena Skiras there must also have been one of those hero's shrines, so common in ancient Greece which was conveniently named together with the name of the place by this legend. But these three mythical personages get us no nearer a derivation for Skiraphorion. Is it possible that the name itself is a figment in the sense that the original festival was simply the *Skira*, but by false analogy with the *Thesmophoria*, the *Oschophoria* and the other similar titles it was mistakenly expanded and so also was the name of the month? Then at a late date the explanations of the objects carried were created to account for this erroneous name?

Two days after the *Skira*, on the 14th of Skirophorion, there took place on the Acropolis the most peculiar of Attic festivals, the *Dipolieia*. Already by the time of Aristophanes it was regarded as utterly antiquated and out of touch with contemporary thought. In *The Clouds* when the virtuous youth describes the moral upbringing of the good old days, the vicious youth exclaims: 'These things are archaic and like the *Dipolieia* and stuffed full of cicadas ... and the *Bouphonia*.' The *Bouphonia*, which is included in this list of out-of-date practices was the particular ceremony of the *Dipolieia* that was most recorded. The deity concerned was Zeus in his special aspect as god of the city. Hence just as Athena as protectress of the city had her temple on the Acropolis, Zeus Polieus had an altar there, which was the scene of the *Bouphonia*. This name ominously meant the slaying of an ox and applied the same word for killing the animal as would ordinarily have been used for the killing of a man. The implication was that the act was not the ordinary routine of sacrifice, but a deed with moral overtones, and the ritual employed exactly fitted this interpretation.[212]

The simplest account of the ceremony is in Pausanias, the guide-book writer. In his description of the Acropolis he mentions the sanctuary of Zeus Polieus, adding: 'I shall record the procedure with regard to his sacrifice, but not the reason which they tell with reference to it.' (This kind of reticence in Pausanias usually implies the presence of some religious mystery or taboo.) He continues:

> They place on the altar of Zeus Polieus barley mixed with wheat and do not protect it at all. But the ox which they have kept prepared for the sacrifice goes to the altar and touches the grain. They call one of the priests the Bull-slayer who kills the bull and throws down the pole-axe there and runs away in flight. For this is their traditional practice. Then the others, as though they did not know who had done the deed, bring the pole-axe to trial.

Later in his tour of Athens Pausanias mentions the court at the Prytaneion where inanimate objects were tried, and states that the trial of the axe used by the Bull-slayer still took place there every year. Actually as we know from a speech of Aeschines this apparently extraordinary judicial proceeding was strictly in accordance with the principles of Attic law. For he reminded the jury that 'wood and stones and iron though without voice or reason, if they fall on a person and kill, are banished beyond the frontiers'. The method usually used was to throw them in the sea. So the axe that slew the ox in the *Bouphonia* was treated as though it were guilty of shedding human blood.[213]

One may well ask why the sacrifice of an animal – such a usual feature of Greek cult – should on this occasion bear this awful significance. The traditional explanation, known to Pausanias, was that it had been early in Attic history under King Erechtheus that the first ox was offered in sacrifice and that the historic *Bouphonia* was a repetition of this event in memory of it. This idea that blood-sacrifice was not the original ritual, but that it had been developed later, was part of the regular Greek myth of a Golden Age of primitive innocence and simplicity. It had no historical justification, as the *Bouphonia* cannot really have stretched back in tradition over millennia in the past. But it was in another unrelated myth treated as the first sacrifice of a bull. It was told that to the famous contest between Athena and Poseidon for the lordship of Athens Athena appealed to Zeus to vote on her behalf and promised in return that the first victim would be offered at his altar as Polieus. How Zeus could vote on the issue which was to be decided by the people of Athens is not explained. But evidently the purpose of the myth was to explain the presence of an altar to Zeus on the Acropolis and to associate it with the first animal sacrifice. (Plate 63)

Actually, as Deubner has correctly argued, it is not likely that the worship of Zeus on the Acropolis was very ancient. Athena as a Mycenaean palace goddess was certainly his predecessor, and her only rival in the second millennium may have been Poseidon, who also was worshipped in that period. By the time of the epic the possibly conflicting claims of Zeus and Athena had been reconciled by the myth which gave Athena a very special relation to the king of the gods as having sprung direct from his forehead. It will have been by the accepting of such a relationship that Zeus, in his capacity of sharing with Athena the protection of the city was assigned an altar on the Acropolis.[214]

The curious ritual of the *Bouphonia* involves the mixture of two different motives. One is the need for the victim to indicate by some action its appropriateness for sacrifice. This occurs elsewhere in Greek ceremonies and other examples show that there was no objection to inducing the animal to give the sign by a certain degree of human stimulus. For example at Delphi the goat which was offered before consultations began was required to shake its head. Plutarch was prepared to believe that this was a sign that the spirit which inspired the Pythia was in operation, but in a simpler age it may merely have been looked for as an indication that the victim agreed to be offered. Anyway the required movement was induced by sprinkling water on the goat's head till it shook it, and the procedure was, if necessary, repeated again and again till the result was achieved.[215]

Athens was not the only place where the victim for Zeus Polieus had to indicate its appropriateness by an action. On the island of Cos in the fourth century the bull to be offered to Zeus was selected out of a successive series of animals, which were driven in threes into the marketplace where the priest in his robes with two other officials sat at a table. The regulations provided for more than twenty-seven bulls to be submitted to the test, which appears to have consisted in the animal to be chosen bowing its head, probably towards food spread on the table. One difference from Pausanias' description of the Athenian *Bouphonia* lies in the fact that he wrote as though the animal at Athens was already selected and prepared in advance. It had only to give the sign that it was ready for sacrifice by eating the grain. However, a much longer and more elaborate account of the ceremony which was given by Porphyry actually describes certain men called the Prickers (*Kentriadai*) as driving the oxen appointed for the ceremony round a bronze table with sacred cakes on it. The animal that tasted the cakes was slaughtered. This version of the ceremony would be approximately the same as that on Cos in this respect if we can trust Porphyry rather than Pausanias to describe the Athenian *Bouphonia* correctly.[216]

Again the Coan ceremony has no element of the trial of the axe. But Nilsson has pointed out that it shows considerable traces of a feeling of guilt connected with the sacrifice. It was associated with elaborate purifications and a sexual taboo and the slaughterer of the bull was not the priest, but was selected by the heralds from those present on the occasion. We see in this the same feeling towards the sacrifice which expressed itself in Athens in the flights of the Ox-slayer and the legal transfer of the guilt to his axe.

Since the nineteenth century anthropologists have discussed this aspect of the *Bouphonia* and have offered various explanations to account for this feeling of guilt. It could be explained on a theory of totemism, but there is nothing otherwise to suggest that the bull was treated as a totemic animal in Attica. Again, analogies have been sought with the practice of hunters placating the spirit of their dead prey. But this does not tally with a domestic animal as victim. Stengel proposed the explanation that the bull was a substitute for a human victim, and that the legal transfer of the guilt survived from the days of human sacrifice. But this is an arbitrary guess, and is hard to reconcile with the evidence that the flesh of the bull was eaten, unless we are to suppose that the human sacrifice was originally followed by cannibalism.

Deubner is probably right in his theory that the bull was not an ordinary animal from the herd, but was a yoke-ox. Greek and Roman literature contain many references to show that the animal which drew the plough and worked at other agricultural tasks was regarded with special affection as a companion and helper of the farmer. The *Bouphonia* fell at the time of harvest – the end of the oxen's labours – and the season called for a special offering in sacrifice in return for its fruits. To kill a yoke-ox was no ordinary act of ritual. Hence originally it had to be justified by the act of the ox itself. Its eating of the sacred grain could be regarded as an impiety which at least explained if it did not fully excuse its killing. What was the earliest form of the ritual in Athens can scarcely be conjectured. But the trial of the axe as described by Pausanias was probably worked-up in the seventh century at the time when the concept of blood-guilt won fuller acceptance in Greece and was embodied in the regulations of Dracon governing trial for murder. If we are to believe Porphyry, whose fuller account of the *Bouphonia* we have already mentioned, there was a much more elaborate transfer of the responsibility. The first to be charged were the girls who fetched the water used in sharpening the sacrificial tools. They blamed those who sharpened the tools. They blamed the man who applied the pole-axe, and he blamed the man who cut the victim's throat. Finally the sacrificial knife was accused and convicted. This account differs from that of Pausanias on the basic point that none of the human agents flee. Instead they stand their ground and pass on the responsibility from one to another until at last the charge falls on the knife, not on the pole-axe. Also, Porphyry adds one further interesting piece of ritual which does not appear in any other reference to the *Bouphonia*. After those concerned in the sacrifice had feasted on the ox, its hide was sewn up and stuffed with hay and was stood up as though alive and yoked to a plough. This restoration to life of the ox was motivated in Porphyry's narrative by a Delphic oracle. Also the story was filled out with circumstantial details about the first man to slay the ox. He had been a resident alien named Sopatros and had fled to Crete at the consciousness of his guilt. His return and the establishment of the annual ritual of the *Bouphonia* had been necessitated in the usual manner of myths by a plague which had to be relieved in accordance with the Pythia's response.[217]

The discrepancies between Porphyry and Pausanias have given rise to much debate. Though Pausanias does not name any persons in his account, which fails to give the reason for the rite, it is probable that it corresponded to a version in which the Ox-slayer was hereditarily a member of the aristocratic family of the Thaulonidai, whose ancestor Thaulon was the first to strike the ox. Though Porphyry's main narrative was about an alien called Sopatros, he also gave a briefer account in which the first ox after its guilty act in eating a sacred cake was slain by Diomos, the priest of Zeus Polieus, with the assistance of those present. The different legends would not cause much surprise; the problem is the difference in ritual which they imply. The legend of Diomos is the only one to state that the killer was the priest of Zeus. The other two versions with a special individual as the Ox-slayer are more plausible and correspond to the ritual in Cos. But more difficult to decide is the question whether Pausanias or Porphyry is more correct in his picture of the question of assigning the guilt. Either of two theories is possible. It may be argued that Pausanias gave an abbreviated version to suit his guide-book and the longer and more complicated story of Porphyry is correct; or one can argue that Porphyry has reproduced a sophisticated philosophic narrative in which the simpler ritual and legend were worked up for dramatic effect. It is true in this second alternative that the quotations from Porphyry come from a lengthy work on vegetarianism and in turn are probably derived from a work by Theophrastus, *On Piety*. While Pausanias was generally an accurate reporter of ritual and its associated legends, Theophrastus may well have felt at liberty to incorporate in his narrative features derived from more than one direction, provided they helped toward the philosophical and moral purpose of his treatise. So he might have chosen to amplify the picture of the transfer of guilt from one party to another. The one point where he sounds to be reproducing some genuine ritual not found elsewhere is the ceremony of restoring the ox and yoking it again to a plough. This has all the air of a genuine primitive device to get round the painful fact that the ox had been slaughtered. In one way, of course, it is completely inconsistent with the rest of the *Bouphonia*. For there would be no point in trying the pole-axe which struck the ox, if the animal had recovered. On this account one may wonder whether Theophrastus, if he was Porphyry's source, was borrowing a piece of ritual from some other *Bouphonia*, and attaching it arbitrarily to the Athenian festival. But though this is possible, one cannot be sure that such rational principles apply in the sphere of religious rites. Two mutually inconsistent, but satisfying, acts such as condemning the pole-axe to banishment and resurrecting the ox may both have been practised. However, it is easy to see how in the fifth century the up-to-date young Athenian must have regarded this conventionalized ritual performed by some hereditary officials on the Acropolis and at the Prytaneion as nothing but ridiculous, antiquated, mummery. On the other hand a deeply thoughtful philosopher writing a century later might see in it all some lessons to be learnt about primitive piety.

Towards the end of the same month another festival of Zeus was held which must have been in form and spirit the very antithesis of the *Dipolieia*. This was the *Diisoteria* or festival to Zeus as Saviour. It was held in the Peiraeus, and does not appear much in classical literature, but is frequently recorded in Hellenistic inscriptions. As with other more recently founded cults, it was under the management of the archon. It is reasonable to suppose that it was not older than the foundation of the Peiraeus in 492 B C. The temple with colonnades surrounding it was the chief sanctuary of the Peiraeus. Athena the Saviour was associated with Zeus in worship there. As this title of Saviour is usually applied to

Greek gods with a specific reference, may one conjecture that the original foundation may have been after the Persian wars on the recovery of the port of Athens from the hands of the enemy?[218]

The festival had the usual features of a classical celebration. There was a procession through the streets with a maiden carrying a basket and in the Hellenistic period at least the Epheboi in military training also took part. Sacrifices were offered to Zeus and Athena and also to other deities worshipped in the Peiraeus, such as Asclepius, and a couch and a table were furnished for the gods to banquet. As at the other local festival of Artemis, the Epheboi held a regatta and raced round the cape to the harbour of Munichia. The victims killed were bulls, and the fourth-century accounts show that they were sacrificed in large numbers. Another indication of the large scale of the festival is found in the story told about Demosthenes. Towards the end of his career he had been convicted of defalcation to the extent of 50 talents, and had taken refuge in exile. But after an interval he was recalled and returned in triumph. However, the Athenian state could not legally remit the 50 talents for which he was in debt. So, on the proposal of a relative of his the state paid him this amount under the nominal heading of erecting and equipping the altar of Zeus Soter. This was an annual expense which the state reimbursed to those who undertook it. Presumably Demosthenes carried out the work for much less than this sum at his own expense and transferred the 50 talents to pay his fine. It is not possible from this story to arrive at a figure for the normal annual expenditure on the altar, but it must have been a quite considerable sum or the state would not have needed to make this arrangement to meet it. We would probably be justified in picturing the *Diisoteria* as the biggest annual occasion in the Peiraeus.[219]

At the end of the month on the last day of the year there was a sacrifice to Zeus the Saviour. It was performed in Athens, probably, as Deubner suggests, at the statue of Zeus in the Agora in front of the colonnade named after him. The city magistrates and the council took part, led by the King Archon. The purpose of the ceremony was to act as an introductory service to the new year, when a fresh set of magistrates and a fresh council took office. But also one may assume that it was both a thanksgiving for the preservation of the state through the year that was past as well as a supplication for the protection of the gods in the year about to begin. As in the Peiraeus, Zeus the Saviour had associated with him Athena the Saviour. The earliest reference to the ceremony occurs in a speech of Lysias dated to 382 BC. There the

orator, as suits his pleading, refers to it as an ancestral sacrifice. But it
need not have been established before the founding of the Cleisthenic
council at the end of the sixth century or perhaps even later. It was the
only Athenian festival to mark the end of the old year and the beginning
of the new, and there is nothing to suggest that it was something in
which the citizens generally took part. Lysias refers to the law-courts as
closed for the day, but this was less as a public holiday than because all
the presiding magistrates would be otherwise engaged by the sacrifice
to Zeus. In fact, as we have already noticed, the Greeks generally did
not take much notice of the passing of the year as a personal event. It
naturally concerned the officials who were due to leave office or take
up office, but to the rest the change of the month was as significant.[220]

Part Two

OTHER FESTIVALS, UNPLACED IN
THE CALENDAR OR LOCAL

We have surveyed the calendar of the Athenian festivals in so far as they can be placed on approximate dates throughout the year. There remain, however, a number of festivals, some evidently of considerable popularity, whose place in the calendar remains quite uncertain. Three of these were all notable by containing as their most important feature a torch-race. We have already seen how the sacrificial fire at the *Panathenaia* was lit by a torch brought by a runner, and the feast of Bendis was remarkable for a relay race of torch-bearers on horseback. But neither of these will have been the prototype of what was apparently an Athenian institution. Torch-races were also run at the festivals of Prometheus (*Prometheia*), of Hephaestus (*Hephaisteia*) and of Pan. The first two deities were closely associated with fire and this was evidently the reason why this particular form of contest should be held in their honour. Of them Prometheus is the more special to Athens. He appeared constantly in Greek mythology as the god who stole fire from heaven and brought it to men, but evidence for his worship outside Athens is lacking. Hence it is natural to suppose that his altar in the precinct of Academus outside Athens was the original centre of the Athenian institution of the torch-race. To ancient scholars his worship there was reckoned to be older than that of Hephaestus who also had an altar in the same precinct. We have already described how at the *Panathenaia* a race was run from the same place to the Acropolis in order to light the sacrificial fire. No doubt the races in the *Prometheia* and the *Hephaisteia* had the same general starting point, but what course they traversed is quite unrecorded. Again we are not told whether they were like it in being races of single runners or relay races. It is more likely that one of them at least was run by a team of runners, for in the fifth century both Aeschylus and Herodotus were evidently acquainted with this style of contest and the careful way in which Pausanias describes how the Panathenaic race was run by individuals points to his needing to distinguish it from other and more familiar examples.[1] (Plate 64)

The *Prometheia* at all events is likely to be a primitive festival in origin, and since Hephaestus, though perhaps introduced at some early period from Asia, was long associated with Athena, the *Hephaisteia* in some form was probably of considerable antiquity. An inscription is extant dated to 421/20 B C, which has sometimes been interpreted as ordering the institution of the festival, but it is more plausibly explained as establishing a major celebration every fourth year. The document is very fragmentary, but it can be seen to contain provisions for the torch-race to be run on the same lines as those used by the organizers of the *Prometheia*. Also it provided for another instance of the extraordinary practice of 'lifting' the bulls, which we have already come across at the *Herakleia* and the *Proerosia*. Two hundred Athenians were to be chosen from the Epheboi (the youths beginning military service). They were presumably arranged in teams each assigned in turn to one bull. But unfortunately the inscription does not state how many victims there were. The regulations, however, provided for three bulls to be assigned to the resident aliens (Metoikoi) and the flesh distributed to them raw. Evidently, as Mommsen remarks, the citizens would receive a much larger number. So one might, for example, conjecture a minimum of ten bullocks with teams of twenty to cope with each. Evidently it was designed as a large and popular celebration and, as Hephaestus was a god of the fire used in handicrafts, it is significant that the non-citizens were a prominent fraction of his worshippers.[2]

The torch-race in honour of Pan is not often mentioned in literature, but its origin is recorded in Herodotus. Philippides, the long-distance runner, was carrying to Sparta the news of the Persian landing at Marathon. While he was crossing Mount Parthenion in the Peloponnese he heard Pan calling him by name. The god bade him give a message to the Athenians that they took no heed of him although he had good will to them and had often in the past been of service to them and would be again in the future. Philippides duly reported this divine warning and the Athenians believed him; so when the war was over they made a sanctuary for Pan in a cave under the Acropolis and appeased him with annual sacrifices and a torch-race.

Herodotus' story can be taken as founded on contemporary sources. Up till 490 B C Pan had been an Arcadian god of goatherds worshiped in the mountainous regions. Philippides' report of his experience may be taken as quite sincere. There are enough examples known from other times which show that men under severe physical stress, such as Philippides underwent, have the experience or hallucination of supernatural companions or supporters. The Athenians acted strictly in accordance with Greek religious practice in establishing a shrine and an annual festival. What date was chosen is not recorded. The reasonable one would seem to be the anniversary of the epiphany of the god, which would be the 9th of the lunar month, probably Boedromion. To honour Pan with a race was a bright idea derived from his interest in Philippides. That it took the form of a torch-race was probably due to the general liking of the Athenians for this kind of contest. What was the course is not recorded, but one would surmise that it ended at the altar of Pan under the Acropolis cliff.[3]

Other deities of Peloponnesian origin who were worshipped in Athens were the Dioscuri, Castor and Polydeuces. They had a sanctuary in the city and a festival. Perhaps they may have had some native cult with which they were combined, For the Athenians addressed them with the title Anakes which was not used elsewhere, meaning probably 'kings'. One late source records that the sacrifice was what was known as a *trittya* – a triple offering – meaning that three different species of victim were offered on the one occasion. But neither the date, nor any further details of the festival are known. The Athenian myths were not particularly favourable to the Dioscuri. It was told that Theseus had carried off the youthful Helen before her marriage to Menelaus and had hidden her at Aphidnai, but that her brothers came on an expedition and rescued her. The late commentator, who mentioned the triple sacrifice, also tried to explain the title Anakes as meaning prudent, and being applied to the Dioscuri because of their moderate behaviour when invading Attica. Clearly the myth and the Athenian cult had no original connection. A fragmentary inscription from the late fifth century on the subject of the Anakia by its references to nautical subjects indicates that by that date at least the function of the Dioscuri may have been particularly as twin stars to protect seafarers. As Nilsson points out, they were less the object of worship by the community than by individuals needing their help.[4]

Besides festivals belonging to deities not otherwise worshipped, some of the most familiar gods and goddesses had occasions which are virtually only known by name. For instance there is a lexicographical reference to the *Epikleidia* as a feast of Demeter at Athens. The name might have some philological connection with the word for 'key' and keys were traditionally associated with the Mysteries. But no more can be said about it.[5]

Again, the same lexicon records the *Galaxia*: 'a feast at Athens, held in honour of the mother of the Gods, on which they boil the *galaxia*: it is a porridge made from barley cooked in milk.' Deubner has conjectured that it took place in the month of Elaphebolion since in Delos

a month with the name Galaxion fell at that point in the calendar. This
is possible, but such synchronisms cannot be regarded as anything more
than supposition.

Another virtually unknown festival is the *Theoinia*. As we have seen,
the group of women known as the Gerarai at the *Anthesteria* were required to swear in their initiatory oath that they would celebrate 'the
Theoinia and the *Iobaccheia* in the ancestral manner and at the appropriate times'. The *Iobaccheia*, though it must have existed in classical
times, is not known till the second century A D when a religious guild
calling themselves the *Iobacchoi* occupied the site which Dörpfeld
identified as the former temple of Dionysus in the Marshes and held a
series of religious rites there which are recorded in a lengthy and detailed inscription.[7] What relation they bore to the classical festival of
the *Iobaccheia* is quite uncertain, and their rites and ceremonies are an
example of the working of a religious guild of late Roman times, but
cast no direct light on the subject of the present investigation. The
Theoinia seems only to have been known to ancient commentators
because it was involved in a legal dispute in the fourth century B C
between two related clans at Eleusis (the Krokonidai and the Koironidai).
So it was probably in origin a festival at Eleusis managed by the local
families and will have been taken over to some extent by the Athenian
state together with the other major cults of Eleusis. At this point the
Basileus and his wife together with the Gerarai will have taken a part
in the ceremonies. But when they were held is not recorded. There is
only one reference surviving to a *Theoinion*, which suggests that somewhere the cult had a special sanctuary of its own. For the rest, Aeschylus
addressed Dionysus in a lost play as 'Father Theoinos (God of wine),
leader of the team of maenads', which suggests that women devotees
may have been prominent in the cult.[8]

As we saw much earlier, in discussing the *Synoikia*, the few fragments
that have survived of the code of religious regulations drawn up by
Nicomachus only serve to show how incomplete is the picture of
Athenian festivals which can be reconstructed from our literary sources.
But even if we were able to recover all the information needed about
the state festivals of Athens it is worthwhile to remind ourselves that
this would not describe fully the religious practice of Attica. It would
be as though we were to try to reconstruct the religious life of a modern
country by using only the list of services held in the metropolitan
cathedral. To many of the inhabitants what goes on in St Paul's or
Westminster Abbey is normally of little significance compared with

the local festivals of his parish church. In Greece with its notable lack of a centralized religious organization, though the festivals of the *polis* concerned all the citizens of the state, they had also their local rites and deities. This was specially true in Attica with a quite extensive territory which had once been split up into several independent districts. The *demes* as organized by Cleisthenes in the last years of the sixth century were separate local communities, not merely for politics, but also for religion, and their religious traditions evidently reach back in places to periods of archaic independence. (Plate 66)

Our literary sources are basically oriented toward Athens itself, and so give us only very occasional references to the activities of the *demes* whether political, social or religious. The rural *Dionysia*, which we have already discussed, offer a partial exception. But inscriptions have yielded at times sudden lumps of detailed information from which a more general picture can be dimly guessed. The *demes* were run as little democracies on the model of Athens itself, and accordingly they published religious regulations and calendars of sacrifices as required for their local communities. From these we can see that in the fifth and fourth centuries there was a thriving and varied pattern of local festivals observed by each of the more important communities at least. None of these records is entirely comprehensive, but they give an indication of the wealth of detail needed to complete our account of Athenian festivals.[9]

For instance some time in the 1940s there was accidentally discovered at the village of Spata, some 20 kilometres (12½ miles) east of Athens a magnificent marble *stele*. It was inscribed in five columns of over sixty lines each with a list of sacrifices spread roughly over the year. This document was headed in large letters with the rather mysterious title the *Greater Demarchia*. The stele itself is practically complete but its title evidently implies the existence of some other list, presumably described as the *Lesser Demarchia*. What the word '*Demarchia*' means in this context is somewhat obscure but the original editor, Georges Daux, was right in suggesting that the heading should be translated 'Principal list of the sacrifices to be performed under the authority of the *demarchos*' (i.e. the annually elected president of the *deme*) and that there must also have been some form of complementary list.[10] (Plate 65)

The catalogue is impressively complicated and comprehensive. If we count the gods and goddesses, heroes and heroines, treating each one with a different epithet as separate, there are no less than thirty-nine.

Fifty-seven sacrifices are listed, but they are assigned to only twenty-five days in the year with sometimes as many as four sacrifices, and once even six, on one day. The distribution of the festivals over the months is also very uneven. The two months with the largest number, Gamelion with twelve, and Metageitnion with nine, are curiously months which were not furnished with much festivity in the Athenian state calendar. But they agree in treating the winter month of Maimakterion as a dead season. In fact the local record gives no festival or sacrifice for that month.

The *deme* responsible for erecting this calendar of sacrifices was evidently Erchia, in the inland plain east of Athens. This is clear from the frequent recurrence of the local place-name in defining where the sacrifice was to be offered. Fifty of them took place within the territory of the *deme*. Sometimes it was at a sanctuary named after the deity – the precinct of Hera or of Apollo Delphinios or Apollo Pythios; at other times the general locality was named: 'on the Acropolis' or 'on the Agora'. For Erchia like a miniature Athens had its one strong point on a hill and its own market-place. Sometimes place-names are given: 'at Pagos' ('the Hill'), 'at Petra' ('the Rock'), 'at Schoinos' ('the reeds'?), even 'at the property of the Sotidai'. Used on one occasion is the curious expression 'In Erchia in the direction of the Paianians', who were a large neighbouring *deme*. It appears as if the sacrifice was made at some spot near the common boundary of the two communities. In one instance a sacrifice was offered in Attica outside the *deme* of Erchia. This was to Zeus on the Height (Epakrios) on Mount Hymettus which was the nearest high place. The only other sites for sacrifices outside the *deme* were at Athens, and the occasions suggest some interesting conclusions. One was in Anthesterion, at the *Diasia* when the men of Erchia were to offer a ram to Zeus Meilichios at his sanctuary in Agrai on the banks of the Ilissos. As we have seen, it was the greatest feast of Zeus in Attica and had a special character as an occasion for offerings of atonement to appease the anger of the god. It is appropriate in this connection that the regulations specify that there is to be no drinking till after the entrails are burnt. One may notice that, though the *Diasia* was a penitential feast, it appears that men of Erchia did not have to make a whole burnt-offering of their ram. Only its entrails were burnt, but until this ritual of appeasing Zeus was completed, they might not indulge in wine. However, as we have seen, the *Diasia* was not without its festive side also and one may picture them as ending the day with roast mutton washed down with drink.

The *Diasia* is the only Athenian festival named on the calendar of
Erchia. All the other sacrifices which they offered in Athens took place
on one single day and did not coincide with any known religious
occasion. It was on the 12th of Metageitnion in high summer that the
demesmen must have made a special expedition to Athens with the
appropriate animals to be offered. In what order the proceedings took
place we do not know, but four entries for the one date appear in the
regulations. A ram was offered in the city to Apollo Lykeios. The exact
place where this sacrifice was made is not recorded; the gymnasium
which was to become famous in the late fourth century as the school
of Aristotle's teaching had a shrine dedicated to Apollo under this title.
But it is possible that the sacrifice could have been given at other
Apolline shrines. The other offerings raise less problems. A ewe was
to be sacrificed to Demeter at the Eleusinion on the way up to the
Acropolis. On the Acropolis itself a ram was offered to Zeus the City
God (Polieus) and a ewe to Athena the City Goddess (Polias). The
practice of having more than one sacrifice on the same day at different
places was not unique to this entry in the calendar. For instance on the
21st of Hecatombaion at Erchia two sacrifices were to be made at
the property of the Sotidai and two on the *deme's* acropolis. It is
not indicated whether either in the sacrifices at Erchia or at Athens the
same officials and members of the *deme* took part in all the ceremonies on the same day. One other detail may be mentioned. After
recording the rams to be sacrificed to Apollo Lykeios and Zeus Polieus,
the entry occurs 'no carrying away' (*ou phora*). This must refer to the
sacrificial meal, and must mean that none of it was to be removed from
the precinct. This did not require the sacrifice to be a whole burnt-
offering: a term which is explicitly used elsewhere in the calendar. It
need only mean that the animal must be roasted and consumed on the
spot or else left behind as a perquisite to the priest.

The inscription is in such a form as to give no indication of what
purpose the sacrifices served. In the case of those in Athens reasons may
be conjectured. The *Diasia* was a religious occasion of such general
importance and gravity that the community of Erchia could feel that
it must play an official part in the service of atonement. The other
group of sacrifices in Metageitnion give the impression that they were
designed to provide once a year a composite service of homage to the
great gods of Athens. On the Acropolis both the city's goddess and Zeus,
her father and often her associate in worship, each received a sacrifice.
Also the Demeter of Eleusis, who since the sixth century held such an

important position in the religion of Attica, was honoured in her convenient sanctuary in Athens, and finally Apollo to all Ionians had a claim for recognition. Zeus, Athena and Apollo were also worshipped at Erchia itself, though Apollo only under various other titles. Demeter, however, is not otherwise mentioned in the *Greater Demarchia*, and one might therefore be correct in supposing that she was not worshipped in Erchia. Instead, on no less than six occasions there is a sacrifice to Kourotrophos ('The Nurturer of the Young') who is often identified with the Earth Goddess or Demeter. But, as in Athens where Kourotrophos received sacrifices, the men of Erchia only made offerings to her as a preliminary before sacrificing to other divinities such as Artemis or Apollo. If the *Greater Demarchia* could be regarded as a comprehensive list of the *deme*'s worship, which it is probably not safe to maintain, then the evidence would show that Demeter was not worshipped locally and this is possibly true.[11]

But, even apart from the question of the comprehensiveness of our evidence, a certain relation between the city calendar and the local calendar seems clear. The dates of the festivals in Erchia never clash with the major celebrations in Athens. No citizen of the *deme* need have been prevented from attending the *Panathenaia*, the Mysteries or the *City Dionysia* because of a local rite on the same day. Sometimes this avoidance of a clash looks as if it was contrived. For instance, if we take it that the *City Dionysia* ran from the 8th to the 13th of Elaphebolion inclusive, the one sacrifice to Dionysus recorded in the *Greater Demarchia* fell on the 16th, allowing the member of the *deme* two clear days in which to return to Erchia and get ready for the local festival. The only clashes that can be identified look as if they can be explained. On the 4th of Munichion the *deme* offered a sacrifice to the Herakleidai. This date coincided with the festival of Eros at Athens known only from the mid-fifth-century inscription below the Acropolis. It was evidently a small local rite, perhaps first instituted at the time the inscription was set up. The *deme* was unlikely to have wanted to participate in it. Again on the 19th of Thargelion the *deme* offered a ram to a local hero Menedeios. This fell on the same date as the *Bendidia*. But as we have seen, the festival in the Peiraeus was only introduced in 429 BC. No doubt the local cult in Erchia long antedated this innovation and would not be altered to suit with it. The only coincidence which is without any obvious explanation is a curious offering to Epops which occured on the 5th of Boedromion. As we have seen, this date at Athens was assigned to the *Genesia*, the somewhat obscure festival in honour of the dead. There seems to be no obvious connection between these two. Epops, who is not elsewhere known as a divinity, is by derivation the bird known as the hoopoe. Presumably he was a local hero and his ritual was mournful – a holocaust offering of a pig at which wine was forbidden. So it would not be out of keeping with the spirit of the Athenian festival. But we do not really know how far the *Genesia* involved a central ceremony in Athens or was held at local burial-places. So it is possible that no inconvenience would be caused by the coincidence of the ceremonies.[12]

As for the local worship in Erchia, if we take the *Greater Demarchia* as comprising the main services, the typical deities who were worshipped in Athens appear here also. The exception, as we have seen, is Demeter. Otherwise, the *deme* had an acropolis on which Athena, goddess of the city, and Zeus, god of the city, were worshipped and were associated with Kourotrophos, Aglauros, Erse and Poseidon. This reproduced exactly the pattern of worship on the Acropolis at Athens and must have been modelled on it. The great occasion was the 3rd of Skirophorion when the offerings were a ewe described as 'in place of a cow' for Athena, a ram each for Zeus and Poseidon and probably a ewe for Aglauros and Erse and a pig for Kourotrophos. This seems to have been what one could describe as the patronal festival of the *deme*. Another major festival at the temple of Hera on the 27th of Gamelion honoured the goddess together with Zeus the Accomplisher (Teleios), Kourotrophos and Poseidon. As was appropriate to the Month of Marriage this was a festival in honour of wedlock and the family. The presence of Poseidon seems to be an unexplained intrusion, as though he had come in as a partner of Zeus. Zeus also had a major festival of his own on the 16th of Poseideon when he received two sacrifices, one as the god of boundaries (Horios). Presumably it was for the protection of the community from intrusion by its neighbours, a thought always present in Greek minds. Also on the 25th of Metageitnion he had a sacrifice under the obscure and unusual title of *Epopetes*. Hera besides her festival with him had a sacrifice alone on the 20th of the same month under a title which seems to mean 'Goddess of Charm' (Thelchinia). So in Erchia she may have included in her sphere the functions of the classical Aphrodite who was not worshipped in the *deme*. Apollo was popular: he had one major festival in his favourite month, Thargelion, on the 4th, so that it did not clash with the *Thargelia* in Athens on the 6th and 7th. He had one sacrifice in his Pythian precinct together with his mother Leto and another 'on the Hill' together with Zeus. It is impossible to tell whether there is some religious significance in the fact that on the same day also there was a sacrifice to Hermes in the market-place, appropriate to the god of trade, and to Castor and Polydeuces under the title of Anakes in an unspecified place. Apollo also had a major festival in Gamelion on two successive days – his traditional 7th and the 8th. He was worshipped under four different titles in at least two separate places of sacrifice and was associated on one day with Kouro-trophos, on the other with the Nymphs. These partners in worship and the choice of the month of Marriage perhaps imply that he was being approached as the god of human offspring. The only other major deity worshipped in Erchia was Artemis who had two festivals, like her brother; one on the 21st of Hecatombaion in association with Kouro-trophos, and one on the 16th of Metageitnion again in association with Kourotrophos but under the title of Hecate.

Besides the major deities, minor gods and heroes and heroines played numerically quite a prominent part in the local ritual. The god of craftsmen, Hephaestus, who was important in Athens does not appear in the *Greater Demarchia*, but instead we find various spirits of the countryside and of localities. As we have seen, the Nymphs were wor-shipped with Apollo: they also had a festival on the 27th of Boedromion in association with the Earth Goddess, Hermes, Acheloös (as the primary river god) and a mysterious Virgin (*Alochos*). Another nameless group of female divinities were the Heroines who were worshipped on the 14th of Pyanepsion. Male heroes also appear in vague plurals – the Herakleidai on the 4th of Munichion and the Tritopatores, who were worshipped also elsewhere in Attica, on the 21st of the same month. But also there are single unknown heroes. Two have appropriate names – 'He of the White Shield' (Leukaspis) and 'He who resists the Foe' (Menedeios). The curious, otherwise unknown, cult of Epops, the hoopoe, has already been mentioned.

This is as far as the *Greater Demarchia* can take us in positive evidence. As Georges Daux has warned us in his original publication, there may have been a lesser list of sacrifices obligatory on the demarch and also possibly further ceremonies which were the responsibility of other officials or associations. The absence of Demeter has been noted. Also there is no regulation for a rural *Dionysia* at the usual date. But perhaps some of these cults may have been left to private landowners or families of the locality. But in spite of the defects of our evidence we get a general picture of religious festivals basically similar to those of Athens performed locally in such a pattern as not to clash with the great City festivals. At the same time the community had its local character and its special local cults.

Other inscriptions from other *demes* give the same picture. For instance the men of the *deme* Plotheia about 400 BC regulated by decree the money derived from investment which was to be spent on festivals. The investment typically was in rents of lands and was to be used on 'the sacred rites of the community at Plotheia and the sacred rites at Athens on behalf of the community of the people of Plotheia and on the festivals once every four years'. The festivals listed were in honour of Heracles, Aphrodite, the Anakes, and Apollo, and also the *Pandia* which is the only festival in Athens that can be identified from the catalogue.[13]

Again, Marathon and three neighbouring demes formed a league known as the Tetrapolis ('The Four Towns'). Parts of a calendar of their festivals have been preserved in a fragmentary form.[14] They listed the feasts of each of the four communities in turn under the officials responsible, giving annual ceremonies and then those occurring biennially in their successive years. Internally the years are each divided into four quarters as well as into months. The document set up in the first half of the fourth century may have been influenced by the great inscription of the religious code lately set up in Athens. Not enough of any one year is preserved to get the annual pattern which we can to some extent detect for Erchia. But the relation to the city calendar shows itself in one interesting type of entry. Twice it is recorded that sacrifices are to be made before important state festivals. In Boedromion 'before the Mysteries' the demarch of Marathon was to offer to a deity whose name is lost a bull costing 80 drachmas and a sheep costing 12: also to Kourotrophos another victim missing from the record. Again in Skirophorion 'before the *Skira*' the demarch was to make offerings to various minor deities: 'To Hythenion, the seasonal offering' (presumably ripe corn) and 'a sheep, twelve drachmas; to Kourotrophos a pig, three drachmas; to the Tritopatreis, a sheep; to the Untiring Heroes (Akamantes) a sheep, twelve drachmas.' The priests were allowed a fee of two drachmas on each of the last three sacrifices. So there is no sign that the men of the Tetrapolis as a community took part in the Mysteries or the *Skira*. Instead they recognized their importance by holding a preliminary service of their own, and then were presumably free to join as individuals in the festivals in Athens which followed. Only one clash in the calendar seems to occur. The 10th of Elaphebolion should have been one of the days of the *City Dionysia*. But on it the demarch offered a black he-goat to the 'earth goddess at the oracle-centre'. This local divinity appears again earlier in the inscription. She can have had no association with Dionysus. But also the scale of the offering and the character of the goddess suggests some primitive local ceremony probably dating back long before the establishment of the City festival. The traditional rite was evidently maintained, even if it may have prevented a few Marathonian officials from seeing the tragedies on that day once a year.

These details of the local rites of Attica serve to expand our view of the festivals, but what they do not tell us was how important these celebrations were to the local inhabitants. For the purpose of official regulations all festivals are of equal importance. At most the evidence for a number of more expensive victims may suggest a greater significance in the ceremony. But even then how far it is an index of popular interest in the small scale of local ritual is difficult to tell. All we can notice is that in some instances local officials went to great trouble to organize the calendar of their feasts and publish it on marble with careful lay-out and script. The existence of some pious individuals responsible for all this patient work cannot be doubted, and in so far as their efforts involved public expenditure, they must have received the backing of their communities.

CONCLUSION

The festivals of the Athenians, which we have surveyed exhibit an extraordinary variety of activity associated with different religious cults. At the one extreme a ceremony such as the descent of the Arrephoroi to the sanctuary of Aphrodite was secret and magical and confined in its operation to the minimum number of specially chosen participants. At the other extreme the Panathenaic or Dionysiac processions could involve almost all the residents in Athens as performers or spectators in an open-air public act of worship. Again, to the modern world the wine-drinking contest of the *Anthesteria* may seem to contain little or no spiritual content. But the Eleusinian Mysteries, whatever their innermost secret, do suggest a rite capable of moving the souls of those taking part.

This diversity of character is partly due to the different sources from which the ceremonies came. The Arrephoroi were probably derived from the little girls of the royal family in the Mycenaean period, performing the private ritual of their palace goddess. Because of the magical and secret character of these ceremonies, even when taken over by the Athenian state, they have remained fossilized throughout the centuries. The Panathenaic procession, in contrast, had always been an open and popular ceremony. To bring the goddess a new dress annually had probably been begun in archaic times when Athena had developed from a palace goddess into the chief divinity of the *polis*. But the procession and its surrounding festival had first been expanded in the sixth century by the aristocrats and the tyrants, and then in the fifth century by the democratic leaders, so as to make it a fuller and fuller expression of the spirit of the community. The *Anthesteria* represented the taking over by the community of what had been originally the vine-grower's inauguration of his new wine, but, as was typical of some Athenian festivals, it had become a complex of different elements: the opening of the jars and tasting of their contents, the arrival of the god Dionysus and his acceptance into the community. But because of the proximity to the festival of All Souls the celebration became contaminated with its influence and had taken on a curiously distorted character. Again, the Mysteries had started from the private rites of another local Mycenaean palace at Eleusis. But the usual enough association of fertility cults with secret rites had there acquired a remarkable deepening of meaning. The life of the hereafter, which otherwise played little part in Attic religion, had become associated with the corn goddess and her return to the upper world. Carefully shielded by a hereditary priesthood, these solemn ceremonies were developed and expanded so as to be incorporated in the Attic state and ultimately to take on a completely Panhellenic and even fully Greco-Roman comprehensiveness.

Festivals so diverse in origin, so different in development and so individual in character cannot be viewed from one standpoint or summed up in one formula. Polytheism accepted and approved of this extraordinary variety of religious expression without being conscious of an inconsistency between the different rites as approaches to the divine. Theological speculators would have maintained that the gods themselves were very diverse in character and that man did not really know them or understand their nature. So conservatism preserved fossilized practices from the past on the principle that it was safer to continue the customs of one's ancestors rather than to break with them. But also since the Greek's conservatism in religion was based more on fear than on faiths or creeds, it did not present any complete obstacle to the introduction of new cults or the enhancement of those already accepted.

If we try to find common elements of classification in the Athenian festivals, one feature can be generally traced in many of them. It concerns what can be called the patronal festivals of their particular deities. As we have seen, temples and precincts were not necessarily open daily for private worship. Some, indeed, were only open once a year. At any rate, even if available on other occasions, it was usual for a divinity to have one day in the year specially set aside in his or her honour. The 28th of Hecatombaion was such a date for Athena the City Goddess (Polias). Legend by making it her birthday justified the choice of this day for her festival, and the annual provision of a new robe gave a convenient central motive for the celebration. Round this date then accumulated such amplifications as the Panathenaic games, the torch-race and the musical contests. Similarly the *Anthesteria* was basically the patronal festival of Dionysus in the Marshes, which at the same time celebrated the god's arrival by sea, his marriage into the Athenian state, and the opening of the new season's wine-casks. Even the Great Mysteries of Demeter could from one aspect be regarded as the patronal festival of the goddess of Eleusis, celebrating her arrival there when wandering in search of her daughter. Out of some forty-five festivals which we have discussed, more than half, some twenty-five, could be classed as in origin patronal. This implies the existence of some twenty-five different precincts dedicated to divinities and recognized by the Athenian state as deserving a place in the calendar. Actually there were no doubt quite a number more of shrines where public sacrifices were made on at least one day in the year, and the local communities added vastly to the list with their smaller celebrations.

Athena was worshipped in her complex of sites on the Acropolis and in the shrine of Athena Skiras near Phaleron. Dionysus had patronal festivals connected with his shrine in the Marshes, his shrine at the Lenaion and his temple beside the Theatre. Zeus had special cults on the Acropolis as City God, outside the walls as the god of appeasement and in the Peiraeus as a local form of Saviour god. Artemis was worshipped separately as the huntress on the banks of the Ilissos, on the hill of Munichia and at Brauron or in its dependent shrine on the Acropolis. Her local cults are clearly defined, each with its patronal festival. Curiously her brother Apollo is much more vague and unlocalized in his worship. He had a shrine in the Agora as Ancestral God (Patroös) and one on the banks of the Ilissos as 'Pythios' and another near it as 'Delphinios' (Dolphin God?). Also he was worshipped at the gymnasium called 'Lykeion' after his title 'Lykeios'. But of these four only the Delphinion was clearly associated with a particular festival – the procession of maidens on the 6th of Munichion. Instead, as we have seen, the Athenian calendar contains three Apolline festivals, which gave their names to months, but were actually of little prominence in the religious year and without any specific connections with individual shrines. Such are the *Hecatombaia*, the *Metageitnia* and the *Boedromia*. In contrast the *Pyanepsia* and the *Thargelia* were prominent feast days of Apollo with important ceremonies, but even they are not closely linked to particular temples. The explanation is probably to be found in the fact that all these five festivals are known elsewhere in Greece, particularly in Ionia. They were evidently not local developments in Attica, but were part of the general agglomeration of cult practices which came to Athens when Apollo was first accepted there, probably early in the geometric period. The different Apolline shrines may point, as with Dionysus, to the introduction of the god from different directions. But if so, there is no sign that particular festivals came in exclusively with one form of the god only. His cult seems to have been fully evolved, presumably in Ionia, before it ever entered Attica.

Here it is interesting perhaps to compare and contrast the situation

in the two cults introduced in the fifth century, of which we have therefore approximately contemporary evidence. Bendis was brought from
Thrace to the Peiraeus, and had one patronal festival on the 19th of
Thargelion, in which worshippers from the Peiraeus and Athens combined. Asclepius, who was also introduced about the same time from
near-by Epidaurus secured the establishment of two festivals in his
honour. The *Asklepieia* on the 8th of Elaphebolion was his patronal
festival, probably on the date when his sanctuary in Athens was consecrated. But he also was worshipped at the *Epidauria* on the 18th of
Boedromion, which was the anniversary of his arrival in Attica. It
would be rash to assert that this double celebration in the year proved
that Asclepius was twice as important as Bendis. But it does appear that
through his recognition by the Eleusinian priesthood and his acceptance
by prominent Athenians of his day he may have won higher regard
than the Thracian goddess.

If we reckon simply by numbers of festivals, Athena was not, oddly
enough, conspicuous by the frequency of her holy days. We might
have expected that as the city's goddess, her place in the calendar would
be much larger than that of other deities, but actually this is not so.
The *Panathenaia* was her patronal festival and also the *Kallynteria* and
the *Plynteria* were concerned directly with her. But these festivals of
cleaning and washing were essentially practical procedures of cult
routine, which never developed into great popular celebrations. Presumably the other temples and statues in Athens had to receive a
periodic spring-clean. But it was only because of the fact that Athena
was the City Goddess that the occasions when she was dealt with
acquired such public recognition. The secret ceremony of the Arrephoroi was linked in some mysterious way with Aphrodite and was
not exclusive to Athena. Also in the somewhat mysterious *Skira* the
fact that her priestess went in procession accompanied by the priest of
Poseidon showed that in that ceremony Athena the City Goddess was
not the only deity concerned. In addition she was associated with other
deities such as Hephaestus in the *Chalkeia* and Zeus the Saviour in the
Diisoteria, but in these rites she was worshipped under other titles than
that of City Goddess.

Dionysus with the extended ritual of the *Anthesteria* and the *City
Dionysia*, or Demeter with the Greater and Lesser Mysteries and the
Thesmophoria and *Proerosia*, occupied at least as much space in the
calendar as Athena or even more. This was partly because they were the
primary deities of the farmer. Though Athens in the fifth and fourth

centuries developed gradually away from the country to the city as the centre of religious as well as of economic life, the calendar was still dominated by the importance of the rites which promoted fertility or acknowledged the gifts of the harvest. Athena, when she was the Mycenaean goddess of the palace on the Acropolis, had concerned herself with all the activities of the kings, and, as the palace records of Knossos and Pylos demonstrate, this will have included extensive receipts of agriculture and animal husbandry. It will have been from this period that the Arrephoroi linking her with Aphrodite in a mysterious fertility cult originated. By the late archaic period she was more and more specialized as a goddess of war, leaving corn to Demeter and wine to Dionysus. In a world in which peace was an infrequent and exceptional condition, Athena with her helmet and breast-plate, spear and shield need not suggest militaristic aggression so much as the guidance and protection of the state. With the development of the Athenian empire in the fifth century the warlike Athena embodied a particularly appropriate form of presiding deity for the head of the Hellenic alliance. Also her aspect as the goddess of handicrafts concerned an increasing branch of her own citizens' activity. But this possible increase and specialization in her importance did not manifest itself in the creation of further festivals in her honour. It showed itself most in the enhanced splendour and elaboration of her patronal festival of the *Panathenaia*.

The agricultural festivals might have been expected to decline in proportion to the increase in other branches of cult activity. But it cannot be said that this shows itself generally as a tendency. The *Kronia*, if it was originally the farmer's 'harvest supper', fell away in importance. The attempt to revive the *Proerosia* after the Peace of Nicias can from one angle be taken as an indication that it was in need of restoration. But this is sufficiently explained by the immediate effects of the Peloponnesian War. The foreign gifts of first-fruits to Eleusis must have been seriously interfered with by hostilities, and the Attic farmer had found it often impossible to harvest his own crops. Hence a revival following on the Peace was very appropriate, and the fact that it was undertaken on such an extensive scale suggests that the priestly authorities still thought that the appeal of Demeter's worship was strong in the Greek world. How effective the response was cannot be proved, and the fresh outbreak of hostilities and the occupation of Decelea by the Spartans must have largely frustrated the attempt.

The other festivals that were agricultural in origin may have continued in popularity for other reasons. For instance those who took part in the drinking contest of the *Anthesteria* need not all or even most of them have been actual producers of wine. Again an enthusiastic number of the audience at the tragedies, while well aware that the festival was in honour of Dionysus, need not have felt much relation between the solemn poetry of Sophocles and the state of the season's grape harvest. Particularly one may surmise that the great female agricultural festivals – the *Skira*, the *Stenia* and especially the *Thesmophoria* – were attractive not only because they procured fertility in the fields, but also because they gave the women of Athens a rare opportunity to assert their independence and escape from the restrictions of the household. It is difficult to tell how far the fifth-century Athenian wife, brought up in a social tradition which to us may seem very oppressive and calculated to produce claustrophobia, was really conscious of this situation and felt the urge to escape from her shackles. But in their different ways Euripides and Aristophanes, though making use of the position of women for their own dramatic and comic purposes, suggest that the women of Athens felt some degree of corporate sentiment and were conscious of their position as a subordinate element in the community. The female agricultural festivals provided a rare outlet and were probably valued accordingly.

Again, another factor that may have worked for the maintenance of certain festivals may have been their associations with particular families or clans. For instance, the *Oschophoria* seems to have been linked particularly with the Salaminians, and the youths who took the leading part in the ceremonial were chosen from the aristocracy of the clan. Other traditional rites, such as the *Synoikia*, seem to be organized on the basis of the old Ionic tribes and must have been celebrated primarily by members of the older Attic families, but what they lacked in popular appeal may have been counterbalanced by the devotion of certain traditional members.

In one way some of the festivals had a popular appeal because the sacrifices offered on the occasion were not wholly consumed as a burnt-offering, but were divided out among the participants, who in some instances were the people as a whole. The most conspicuous example was the *Panathenaia*. We have discussed the regulations governing the distribution at the lesser, annual, festival, and they illustrate *a fortiori* what must have taken place at the great quadrennial celebration. Again it has been calculated that two hundred and forty bulls were sacrificed on a single occasion at the *Dionysia*, which must have meant a free meal of beef for some thousands of Athenians. Besides these public feastings,

festivals were evidently the occasion for special dinners. Strepsiades
treated himself to a haggis on the *Diasia*. Apart from the natural link
between sacrificial offerings and meat meals on holidays, many of these
were occasions also for special vegetable dishes or cakes. The *Pyanepsia*
and the *Thargelia* derived their names from these mixed stews of the
fruits of the earth which were offered to Apollo and also consumed by
men. The cakes are less prominent, and no names of holidays are
derived from them. Pastry was sometimes used to provide substitutes
for sacrificial victims, as in the *Diasia* or the *Elaphebolia*. Again, the objects hung on the bough called *eiresione* were made of pastry. Long
loaves were carried in the Dionysiac procession, and cakes with circles
of candles were offered to Artemis as moon goddess. To some extent
this was all part of traditional ritual, but also it is hard to tell at times
whether it was more religious in feeling than turkeys at Christmas,
hot-cross buns at Easter or barm-bracks at Hallow-e'en.

Some indication of the relative importance in popular esteem attached
to particular festivals can perhaps be gathered by noting which are
mentioned by Aristophanes. While his choice was no doubt influenced
by the opportunities which these occasions gave for humorous
allusions, it is likely that he tended to name festivals which evoked an
immediate response from the audience and omit those without any
popular appeal. So the various Dionysiac festivals and the *Panathenaia*
are mentioned. The special holy days of women appear: in fact in one
instance one provides the setting for a comedy. The *Diasia* in its lighter
aspects is twice named. But there is no mention of the *Oschophoria* or
of the *Synoikia*. The *Dipolieia* is only referred to as something antiquarian and absurd. Even the girls' ritual where it concerns the aristocratic families comes in only once for playful treatment, as reminiscences
of the chorus of old ladies in *Lysistrata*. As we have already suggested,
the Athenian state kept up its ritual ceremonies on the correct dates,
but already in the fifth century some of the ceremonies were felt to be
archaic survivals of no general interest.

It is not entirely clear how far festivals really involved the cessation
of work. Here no doubt the Athenians were ruled by what they would
call *nomos*, which could mean 'law', or could mean 'custom'. It is unlikely that the Solonian code contained anything as specific as the Sun-
day Observance legislation of Great Britain. No prosecutions for
infringement are mentioned in our sources. Though public business
such as meetings of the Assembly should not take place on festival days,
Aeschines implies that Demosthenes could get away with arranging a

meeting on the *Proagon*, but even he does not state that that action was unconstitutional. In the same way there was probably no legal power to compel citizens to close their shops on a holiday, but one can imagine that public opinion basing itself on customary practice would exercise considerable pressure on those who failed to conform. Even so, one must not picture the Athenians as feeling that to abstain from daily work was something required of them by their gods. This sabbatarian attitude derives from Judaism and was so unintelligible to the Greeks that they were inclined to suppose that the Jews must be a peculiarly lazy people if they rested every seventh day. The closing of businesses and the suspension of public services on the occasion of festivals in Athens would not be because these activities were regarded as inconsistent with worship, but simply because they could not be carried on simultaneously with it. People must be free to join in the worship of the gods, but the extent to which this participation was expected varied no doubt with the particular festival. They were not all embraced in one commandment like sabbaths or Sundays. One can imagine that an Athenian, or even an alien resident in Athens, who pointedly disregarded the *Panathenaia*, might call unfavourable notice on himself. But there seems to be no example to prove it, particularly in the classical period. The nearest instance appears to be in the second century A D when Athens was largely a tourist and university centre. Then, if we can trust Lucian (9, 11), the philosopher Demonax found it appropriate to offer a public explanation before the Assembly why he had not partaken in the Eleusinian Mysteries. But perhaps this was because he was regarded as a philosopher in a city where they then represented an important element in the population and were expected to assume and justify their attitude to religion.

In fifth-century Athens the participation in festivals was probably more spontaneous and less self-conscious. Also the emphasis would lie less on the individual conscience and more on the community. The festivals of the Athenian state had been essentially a natural expression of the feelings of the community towards the world and the pattern of its events. As long as Athens satisfied the needs of its citizens politically and socially, their festivals also fulfilled their part in daily life. This expressed mostly a cheerful outlook which did not feel the need often to humble itself in penitence before the gods. Even the *Diasia*, the atonement to Zeus, does not seem to have kept up this grim attitude throughout the whole day. The *Chytrai* was more an occasion of protecting oneself on the one day when malevolent spirits were abroad than a day for joining in appeasement of them. Otherwise it is significant that days of fasting only occurred in the middle of lengthy festivals such as the Mysteries, or the *Thesmophoria*, and so were appropriately balanced by a later feast. The general word for festival – *heorte* – implies enjoyment, and, as we have seen, most of the Greek celebrations developed this aspect. So plays and athletic games were typical special features on these occasions, and in fact they continued to develop after the ceremonies had tended to become more and more formalized and antiquarian in feeling.

With the decline of the city-state the religious cults connected with it became more and more stereotyped. The traditional festivals were not abandoned. In fact, as the inscriptional records show, they were clung to and preserved officially as part of the essential nature of Athens in a world in which the Athenians had little left them except their past as expressed in their traditions. Officials again and again are recorded as earning the gratitude of their fellow citizens by performing correctly their part in the state ceremonial. As public funds dwindled these activities must have depended more and more on the patriotic loyalty of private individuals: and patriotic loyalty rather than deep religious feeling became the ruling motive. The Eleusinian Mysteries alone seem to have been capable of taking on a new spirit of revival. In the second century AD it is probably not merely antiquarianism which makes Roman emperors such as Hadrian and Marcus Aurelius accept initiation. That elusive spiritual element, which had been present at Eleusis from the earliest periods known to us, still manifested itself in the festival even in its later stages.

At last with the fall of paganism the ancient festivals ceased, and in the Byzantine period the lexicographers patiently recorded their names, each with a brief explanation, because they were still part of the heritage of Greek literature. Also their mark on Greek art survived in such works as the Parthenon frieze. It is from these literary and artistic sources that we have tried to picture as a living activity the festivals of the Athenians.

NOTES

INTRODUCTION

(Abbreviations of ancient sources as in Liddell and Scott and of modern authors as in the select bibliography, p. 202.)

1 Lys. 36. Sokolowski, *Suppl.* No. 10; Sterling Dow, *Historia*, 9 (1960), 270 ff., *Hesperia*, 30 (1961), 58 ff.; J. H. Jeffery, *Hesperia*, 17 (1948), 106 ff.
2 The fragments arranged with detailed commentary, Felix Jacoby, *Fragmente der griechischen Historiker*, III, B., and discussed by him in *Atthis* (1949).
3 The best comprehensive survey is still P. Stengel, *Die griechische Kultusaltertümer*² (1910).

4 I *Ep. Cor.* 8. Pliny, *Ep.* 10, 96, 10.
5 Pol. 10, 5, 2, with Walbank's commentary; Livy, 26, 19, 5.
6 Menander, *C.A.F.* 3, fr. 292. = Ath. 14, 659D.
7 I. T. Hill, 34 ff., Travlos, 477, who believes the small rooms were also used for living quarters for the guard and as dining-rooms.
8 Ar. *Ec.* 730 ff., with the commentary by R. G. Ussher. For the Panathenaic Pompe, see pp. 37–44 infra.

I FESTIVALS IN THE CALENDAR

1 Hecatombaia, as derivation of Hecatombaion, *E.M.* 321, 5. As a festival elsewhere, Nilsson, *Feste*, 43, 138, 174. For the New Year festival as a Roman intrusion in Greece, Nilsson, *G.R.* 2, 358.
2 Cf. infra p. 168. *IG.* 2², 689, 20 and 690, 3.
3 Kronion, Plu. *Thes.* 12, 1. *E.M.* 321, 4. Kronion in Samos, Nilsson, *Feste*, 37. As harvest supper, Philochorus, *F.Gr.Hist.* 328 f 97 = Macr. *Sat.* 1, 11, 22. As out of date, Ar. *Nu.* 397 with Sch. As state holiday, D. 24, 26. As slaves' holiday, Plu. 6, 1098B.
4 Th. 2, 15, 2. Plu. *Thes.* 24, 4.
5 *Hesperia*, 4 (1935), 21. Sokolowski, *Suppl.* No. 10.
6 *IG.* 1², 188, 60.
7 Eirene, Hes. *Th.* 902, Ar. *Pax*, esp. 1017 ff. with Sch. The cult in the Agora, Isoc. 15, 109, Nepos, *Tim.*, 2, 2, Did. *in D.* 10, 34 = Philochorus, *F.Gr.Hist.* 328 f 151, Paus. 1, 8, 2.

Contrast Plu. *Cim*, 13.6. Accounts of 333 BC., *IG.* 2², [1496] Aa 94 following.
8 Athena's birthday, Callisthenes, *F.Gr.Hist.* 124 f 52 = Sch. Lyc. 520. Sch. BT. *Il.* 8, 3q. The Peplos, Ar. *Av.* 827 with Sch., Pollux, 7, 50, Harpocration, πέπλος.
9 The *Athenaia* legendarily founded by Erichthonios, Apollod. 3, 190, Marmor Par. A10, Harpocration, Παναθήναια (with references to Hellanicus, *F.Gr.Hist.* 323ᵃ f 2, Androtion, 324 f 2 and Istros, 334 f 4). Called *Panathenaia* by Theseus, Plu. *Thes.* 24, 3. Paus. 8, 2, 1, Sud. and Phot. Παναθήναια. Hippocleides' archonship as foundation date of athletic festival, Pherecydes, *F.Gr.Hist.* 3 f 2 = Marcell. *Vit. Thuc.* 2, 4, Euseb. *Chron ab Abr.* 1451 = Ol. 53. Hom. *Il.* 2, 547 describing a periodic festival at Athens may allude to it.
10 Hippocleides, Hdt. 6, 127, 4 ff. Peisistratus, Sch. Aristid. p. 323.

11 For four days as the duration in the 2nd century AD, Sch. Aristid. 98, 31 and 196, 30. Ditt. *Syll.*³ 1055.
12 Danced by Athena, D.H. 7, 72. As a liturgy, Lys. 21, 1. The boys' pyrrhic dance, Ar. *Nu.* 988.
13 X. *Mem.* 3, 3, 12. Philochorus, *F.Gr.Hist.* 328 f 102 = Harpocration, εὐανδρία. Arist. *Ath.* 60, 3.
14 Cf. p. 45 infra.
15 Cf. pp. 138 and 168 infra.
16 Pi. *N.* 10, 35.
17 For the frieze, see A. Michaelis, *Der Parthenon*, 211 ff; A. H. Smith, *The Sculptures of the Parthenon*, 50 ff; P. E. Corbett, *The Sculptures of the Parthenon*, 15 ff.
18 Ergastinai: Hsch, s.n.; Sud. Χαλκεῖα, 35; EM. 805, 43; Ditt. *Syll.*³ 718. The subjects: E. *Hec.* 468 with sch.; sch. Ar. *Av.* 827.
19 The peplos and its ship-car, sch. Ar. *Av.* 827. Phot. ἱστὸς καὶ κεραία. Strattis, *C.A.F.* fr. 30 = Harpocration, τοπεῖον. The ship's dock, Paus. 1, 29, 1.
20 Arist. *Ath.* 49, 3.
21 Ditt. *Syll.*³ 374. Plu. *Demetr.* 12.
22 Arist. *Ath.* 54, 7, 60, 1 ff., 62, 2.
23 For military in the Panathenaic procession. Th. 6, 56, 2; Arist. *Ath.* 18, 4. Apobatai, Plu. *Phoc.* 20, 1; Harpocration, ἀποβάτης.
24 Kanephoroi, Arist. *Ath.* 18, 2; Philochorus, *F.Gr.Hist.* 328 f 8 = Harpocration, s.n. Diphrophoroi, Hsch. s.n. For comic parodies Ar. *Ec.* 734 and *Av.* 1508, where it is implied that the Diphrophoros should carry a sunshade. Lycurgus: Paus. 1, 29, 16; [Plu.] 5, 852B.
25 Thallophoroi. X. *Smp.* 4, 17; Ar. *V.* 544 with sch. (Philochorus, *F.Gr. Hist.* 328 f 9, etc.); Hsch. s.n.; Eustath. *Od.* 1557, 25.
26 Skaphephoroi: Men. *C.A.F.* fr. 1064 = Phot. σκάφας. Harpocration, s.n.; Pollux, 3, 55; Zenob. συστομώτερον σκάφης; Sud. id.
27 Bekker, *Anecd.* 1. 242, 3.
28 Offerings for the *Panathenaia* required: Meiggs-Lewis, no. 40, l.3 ff. (Erythrai); no. 46, l.42 ff. (decree of Cleinias); no. 49, ll.11 ff. (Brea); no.

69, ll.56 ff. (tribute reassessment, 425–4 BC).
29 Plu. *Sol.* 1.7. (torches lit from altar of Eros founded by Peisistratus); Paus. 1, 30, 2 (race from the altar of Prometheus in the Academy); Ar. *Ra.* 129 with sch.; Harpocration, λαμπάς. Arist. *Ath.* 57, 1 (the Basileus responsible). For the prizes, cf. p. 35 supra.
30 Ar. *Ra.* 1089 ff.
31 Hegesandros, *FHG.* 4, fr. 8 = *Ath.* 4, 167F.
32 Ditt. *Syll.*³, 271.
33 E. *Heracl.* 777 ff.
34 Ar. *Nu.* 386 with sch.
35 Lysimachides, *F.Gr.Hist.* 366 f 1 =Harpocration, Μεταγειτνιών Plu. 3, 601B (who regards it as referring to removal of dwelling); Deubner, 202; Nilsson, *Feste*, 468.
36 Ar. *Ra.* 651 (referring to Kynosarges as in the *deme* Diomeia); Harpocration, Ἡράκλεια. Alcibiades' decree, Polemo, *FHG.* 3, fr. 78 = Ath. 6, 234E. On lifting the bull, Theophr. *Ch.* 27, 5; Ziehen, *Hermes*, 66 (1931), 277. Cf. infra pp. 74 (*Proerosia*) and 171 (Hephaistia).
37 Philochorus, *F.Gr.Hist.* 328 f 13 = Harpocration, Βοηδρόμια; *EM.* 202, 49. For an alternative legend deriving the festival from Theseus' war with the Amazons in Attica, Plu. *Thes.* 27. Demosthenes' allusion, 3, 31. For the title Boedromios used by many of Apollo, Call. *h. Ap.* 69. At Thebes, Paus. 9, 17, 2. No festival outside Attica under this name is recorded by Nilsson.
38 The discussion in Deubner, 229 is largely superseded by the article by Jacoby, *Cl.Qu.* 38 (1944), 65 ff. where the ancient evidence is printed *in extenso* in the appendix.
39 Th. 2, 34 (trans. Rex Warner (Penguin), p. 115).
40 The temple and the local legend, Paus. 1, 19, 6. The vow before Marathon, X. *An* 3, 2, 12. 6th Boedromion as the date of Marathon, Plu. *Cam.* 19, 3, but cf. *C.A.H.* 4, 238. Losses at Marathon, Hdt, 6, 117, 1. The Polemarch, Arist. *Ath.* 58, 1. The Ephebes,

IG.2², 1058, 8. Plu. 5, 862A seems to assign the Pompe to Hecate in Agrai.
41 Arist. *NE*. 3, 1111ᵃ, 10 with sch.
42 The Homeric Hymn to Demeter (*h. Cer.*). The edition with commentary by N. J. Richardson (Oxford, 1974) appeared too late to be used extensively here. It contains a detailed discussion of relation of the *Hymn* to the Mysteries.
43 Hierophantes, Mylonas, 229 ff. and Diaduchos, 232 with references.
44 Vestments, Ath. 1, 21 E. Callias Lakkoploutos, Plu. *Aristid*. 5, 6.
45 The taboo on the personal name, Mylonas, 155. Chastity, 230, and Jul. *Or*. 5, 173D.
46 Pl. *Gorg*. 497C with sch. Plu. *Demetr*. 26, 1. Polyaen. 5, 17, 1. Bekker, *anec*. 1, 326, 26 (Cleidemus, *F.Gr.Hist*. 323 f 9). Steph. Byz. *Ἄγρα*.
47 On the site of the Eleusinion, Travlos, 198 ff., Mylonas, 247. On the relations with Eleusis, Nilsson, *G.R*.², 1, 712.
48 The Cistai and the ribbons, Plu. *Phok*. 28. Mylonas 84 and 274.
49 The Rheitoi, Paus. 1, 38, 1 and *IG*. 1², 81.
50 Ditt. *Syll*.³ 885, l.16.
51 Hsch. Ἀγυρμός, Isocr. 4, 157, Liban. *Declam*. 13 (Vol. VI, p. 20 Forster), Celsus ap. Orig. *Cels*. 3, 59. Theo Smyrn. p. 14 (Hiller).
52 Ditt. *Syll*.³ 42. Revised Text, Meritt, *Hesperia*, 14 (1945) 77, *SEG*. 10, 6 and Sokolowski, *Suppl*. No. 3. *IG*.2², 1672, l. 207 (15 drachmai).
53 Mylonas, 244.
54 Mystagogos, P.W. s.n. and Mylonas, 237. Andocides as initiator, 1.132. Prohibition of group initiation, Sokolowski, *Suppl*. No. 3, C.22.
55 Hsch. ἅλαδε μύσται.
56 Ditt. *Syll*.³ 540, 20 (control of the procession). The shark, Sch. Aeschin. 3.130. Plu. *Phok*. 28 may refer to the same event, but, if so, appears to give it a different date.
57 'Hither the victims', Philostr. *VA*. 4, 18. Cf. Lys. 6, 4.
58 Arist. *Ath*. 56, 4.
59 Edelstein, T.170.

60 Paus. 2, 26, 8. *IG*. 2², 974.
61 Deubner, 73.
62 Iacchagogos, Paus. 1, 2, 4, Polydeukes, 1.32. Myrtle garlands, sch. Ar. *Ran*. 333. Bacchoi, Sch. Ar. *Eq*. 406.
63 'The donkey brings the mysteries', Ar. *Ran*. 159. The yellow band, Phot. κροκοῦν, Krokidai, Paus. 1, 38, 2. The men on the bridge, Hsch. γεφυρίς, γεφυρισταί (where the bridge is over the Eleusinian Kephisos). Strabo, 9. C.400, places the happening on the Attic Kephisos. The identity of the rivers' names was a natural cause of confusion to our sources. Similar practices may have occurred on both, but I follow Mylonas (p. 256, note 150) in supposing that on the outward journey at least the Eleusinian Kephisos was the scene.
64 All night celebration, E. *Ion*, 1074; *IG* 2², 847, 21. Kernoi, Polemo, *FHG*. Vol. 3, fr. 88 = Ath. 476F and 478D. Mylonas, 257.
65 Nilsson, *Minoan – Mycenaean Religion*,² 452. Mylonas, 17.
66 Hdt. 8, 65. For 30,000 as the Athenian male population, Hdt. 5, 97, 2.
67 X. *HG*., 4, 20, Plu. *Alc*. 34, 4.
68 Arr. *An*. 1, 10, 2.
69 The Pelanos, Ditt. *Syll*.² 587, 280; *Syll*.³ 83, 36 and 200, 17; Mylonas, 258. The Kykeon, *h.Hom.Cer.* 208 with Richardson, Appendix IV; Clem. Al. *Protr*. 21, 2.
70 For a detailed discussion of the literary and archaeological evidence for the Telesterion, see Mylonas, 67 ff., 78 ff., 113 ff.
71 For discussion of the secret of the Mysteries, see Deubner, 78 ff., Nilsson, *G.R*. 1², 659 ff., Mylonas, 261 ff. and Appendix, 287 ff. Hippolytus, *Phil*. 5, 8, 39.
72 The Anaktoron only entered by the Hierophantes, Ael. fr. 10. The sudden light when the Anaktoron was opened, Plu. 1, 81E.
73 Arist. fr. 15 (Rose); Dio C.12, 33; Themistius ap. Stob 5, 1089 (Heuse), wrongly assigned to Plutarch (Bernardakis, 7, p. 23 – see Nilsson, *G.R*. 2,

p. 652, note 3); Deubner, 87, note 5. None of the ancient sources refer to Eleusis by name.

74 Plemochoai, Ath. 11, 496A; Pollux, 10, 75.

75 Mylonas, 279. Sch. Ar. *Plu.* 845 (Melanthius, *F.Gr.Hist.* 326 f 4).

76 Parke and Wormell, *Delphic Oracle*, 2, No. 164. Since this publication, I am more inclined to believe that there was a historic response to this effect in the early sixth century. For the revival, *c.* 420 BC, Meiggs-Lewis, No. 72. For archaeological evidence of grain stores at Eleusis, Mylonas, 97 (Peisistratean), 126 (later fifth century), 150 (fourth century).

77 The proclamation of the *Proerosia*, *IG.* 2², 1363, 2; Ditt. *Syll.*³ 1038. The lifting of the oxen, *IG.* 2², 1028, 28; cf. p. 172 infra. Private cult, Max. Tyr. 292, 17 (Hob.). The scene of the *Supplices*, E. *Suppl.* 1 ff. For the legend that corn was first given to Triptolemus by Demeter as developed by the Athenians from the mid-sixth century, see Richardson on *h.Cer.* 153.

78 *IG.* 2², 1363, 7; Deubner, 199.

79 For the derivation, Harpocration, *Πυανόψια*; Phot. *Πυανέψια*; Pollux, 6, 61. For the *Aition*, Plu. *Thes.* 22, 5 and cf. 18, 1.

80 Eiresione, Plu. *The.* 22; Suda, s.n. and *διακόνιον*; Hsch. *διακόνιον*. At the house door, Ar. *Eq.* 729 and *Ec.* 1053.

81 Deubner, 200.

82 Istros, *F.Gr.Hist.* 334 f 8 = Harpocration, *ὀσχοφόροι*; Suda, *ὠσχοφορία*; Phot. *ὀρχοφορεῖν*; Hsch. *ὠσχοφόροι*.

83 Plu. *Thes.* 22.

84 Deipnophoroi: Plu. *Thes.* 23, 4 (Demon, *F.Gr.Hist.* 327 f 6); Hsch. s.n. and *ὠσχοφόριον*; Suda, s.n.; Harpocration, *δειπνοφόρος*; Bekker, *Anec.* 1, 239, 11 (Philochorus, *F.Gr. Hist.* 328 f 183).

85 Plu. *Thes.* 23, 2 ff.

86 Plu. *Thes.* 22, 2 ff.

87 Ferguson, *Hesperia*, 7 (1938) 1 ff., Nilsson, *H.J.Th.* 59 (1938), 385. On the *Oschophoria* generally, see Jacoby's commentary on Philochorus, *F.Gr. Hist.* 328 f 14–16.

88 Plu. *Thes.* 17, 6.

89 Parke and Wormell, *Delphic Oracle*, 2, no. 214. Plu. *Thes.* 34, 4.

90 Phytalidai, Plu. *Thes.* 23, 5 and Arist. *Ath.* 15, 4; Deubner, 224. The sacrifice and procession, *IG.* 2², 956, 4 and 1496 A c134. Athara, Ar. *Plu.* 627 with sch. Four shrines in Attica, Philochorus, *F.Gr.Hist.* 328 f 18ª.

91 Ditt. *Syll.*³ 667, 43 ff.

92 The chief source on this question is the scholia to Lucian (pp. 275 ff. Rabe), reproduced and discussed by Deubner, 40 ff.

93 Hdt. 2, 171. Ar. *Thesmophoriazousai*, passim: esp. the interrogation of Mnesilochus, 626 ff. and the choric hymns, 969 ff. and 1136 ff.

94 Three days of the festival, sch. Ar. *Thesm.* 78; Alciphr. 2, 37, 1. Contrast Plu. *Dem.* 30, 5. Tent-mates and gangways, Ar. *Thesm.* 624 and 658 with sch. Local officials, Isaeus, 8.19. The site of the Thesmophorion is disputed.

95 Public business stopped, Ar. *Thesm.* 78. Fasting and sitting on the ground, Ar. *Av.* 1519; Plu. 2, 378E; Ath. 7, 307F. Demeter's refusal of a chair and the episode of Iambe, *h.Hom.Cer.* 193 ff. Richardson believes that this passage was connected with ritual in the Mysteries of Eleusis. This is likely, but would not exclude the parallel occurrence in the mystery of the *Thesmophoria*, just as Iambe has a parallel in Baubo. Apollod. 1, 5, 3.

96 Abuse, Apollod. l.c.; Hsch. and Phot. *Στήνια*; Cleomedes, *de motu circul.* 2, 1; Deubner, 53 and 57. Nilsson, *Feste*, 322 ff. The lexicographers refer it to the *Stenia*, but it was probably customary at both festivals.

97 Ar. *Thesm.* 372 ff. Torches, id, 281 and 1152.

98 Chalcidicon Diogma, Hsch. s.n. and Suda, s.n. (Semus, *F.Gr.Hist.* 396 f 21).

99 *Stenia*, Hsch and Phot. s.n. (Eubulus, *C.A.F.* 2, fr. 148). General references in Ar. *Thesm.* 834 with sch.

100 Plu. *Sol.* 8, 4; Clem. Al. *Protr.* 2, 34, 2. For a parallel legend Aen. Tact. 4, 8.

101 Sch. Ar. *Ach.* 146; Proclus, 1, 88, 11, commenting on Pl. *Tim.* 21B, Harpocration, μεῖον; Bekker, *Anec.* 1, 273, 2. Demotionidai, Ditt. *Syll.*[3] 921.

102 Deubner, 232, note 1.

103 Parke and Wormell, *Delphic Oracle*, 2, no. 214. As a common festival of the Ionians, Hdt. 1, 147.

104 Hsch. κουρεῶτις; Suda, κουρεώτης.

105 Lys. 23, 3.

106 Epibda, Hsch. ἐπιβάδαι; Pi. *P.* 4, 140.

107 Harpocration, Χαλκεῖα (Apollonios of Acharnai, *F.Gr.Hist.* 365 f 3, Phanodemus, 325 f 18 and Menander, *C.A.F.* 3, fr. 509 and 510); Suda, Χαλκεῖα, 35 (the peplos); Pollux, 7, 105; Eustath. *Il.* 284, 35. Harpocration's two quotations of Attic authorities illustrate the dispute between the attribution of this festival to Athena (Apollonios) and to Hephaestus (Phanodemos). Deubner, 35, is all for Athena. Athena's statue in the temple of Hephaestus, Paus. 1, 14, 6; Travlos, 261. Athena Archegetis, *IG.* 2², 674, 16. Ergane, Soph. fr. 760N.

108 Lysimachides, *F.Gr.Hist*, 366 f 2 = Harpocration, Μαιμακτηριών.

109 Maimactes and Meilichios associated, Plu. 3, 458C; cf. Hsch. μαιμάκτης; Nilsson, *Feste*, 6. The Dion Koidion, Polemo, *FHG.* 3 fr. 87 = Hsch. s.n. and Suda s.n. Cf. compound verbs, such as ἀποδιοπομπέομαι, Eust. *Od.* 22, 481. For the *Diasia*, cf. p. 120 infra and for the Fleece in an Eleusinian context, *h.Hom.Cer.* 196.

110 Local evidence, *IG.* 1², 190, 8 and 2², 1367, 16 ff. The *Penteteria*, Hdt. 6, 87; Lys. 21, 5; Deubner, 215.

111 Elsewhere in Greece, Nilsson, *Feste*, 69 and 82 ff. Poseidon as supreme god, Nilsson, *G.R.* 1², 444 ff and Schachermeyer, *Poseidon*, passim.

112 Philochorus, *F.Gr.Hist.* 328 f 83 = Harpocration, Ἅλῳα; Eust. *Il.* 772, 26; Bekker, *Anec.* 1, 384, 31; Deubner, 60 ff., Nilsson, *G.R.* 1², 466 ff.

113 Sch. Lucian, 279, 24 (Rabe).

114 Cook, *Zeus*, 1,685, fig. 510a. Deubner, 65 and pl. 3.3.

115 [D.] 59, 116. For Archias and the Theban oligarchy, Plu. *Pel.* 10, 3.

116 For Poseidon, cf. Eustath. and Bekker. *Anec.* cit. supra note 112, and *IG* 2², 1299.

117 Plu. 3, 527D.

118 Ar. *Ach.* 247 ff.

119 For the participation of slaves, Plu. 6, 1098B, mentioned in connection with the *Kronia*, supra p. 29. Askoliasmos, Pollux, 9, 121; Suda, ἀσκωλίαζε = Eubulus, *C.A.F.* 2, fr. 8; sch. Ar. *Plu.* 1129.

120 D. 18, 180 and 262.

121 For inscriptional evidence for the *Dionysia* in the Piraeus, see Deubner, 137. The Demarch appointed, Arist. *Ath.* 54, 8. The Colophonian embassy entertained, *IG.* 2², 456, 32.

122 Hsch. ἱερὸς γάμος; Phot. ἱερὸν γάμον.

123 Hsch. ἐπὶ Ληναίῳ ἀγών, and similarly in the other lexica, Ar *Ach.* 504. On the difficult question of the site of the Lenaion the latest discussion is Wycherley, *Hesperia*, 34 (1965), 72.

124 Suda, ἐξ ἁμαξῶν; sch. Clem. Al. *Protr.* 297, 4.

125 The Basileus and the Epimeletai, Arist. *Ath.* 57, 1. The ritual, sch. Ar. *Ra.* 482.

126 Lenai, Deubner, 126. The Vases, 127. The Delphic Thyiades, Plu. 5, 953D. The Athenian excursion to Delphi, Paus. 10, 32, 5.

127 Children crowned with flowers, Philostr. *Her.* 12, 12, p. 187, 20 (K). The derivation of Anthesterion, *EM.* 109, 12. Miniature Choes, Deubner, 97 and Appendix 1, pp. 238 ff. Teachers' fees, *Ath.* 10, 437D.

128 The three days of the Anthesteria, sch. Ar. *Ath.* 390 (Apollodorus, *F.Gr.Hist.* 244 f 133). The *Pithoigia*, Plu. 4, 655E, cf. 735E; Phanodemus, *F.Gr.Hist.* 325 f 12 = Ath. 11, 465A.

129 Th. 2, 15, 4. For a strong advocacy of Doerpfeld's site with full references to the earlier literature, Jane Harrison, *Primitive Athens*, 83 ff. Recent scholars are more cautious, e.g. I. T. Hill, 192-3, or definitely reject it, Travlos, 274.

130 R. M. Cook, *Greek Painted Pottery*, 227. Miniature Choes, Deubner as cited in note 127.
131 The ship-car is fully discussed by Deubner, 102 ff. In Smyrna, Nilsson, *Feste*, 268. *h.Hom.Dion.* 7.
132 [D.] 59, 73 ff.
133 Pollux, 8, 108; *EM.* 227, 35; Bekker, *Anec.* 1, 228, 9 and 231, 32.
134 Boukoleion, Judeich, 298; I. T. Hill, 103. The Holy Marriage, Arist. *Ath.* 3, 5; Deubner, 116.
135 Ath. 7, 276C; Plu. 4, 613B and 643A. For the arrangements, sch. Ar. *Ath.* 1085.
136 Plu. *Ant.* 70, 2.
137 The legend first appears in E. *LT.* 942 ff., where it is put into the mouth of Orestes himself describing his treatment by the Athenians and mentioning that the ritual has become traditional. So the story was invented before the Atthidographers. Cf. also Phanodemus, *F.Gr.Hist.* 325 f 11 = Ath. 10, 437C; Callimachus, fr. 178 (Pfeiffer); sch. Ar. *Ath.* 961; Suda, *Χόες*. See also the references in note 135 supra.
138 Ar. *Ach.* 1000 ff. with sch.
139 Timaius, *F.Gr.Hist.* 566 f 158. DL. 4, 8.
140 Phanodemus, *F.Gr.Hist.* 325 f 11; Ar. *Ra.* 210.
141 Chytrai, Theopompus, *F.Gr. Hist.* 115 f 347 = sch. Ar. *Ach.* 1076 and *Ra.* 218.
142 Phot. *θύραζε Κᾶρες*. For parallels for the custom, cf. the *Lemuria* (May 9th), Ovid, *Fasti*, 5, 429 ff., and the example in Deubner, 113, note 5. For slaves at the *Anthesteria*, cf. Callimachus, fr. 178 (Pfeiffer).
143 Paus, 1, 18, 7; Plu. *Sul.* 14, 6; Suda, *Ὑδροφορία* = Apollonius, *F.Gr. Hist.* 365 f 4.
144 Parke and Wormell, *Delphic Oracle*, 1, 335 and 2, No. 542. As a festival of the *Anthesteria*, Callimachus, fr. 178. The story was told at length in a poem by Eratosthenes (*Coll. Alex.* fr. 22–27). Also there was a traditional song called Aletis (The Wandering Girl) associated with Erigone and swinging, Pollux, 4, 55 and Ath. 14,

618E. Significantly an attempt was made to link Erigone and Orestes' trial in Athens by describing her instead as his half sister, who prosecuted him for the murder of their mother. On this subject and particularly on the vase, see Deubner.
145 Zeus Meilichios and the fleece, cf. supra, p. 95, Cylon, Th. 1, 126, 6; Parke and Wormell, *Delphic Oracle*, 1, 120 and 2, No. 12.
146 Sch. Th. 1, 126. Pollux, 1, 26 is probably wrong in explaining the sacrifice as incense.
147 X. *An.* 7, 8, 4.
148 Ar. *Nu.* 864 and 408 with sch., where Apollonius of Acharnae (*F.Gr. Hist.* 365 f 5) is cited for an absurd derivation of Diasia, which reappears in Suda, s.n. and *EM.* 270, 14.
149 cf. supra p. 64.
150 Plu. *Demetr.* 26.
151 Heracles and the *Lesser Mysteries*: sch. Ar. *Plu.* 1013. His initiation at Eleusis, D.S. 4, 25, 4 and X *H.* 6, 3, 6. His need for purification, Plu. *Thes.* 30, 5. Mylonas, 212, note 69. Lustration in the Ilissos, Polyaen, 5, 17, 1. The Lovatelli vase and the Torre Novo sarcophagus, Mylonas, 205–8.
152 The sacrifice of stags, Bekker, *Anec.* 1, 249, 9. *Elaphoi*, Ath. 14, 649E.
153 Paus. 1, 38, 8 and 1, 20 3. For the earliest remains at the Dionysiac theatre, see Travlos, 537.
154 Paus. 1, 2, 5. For the *aition* of the phallic processions, sch. Ar. *Ach.* 243.
155 Paus. 1, 29, 2. Pickard-Cambridge, *Dramatic Festivals*[2], p. 60.
156 Pickard-Cambridge, op. cit. 61 ff. Brea, Meiggs-Lewis, no. 49. The *metoikoi* and *askophoroi*, Sud. *ἀσκοφορεῖν*. Obeliai, Pollux, 6, 75. Ath. 3, 111B. *Kanephoros*. sch. Ar. *Ach.* 241 (in the plural), but Gould and Lewis note that the inscriptions *IG.* 2[2], 896, etc. prove that by the second century at least there was only one. Dances, X. *Hipp.* 3, 2.
157 The number of victims in 333 BC., Ferguson, *Hesperia*, 17 (1948), 134. The *Komos*, Deubner, 140, and Pickard-Cambridge, 63.

158 On the development of the dramatic and dithyrambic performances at the *City Dionysia*, Pickard-Cambridge, pp. 70 ff.
159 For the evidence discussed, see Pickard-Cambridge, 264 ff.
160 Admission, etc., Pickard-Cambridge, 266.
161 Theophr. *Char.* 2.11. Aesch. 2, 11 and 3, 76.
162 Philochorus, *F.Gr.Hist.* 328 f 171 = Ath. 11, 464F. Sweetmeats, Arist. *NE.* 10, 1175*b*, 12. Opponents criticized, Ar. *Vesp.* 59 and *Plu.* 797. Aristophanes does it himself, *Pax* 962. Relieving oneself by flying away, Ar. *Av.* 785 ff.
163 For the arrangements, Pickard-Cambridge, 81 ff. The chief evidence is Arist. *Ath.* 56, 3.
164 D.21, 16 ff.
165 Pickard-Cambridge, 67. Aesch. 3, 67 with sch. Pl. *Sym.* 194b. Probably the scene of Ar. *Ach.* 10 ff.
166 The tribute, Isocr. 8 (*de Pace*), 82. The orphans, Aesch, 3, 154.
167 Aesch. 3, 41 ff.
168 Pickard-Cambridge, 272 ff.
169 The inquest, D. 21, 8–10. Penalties, D. 21, 178 and 180.
170 Edelstein, 1, T587 and 590. For hides sold from the sacrifices, *IG.* 2², 1496 Aa 78 etc.
171 Deubner, 176–7. For derivations, Phot. *Πάνδια*. The *deme* Plothia, *IG.* 2², 1172, 9. The tribe Pandion, *IG.* 2², 1140.
172 Plu. *The.* 18, 2.
173 Suda, *῎Εμβαρος*. App. Prov. 2, 54. Eust. *Il.* 268, 24 ff. For the site, *JHS.* 56 (1936), 142.
174 Amphiphontes, Ath. 14, 645A (quoting Philemon, *C.A.F.* 2, fr. 67). Suda, s.n. (quoting Apollodorus, *F.Gr. Hist.* 244 f 152) and *ἀνάστατοι*, Pollux, 6, 75. *EM.* 94, 55.
175 The regatta, *IG.* 2² 1006, 30 (122/1 BC) and in imperial times a sea-battle, *IG.* 2², 2130, 49. For the procession, *IG.* 2², 1029, 13 (AD 94).
176 The sanctuary of Artemis Brauronia on the Acropolis, I. T. Hill, *Ancient Athens*, 179, Travlos, 124–6.

The *Brauronia*, Arist. *Ath.* 54, 7.
177 Harpocration, *ἀρκτεῦσαι*, citing Craterus, *F.Gr.Hist.* 342 f 9, Suda, *ἄρκτος*, Hsch. *ἀρκτεία*.
178 Ar. *Lys.* 641 with sch.
179 Mrs L. Ghali-Kahil, *Antike Kunst*, 8 (1965), p. 21 and Plate 7. On the subject see C. Sourvinou, *Cl.Qu.* 21 (1971), 339 ff., who discusses the passage from the *Lysistrate* and appears to establish the correct reading, but hesitates over taking 'shedding' in its literal sense.
180 The *Arrephoroi*, Harpocration, *ἀρρηφορεῖν*. Sch. Ar. *Lys.* 642 (citing Istros, *F.Gr.Hist.* 334 f 27). Sud. *ἀρρηφορία. EM.* 149, 14 ff. The ceremony, Paus. 1, 27, 3.
181 Broneer, *Hesperia*, 1 (1932), 51 ff., and Travlos, 229 ff. The Basileus' selection, Suda, *ἐπιώψατο*. For parallelism with the *Thesmophoria*, cf. sch. Lucian, 276, 13, where it is suggested that the objects borne by the Arrephoroi were pastry models of snakes and male genitals. But the scholiast is confused and rather undependable. For discussions, see Deubner, 10 and Nilsson, *G.R.*² 1, 441.
182 For Skirophorion, *EM.* 149, 14. For the confusion, Deubner, 13. Jacoby, commenting on the citation from Istros (note 180 above), is probably right in distinguishing between two completely different institutions – the Dew-carrying and the Carrying of Unspoken Things – confused by the verbal similarity.
183 The ban on gold ornaments, Harpocration, *ἀρρηφορεῖν*. Anastatoi, Suda, s.n. The ball-court, [Plu.] 5, 839C. For the game (*κερητίζειν*) cf. S. Casson, *JHS.* 45 (1926), 171–2.
184 Broneer, *Hesperia*, 1 (1932), 44; Sokolowski, *Suppl.* no. 5.
185 Plu. *Phoc.* 37, 1.
186 X. *Hipp.* 3, 10. *IG.* 2², 1291 on the *Anthippasia* at this festival and at the *Panathenaia*. Pritchett, *Hesperia*, 9 (1939), 111, No. 21 – an inscription for a phylarch victorious in the *Anthippasia*. Cf. *IG.* 2², 3130 – the base of Bryaxis' monument. The hide

account, *IG.* 2², 1496 A82 – 631 drachmai (334/4 B C).

187 Nilsson, *Feste*, 105 ff.

188 For a classic discussion of the institution of Pharmakoi, see Gilbert Murray, *Rise of the Greek Epic*, Appendix A, 317 ff. The chief ancient sources for Athens are Harpocration, φαρμακός (citing as authority, Istros, *F.Gr.Hist.* 334 f 50 on an *aition*, but probably not for the Athenian festival) and Helladius, Chrestomathy = Phot. *Bibl.* 279, p. 534a, 2 ff. For the 6th Thargelion as a purification and the birthday of Artemis, D.L. 2, 44.

189 Hsch. φαρμακοί. The source appears to be Hipponax. So the city may be Ephesus.

190 Pharmakos as a term of abuse, Ar. *Eq.* 1415, *Ra.* 733.

191 The 7th as the *Thargelia*, Plu. 4, 717D. Thargelos, Phot. Θαργήλια. Bekker, *Anec.* 1, 263, 23. Thalusia, Hom. *Il.* 9, 324 (but not a sacrifice 'made to Artemis' as L. and S.!); Nilsson, *Feste*, 330 ff.

192 Arist. *Ath.* 56, 3; Antiph. 6, 11; D. 21, 10; Lys. 21, 1; Suda, Πύθιον. *IG.* 2², 1138 etc.

193 Isaeus, 7, 15.

194 Philochorus, *F.Gr.Hist.* 328 f 61 = sch. Ar. *Lys.* 835; Deubner, 192.

195 Parke, *Oracles of Zeus*, 149. The relief, Bulle, *Der Schoene Mensch*, no. 278.

196 Pl. *Rep.* 1, 327A with sch., and 328A. Sokolowski, *Suppl.* no. 6.

197 *IG.* 2², 1255, 1324 and 1283.

198 Nilsson, *G.R.*² 1, 835.

199 Phot. *Καλλυντήρια* and *Πλυντήρια* dating the K. to the 19th and the P. to the last but one. But Plu. *Alc.* 34 dates the P. to the 25th, evidently correctly.

200 Plu. *Alc.* 34, 1 (referring to it as ὄργια – ἀπόρρητα). Suda and Phot. *Νομοφύλακες*. Phot. *Καλλυντήρια* and Hsch. *Πλυντήρια* associate Aglauros with these proceedings in a rather unintelligible way. For historic records, e.g. *IG.* 2², 1006, 11. The figs carried Phot. and Hsch. ἡγητηρία; Ath. 3, 74D; Deubner, 19 ff.

201 The Washers, Phot. λουτρίδες. The cleaner, Bekker, *Anec.* 1, 269, 29 (Masculine?).

202 Parke and Wormell, *Delphic Oracle*, No. 124; *IG.* 1², 80.

203 Pollux, 8, 141; Deubner, 22. Similarly E. Fehrle, *Die kultische Keuschkeit im Altertum*, 172 ff., will not accept that this was a mere washing, but insists on a more mystical interpretation. Alcibiades, X. *H.* 1, 4, 12.

204 For alternative deities, see sch. Ar. *Thesm.* 834 and *Eccl.* 18, and Steph. Byz. Σκίρος. For the various ancient derivations, see p. 161, infra with notes. For modern theories, Deubner 45.

205 Ar. *Thesm.* 832 and *Eccl.* 18.

206 Lysimachides, *F.Gr.Hist.* 366 f 3 = Harpocration, Σκίρον; sch. Ar. *Eccl.* 18; Pollux, 7, 174; Deubner, 46.

207 Plu. 1.144A. Deubner's attempt (p. 47) to connect Skiron with a neighbouring cult of Demeter is unconvincing (Paus. 1, 37, 2). For the Byzugai and ploughing, Deubner, 250 and P.W. s.n.

208 Sch. Lucian, 275, 23; Deubner, 40 ff. See p. 83 supra.

209 Philochorus, *F.Gr.Hist.* 328 f 89 = Phot. τροπηλίς, Burkert, *Cl.Qu.* 20 (1970), 10. For the garlic at the *Thesmophoria*, *IG.* 2², 1184, 15, Sokolowski, *Suppl.* No. 124 (the deme Cholargai). That the staters are weights, not currency, cf. L. H. Jeffery, *Hesperia*, 19 (1948), 98, that the cheese in the same inscription is defined by weight.

210 For a collection of all the ancient evidence on the *Skira* in this connection, see Jacoby, *F.Gr.Hist.* 3b, a commentary on the ancient historians of Athens, Vol. 1, 286 ff., commenting of Philochorus, f 14–16. For the race the particular references are Aristodemus the Theban, *F.Gr.Hist.* 383 f 9 = Ath. 11, 495F.; sch. Nikandr. *Alex.* 169 and Proclus, Chrest. (Phot. *Bibl.* 239, p. 332 a 13). The interpretation in the text follows Jacoby in distinguishing the race and the procession as two different events, the first at the *Skira*, the latter at the *Oschophoria*.

211 For the derivation from Skiron the Megarian, Praxion, *F.Gr.Hist.* 484 f 1. The other four derivations all occur in Phot. and Suda, s.v. *Σκῖρος*. For Skiros the Salaminian, Str. 9, C. 393. For Skiros the prophet from Dodona, Paus. 1, 36, 4. *Σκιροφόρια* is only cited by L. S. from lexicographers and scholiasts. *Σκιροφοριών* occurs first in *IG.* 1², 304, 81 and Antiphon 6, 42.

212 Ar. *Nu.* 983 wich sch.; Suda, *Βουφόνια* and *Θαύλων*; Hsch. *Βουφόνια* and *Θαυλωνίδαι*; sch. Ar. *Pax.* 459. In the quotation from Aristophanes 'cicadas' refers to the ornament worn by old-fashioned Athenian men.

213 Paus. 1, 24, 4 and 28, 10; Aesch. 3, 244.

214 Deubner, 158 ff.; Nilsson, *G.R.* 1², 152 ff. Hsch. *Διὸς θάκοι καὶ πεσσοί.*

215 Parke and Wormell, *Delphic Oracle*, 1, 21.

216 The regulations for the sacrifice at Cos, Ditt. *Syll.*³, 1035, discussed by Nilsson, *Feste*, 17 ff. and *G.R.* 1²,

153 ff. Porphyry, *Abstin.* 2, 28, p. 159, 18 and Phot. and Hsch. *κεντριάδαι.* Nilsson, *G.R.* 1², 153 cites an example from Magnesia on the Maeander of a bull selected and fed as an intended victim for some six months, but, though perhaps resembling Pausanias' version in this respect, it has otherwise no analogies (Ditt. *Syll.*³, 589).

217 Parke and Wormell, *Delphic Oracle*, 1, 365 and 2, No. 536. Also Deubner and Nilsson, *G.R.* ll. cit. For the sacrificial priest as *βουτύπος IG.* 1², 839, 8 (Sokolowski, *Suppl.* No. 2, Ac. 10 – a fragment of the sacred laws) and 2², 2291 a2, etc. For heralds at the *Buphonia*, *IG.* 1², 843.

218 The temple, Str. 9, C. 395 and Paus. 1, 1, 3.

219 For the inscriptional evidence, see the fourth century accounts, *IG.* 2², 1496 Aa, 88 f. etc., and the other references in Deubner, 174 ff. Plu. *Dem*, 27, 8 (50 talents) and 846D (30 talents).

220 *IG.* 2², 689, 20 and 690, 3. Deubner, 175. Cf. supra p. 29.

II OTHER FESTIVALS, UNPLACED IN THE CALENDAR OR LOCAL

1 List of three torch-races (*Panathenaia, Hephaisteia, Prometheia*). Harpocration, *Λαμπάς* (quoting Polemo, *FHG.* 3, fr. 6). The Basileus as responsible, Arist. *Ath.* 57, 1. The altar of Prometheus, Paus. 1, 30, 2; Apollodorus, *F.Gr.Hist.* 224 f 147. For *Panathenaia*, see p. 45 supra, and *Bendidia*, p. 150 supra. For early references to relay races, A. *Ag.* 313 and Hdt. 8, 98.

2 *Prometheia*, Isaeus, 7, 36 (proving it was organized on a tribal basis). *Hephaisteia*, *IG.* 1², 84, Sokolowski, No. 13. 'Lifting' oxen, cf. supra, p. 52 (*Herakleia*), p. 74 (*Proerosia*); A. Mommsen, *Feste*, 342.

3 Hdt. 6, 105, 3. Phot. *λαμπάς*. For the date of Philippides' run, see

N. G. L. Hammond, *Studies in Greek History*, 216. For the site of Pan's cave, Travlos, 417.

4 The Anakes – their sanctuary, Th. 8, 93.1. Their festival, Pollux, 1, 37; *IG.* 1², 127, 40. The *Trittya*, Pausanias ap. Eust. *Od.* 1425,62.

5 *Epikleidia*, Hsch., s.n.

6 *Galaxia*, Hsch. s.n. and Bekker, *Anec.* 1, 229, 25.

7 For the site, cf. p. 108 supra. The Iobacchic inscription, Ditt. *Syll.*³ 1109, Sokolowski, No. 51.

8 Harpocration, *Θεοίνιον* (referring to a lost speech of Lycurgus and to Istros, *F.Gr.Hist.* 334 f 3); Lycophr. 1247 with sch. (quoting Aeschylus, fr. 382, Murray); Hsch. *Θεοίνια.*

9 Rural *Dionysia*, p. 100–2 supra.

10 'La Grande Demarchie', Georges Daux, *BCH.* 87 (1963), pp. 683 ff. Sokolowski, No. 18.

11 It is noteworthy that one of the few literary references to Erchia (St. Byz. s.n.) derives the name from 'Erchios who entertained Demeter'. This is somewhat surprising, as one might have expected this legend to be founded on a local cult.

12 Festival of Eros, cf. supra, p. 143 *Bendidia,* p. 149, *Genesia,* p. 53.

13 *IG.* 2², 1172. Wilamowitz-Moellendorf, *Aristoteles und Athen.* 2, 154, n. 23.

14 *IG.* 2², 1358, Sokolowski, No. 20.

SELECT BIBLIOGRAPHY
of most often cited works with the abbreviations used

The *Cambridge Ancient History*, edited by J. B. Bury, S. A. Cook and F. E. Adcock (Cambridge, 1923–39) – *C.A.H.*

Comicorum Atticorum Fragmenta, edited by T. Kock (Leipzig, 1880–88) – *C.A.F.*

Cook, A. B. *Zeus* (Cambridge, 1914–40).

Deubner, Ludwig, *Attische Feste* (Berlin, 1932: reprinted Hildesheim, 1966) – Deubner.

Edelstein, Emma J. and Ludwig. *Asclepius*, A collection and interpretation of the testimonies (Baltimore, 1945) – Edelstein.

Fragmenta Historicorum Graecorum, ed. Car. and Theod. Mueller (Paris, 1885) – FGH.

Fragmente der griechischen Historiker, ed. Felix Jacoby (Berlin, 1923, etc.) – *F.Gr. Hist.*

Greek Historical Inscriptions, A selection of, edited by Russell Meiggs and David Lewis (Oxford, 1969) – Meiggs–Lewis.

Harrison, Jane, *Primitive Athens, as described by Thucydides*, 3rd ed. (Cambridge, 1922).

Hill, Ida Thallon, *The Ancient City of Athens, its topography and monuments* (London, 1953) – Hill.

Mommsen, August, *Feste der Stadt Athen im Altertum* (Leipzig, 1898) – Mommsen, *Feste*.

Mylonas, George E., *Eleusis and the Eleusinian Mysteries* (Princeton, 1961) – Mylonas.

Nilsson, Martin P. *Griechische Feste von religiöser Bedeutung mit Ausschluss der Attischen* (Leipzig, 1906) – Nilsson, *Feste*.

— *Geschichte der griechischen Religion* (München, Vol. 1², 1955, Vol. 2, 1950) – Nilsson, *G.R.*

Parke, H. W. and Wormell, D. E. W. *The Delphic Oracle* (Basil Blackwell, Oxford, 1956) – Parke and Wormell, *Delphic Oracle*.

Pickard-Cambridge, Sir Arthur. *The Dramatic Festivals of Athens*, second edition, revised by John Gould and D. M. Lewis (Oxford, 1968) – Pickard-Cambridge, *Dramatic Festivals*².

Sokolowski, F., *Lois Sacrées des Cités Grecques* (Paris, 1969) – Sokolowski.

— *Supplément* (Paris, 1962) – Sokolowski, *Suppl.*

Travlos, John. *Pictorial Dictionary of Ancient Athens* (London, 1971) – Travlos.

SOURCES OF ILLUSTRATIONS

INDEX